The Southern Elite and Social Change

The Southern Elite and Social Change

Essays in Honor of Willard B. Gatewood Jr.

Edited by
Randy Finley and Thomas A. DeBlack

With a Foreword by James C. Cobb

The University of Arkansas Press
Fayetteville
2002

Manufactured in Canada

06 05 04 03 02 5 4 3 2 1

Designer: John Coghlan

∞ The paper used in this publication meets the minimum requirements of the American National Standard for Permanence of Paper for Printed Library Materials Z39.48-1984.

Library of Congress Cataloging-in-Publication Data

The southern elite and social change : essays in honor of Willard B. Gatewood, Jr. / edited by Randy Finley and Thomas A. DeBlack ; with a foreword by James C. Cobb.
p. cm.
Includes bibliographical references.
ISBN 1-55728-720-1 (pbk. : alk. paper)
1. Southern States—Civilization. 2. Southern States—Social conditions. 3. Southern States—Politics and government. 4. Elite (Social sciences)—Southern States—History. 5. Social change—Southern States—History. 6. Southern States—Biography. I. Finley, Randy, 1954– II. DeBlack, Thomas A., 1951–
F209.5 .S67 2002
305.5'2'092275—dc21

2002000242

Cover illustrations: *(top)* Rev. Richard Harvey Cain *(Courtesy of Moorland-Spingarn Research Center at Howard University); (center)* Emily Newell Blair *(Courtesy Western Reserve Historical Society);* and *(bottom)* James C. Napier *(From the* Nashville Globe*).*

Contents

Foreword

June 1969 was a momentous month in my life. I received my undergraduate degree on June 7, got married on June 8, and scarcely a week later began my graduate study in history at the University of Georgia. As I sat wondering both what my first graduate course, The United States, 1877–1917, would be like and why I was in it to begin with, into the room strode a truly striking figure, clad in a dark blazer and tie (no summer school dress down for this guy), sporting a shock of perfectly groomed white hair, and establishing an atmosphere of dignity and decorum before he even opened his mouth.

This was my first encounter with Willard B. Gatewood Jr., and I knew immediately that this man was what I wanted to be when I grew up. I cannot remember everything that Willard taught me about the period between the end of Reconstruction and American entry into World War I, but I do remember that he taught me a great deal about becoming a professional historian. For example, I recall very well when, with the perfect mixture of understanding and reproach, he informed me that in graduate school we do not refer to Theodore Roosevelt as either Teddy or TR. Needless to say, I have not done so since and no student of mine has done it more than once.

In addition to such nuts-and-bolts suggestions for self-improvement, Willard Gatewood taught me a great deal about professors' obligations to their students. Any of the contributors to this volume will tell you that the likelihood of his coming to class unprepared was roughly equivalent to that of his coming in his undershirt. They would also tell you that when Professor Gatewood graded papers and exams, he got them back to you with an alacrity that made timely fashion seem inexcusably slow. For those who would not have minded more of a breather between crime and punishment, there was at least the consolation that when they received the bad news, they also received a detailed explanation of why the news was bad.

The same values and expectations that made him a great teacher made

Willard a great scholar as well. His productivity has been nothing short of astonishing, and the editors of this volume rightly underscore the remarkable diversity of his contributions. For someone unacquainted with Willard or his work, the quantity and the breadth of his work might suggest hastiness or superficiality. However, anyone who examines even one of his books or articles quickly realizes that, as a scholar, he demands of himself the same diligence, exhaustive research, and objective, thoughtful analysis that, as a teacher, he has always expected from his students.

Although it is well over thirty years ago, I still feel a sense of accomplishment in emerging from Willard's class with an A–. (I wouldn't dare fudge on this because I am sure he still has the grade book.) He left the University of Georgia shortly thereafter, and it was nearly a decade before I saw him again at a meeting of the Southern Historical Association. He managed to make me think he actually remembered me and graciously received my thanks for giving me such a good start in graduate school. Some years later, he even managed to keep a straight face when he introduced me to an audience as someone who had shown striking potential as a beginning graduate student. In addition to shading the truth quite a bit on this occasion, Willard's numerous career-and-spirit boosting kindnesses in the years since our acquaintance was renewed make me feel privileged indeed to have the opportunity to join others who have benefited from both his professional and his personal example to pay him the tribute he so richly deserves.

James C. Cobb

Introduction

A study of southern history from the early days of the Republic to the ascendancy of the Sun Belt exposes major themes and conflicts in American history. The dynamics of liberty, equality, democracy, hierarchy, status, justice, and capitalism become readily evident as each generation of southerners—whites and blacks, men and women, elite and dispossessed—struggled to define these fundamentals for themselves and their age. Analysis of the South through time reveals the rich diversity of the American and southern experience. Although capitalism often subsumes differences and spawns bland homogeneity, southerners have somehow resisted (or tried to resist) the numbing sameness engendered by the cash nexus. They stubbornly balk. Sometimes they lose; at other times a partial victory is gained. But through it all a core of southern values lingers. The southern political and economic elite have most often led the transition of southerners as they endured secession, Civil War, Reconstruction, industrialization, modernization, civil rights movements, and postmodernity.

Southerners often embraced "alternate social visions," which demarcated them as "Other."[1] They resisted ersatz egalitarianism and insisted that hierarchical relationships still fashioned power and identity, opposed the metamorphosis of Christianity into its postmodern aberrant of liberal or fundamentalist narcissism, and labored to create genuine multiracial communities in a nation that repeatedly rejected any other norm save the self. Whites and blacks painfully worked out lasting bonds of affection with each other. Many southerners often championed the Republic over the demos. They clung to the land, if but only in their memory. They behaved anachronistically and felt keenly both alienation and despair. Southerners knew the dance of the dinosaur.

Yet southerners just as often rejected alienation and embraced the prevailing gestalt of the nation. Wrestling with Gordian knots, they often failed even to begin to unravel them. Chattel slavery was abandoned only after a bloody patricide that killed over six hundred thousand. Defeated Confederates lustily embraced bourgeois materialism as the key to a "New South," but in reality this vision aimed to reduce them to little more than a northern clone. Gilded Age southerners endured a poverty so severe that it often maimed both their bodies and their souls. Violations of bizarre rituals and Jim Crow legalities denied black southerners opportunity and individuality and often culminated in unimaginable mutilations and lynchings.[2]

The same psychic specters that compelled southern writers such as William Faulkner, Robert Penn Warren, James Baldwin, Tennessee Williams, Zora Neale Hurston, Eudora Welty, and Flannery O'Connor in the years after World War I to produce one of the South's lasting contributions—the southern literary renaissance—also haunted the southern political, economic, and intellectual elite. The ever-encroaching onrush of capitalism, materialism, and modernity perplexed many in the early years of the twentieth century. Southern politicians embraced or rejected new roles for the government as Franklin Roosevelt's New Deals journeyed to Dixie. After World War II, an irresistible impetus toward modernity, urbanization, industrialization, and globalization heightened southerners' uneasiness over these cataclysmic changes, causing historian Pete Daniel to label the 1940s and 1950s as "a time many people look back on as the Golden Age."[3]

The civil rights movements for African Americans, Hispanics, and women of the 1950s and 1960s forever altered the South. Each of these historically dispossessed groups struggled to gain political and economic power. At times, white southern power brokers supported their demands, while at other times they bitterly opposed them. It was, as with all of southern history, a record of both successes and failures.

In all of these transformations, there remained a South and distinctive southern cultures. Many of the old verities remain. The essays in this book address the impetus of change on a grass-roots level and analyze broad political, economic, cultural, intellectual, and social themes as they fundamentally altered a particular place and time. By focusing on the microcosm, the broader context and contours of American history are revealed. These essays also attempt to counter the recent historiographical trend of studying history only from the perspective of the masses. These essays assert that a southern elite existed, impacting and altering—for better and for worse—the times in which both elite and nonelite lived. A key assumption of these essays is that an elite group of powerful and influential men and women shaped southern life and communities. Although not claiming that the elite ever acted by itself or without the aid of the masses of blacks and whites, men and women, the authors do insist that the elite played a vital role in how southerners consciously confronted change throughout their history.

In the first essay, Whittington B. Johnson questions Gordon S. Wood's assumption that the American Revolution was "the most radical and most far-reaching event in American history."[4] The ringing Jeffersonian cry of "all men are created equal" did not apply to Savannah, Georgia's free African American community. Their freedom was restricted, yet what freedoms the elite possessed—proscribed economic opportunity, religious choices, social choices, educational opportunity, and leadership roles—came about because of the pressures exerted upon the white elite by the black elite.

Next, Thomas A. DeBlack analyzes how one southeastern Arkansas planter, Lycurgus Johnson, adapted to the economic flux and political maelstrom of Jacksonian westward expansion. As if the cotton market's fluctuations were not enough cause for concern, the precariousness of life on the Mississippi River, where the river was the real master, made Johnson's efforts to create a fiefdom even more difficult. Johnson takes part in the American and southern saga of asserting man's dominance over nature by building an impressive plantation house and amassing more and more property. Civil War and Reconstruction furthered the uncertainty and tentativeness of his will to mastery.

Bernard E. Powers Jr. reveals the activism of black leader Richard Harvey Cain who was at the forefront of creating the institutions and upholding the values that sustained free blacks' rights and spirits in a racist antebellum North. With one eye always focused on the possibility of a return to Africa, Cain also focused on ameliorating the prejudice that free blacks faced in the North. As the Civil War ended and Reconstruction began, he journeyed southward and diligently pushed for political, economic, and social opportunities for the freedmen. The role black leaders played in shaping and defining the initially tentative freedom that African Americans gained through emancipation is clearly demonstrated by Cain's political activism.[5] If Reconstruction was, as historian Eric Foner points out, an unfinished revolution, black activists were not at fault.[6]

Then Randy Finley examines the political chameleon Edward W. Gantt of Arkansas. Just like Lycurgus Johnson, Gantt was the embodiment of the self-made man and Jacksonian politico who said or did anything to gain status and prestige. He embodied the values southern whites espoused as they seceded from the Union in 1860 and 1861, then rejected their values completely after he was captured by the Yankees in 1862, metamorphosing by 1863 into a scalawag who upheld emancipation of the slaves and industrialization of the South. As a Freedmen's Bureau agent, Gantt tried to broker relationships between whites and blacks that would offer freedpeople some real hope for economic and political opportunity. His successes and failures help to explain both the ambivalent record of Reconstruction in the South and the complexities of the Civil War's impact.

Bobby L. Lovett examines James Carroll Napier, a Tennessee black leader whose life spanned from the era of slavery to the eve of World War II. A member of what Willard Gatewood calls the South's "aristocrats of color," Napier exemplifies Gatewood's leaders who demonstrated "persistent commitment to racial uplift" and made contributions of "significant and enduring value to the larger black community."[7] Educated at Oberlin and Howard University, Napier served on the Nashville, Tennessee, City Council, constantly pushed for better teachers and educational opportunities for African Americans, privately and publicly opposed Jim Crow laws in the late 1800s, and agitated consistently for racial pride and uplift. Aligning himself with Booker T. Washington, Napier also practiced accommodationism toward white prejudices while attempting to politically and economically discern what changes were realistic in the era of Jim Crow, which saw lynchings at an all-time high. Civil rights historians increasingly emphasize the foundations for the post–World War II civil rights movement laid by earlier activists, and James C. Napier belongs on any list of civil rights groundbreakers.

Jeannie M. Whayne investigates what it meant to be a southern planter in the Arkansas Delta of the late 1800s and early 1900s. She finds a persistence of a hierarchical, paternalistic social and economic system in eastern Arkansas. Crossing over the Mississippi River, Robert E. Lee Wilson found that frontier-like conditions still existed in the region. Just as with previous southern planters, he arduously labored to accumulate capital and power and to imprint his personality on the land and people of the region. His kingdom knew no end as he controlled cotton production, timber operations, a railroad, several area banks, a light company, and numerous stores. Exemplifying the symbiotic relationship between the business elite and politicians, Wilson pressured the state government to push for swamp drainage and flood control levees. When the United States Supreme Court ruled in

1917 that much of the land claimed by Wilson really belonged to the federal government, Wilson rallied U.S. congressmen to help him buy much of the disputed land. Floods in 1912 and 1927, a decline in cotton prices in the 1920s, and the drought of 1931 threatened to sink Wilson's enterprises, but he persevered through luck, hard work, and the aid of the New Deal.

Virginia Laas and Fon Gordon analyze southern women who played key roles in the New Deal and suggest ways in which their activism began to offer new paradigms for southern femininity. Laas investigates Emily Newell Blair of Missouri and documents her rise to political prominence in the 1920s. Actively engaged in journalism that endorsed women's suffrage, Blair consistently pushed the Democratic agenda in the twenties. In the 1932 presidential canvass, she diligently campaigned for Roosevelt in countless campaign speeches and headed the Bureau of Women's Clubs for FDR. With Roosevelt's victory, she sought a government position for her husband rather than for herself. Her husband, Harry Blair, eventually gained a job in the Lands Division of the Justice Department, and Blair herself received a post with the National Recovery Administration. Blair reveals the difficulties southern women encountered, so long perceived as the "Southern Lady" on a pedestal and above the political fray. She also highlights the dynamics of gender relationships in an era when women often chose to push their husbands' careers at the expense of their own.

Fon Gordon also documents the precarious situation an Arkansas black woman faced as she tried to promote a social agenda and gain political power. Spurning the passivity expected of black women of the middle class, Hattie Rutherford Watson insisted on becoming more than just the wife of the president of an African American college. She joined other middle-class African American women in a network of "Southern race women" who supported inculcating bourgeois norms in working-class blacks. As leader of the National Youth Administration Camp in Pine Bluff, Arkansas, in 1937, she created a curriculum that emphasized academics, vocationalism, and health care. The camp became a showplace where white dignitaries visited to observe the successes that blacks achieved when given the opportunity. Hattie R. Watson, just like James C. Napier of Tennessee, was on the vanguard of the civil rights movement before World War II.

In the next essay, Thomas Deaton chronicles the rise of the Sun Belt into Georgia through analysis of the carpet industry in Dalton. Mechanization of the industry accelerated during World War II and was stimulated by the cotton-mill heritage, the proximity of water and electricity, and the strong work ethic still prevalent in the region. By comparing the leaders of the industry—B. J. Bandy, Eugene T. Barwick, Bud Seretean, Guy Henley, Piera Shaheen, and Bob Shaw—it is interesting to see whether they are most like robber barons of northern factories or southern agricultural barons. What distinguishes the carpet industry in Georgia seems to be the persistence of southern paternalism demonstrated by the owners toward their workers and the region itself.

Last, Paula Barnes looks at the civil rights movement in Arkansas during the days of the Little Rock Central High School crisis of 1957. Denying the homogeneity of the Little Rock white community, Barnes emphasizes the moderating influence of activist Sara Murphy who was a bulwark of the Women's Emergency Committee to Open Our Schools of Little Rock. Murphy continually campaigned for moderate political candidates. Sensing that a change in the hearts and minds of people on a grass-roots level was as necessary as Supreme Court orders and mass marches, she joined other women in forming the Panel of American Women, which encouraged interracial group discussions in localities where Jim Crow still reigned. Simply getting blacks and whites together in public forums in southern communities was a first step toward racial reconciliation. Whatever the limitations of her approach, the courage of Murphy, who transcended both racial and gender norms, is beyond dispute.

Each of the essays in this collection emphasizes the impact that a member of a southern communities' elite could make. Whether brokering new understandings of racial, gender, or class relationships, each elite changed the quality of life for southern whites and blacks, men and women, highborn and lowly.

• • •

These essays seek to honor our teacher and colleague Dr. Willard B. Gatewood Jr. Born in North Carolina and educated at Duke University, Professor Gatewood received his Ph.D. in history in 1957. During his academic career, he taught at East Tennessee State University, East Carolina University, North Carolina Wesleyan College, the University of Georgia, and the University of Arkansas. Professor Gatewood also served as president of the Southern Historical Association from 1986 to 1987 and was actively engaged in the American Historical Association, the Organization of American Historians, and the Arkansas Historical Association. As his list of publications demonstrates, few scholars have dealt with such an expansive and diverse array of subjects. His published works span political, intellectual, social, cultural, economic, military, ethnic, and even environmental history. His focus on the impact of the elite in history began with his first published monograph about North Carolina educator Eugene Clyde Brooks and culminated in his *magnum opus, Aristocrats of Color: The Black Elite, 1880–1920.* Such an intellectual interest spurred the authors of this collection, his students and colleagues, to write these essays in his honor.

The authors and editors of this volume are acutely aware of their paltry inability to say thank-you to Professor Gatewood. Memories of his love for learning, of his scholarship, of his deep, warm, and caring personality abound. Students may remember the chemical smell of the seminar room in Ozark Hall in Fayetteville, Arkansas, where he smiled after their first real research papers had been turned in, evaluated, and encouraged "with just a little more changing," he assured, "this will be good." They may remember his walk toward the library with his special note-taking stand to read three more reels of microfilm, ever hunting out the "Aristocrats of Color" or the sound of his North Carolinian voice inquiring over the telephone about their safety after they had endured a tornado. They may ponder all the scholarly essays and manuscripts for monographs he carefully critiqued and improved or imagine all the letters he wrote to help them get a job, a position, or a fellowship in a historical profession where he is truly and deeply respected and treasured. There will be, no doubt, other great teachers and scholars. But all who contributed to this volume are certain that Dr. Willard B. Gatewood Jr. is a profound teacher and scholar. We owe our abiding enthusiasm and respect for history to him.

Randy Finley
Thomas A. DeBlack

Publications by Willard B. Gatewood Jr.

"Eugene Clyde Brooks: Educational Journalist in North Carolina." *North Carolina Historical Review* 26 (July 1959): 307–29.

"James Calvin Hemphill: Southern Critic of Woodrow Wilson." *The Georgia Review* 13 (winter 1959): 378–92.

Eugene Clyde Brooks: Educator and Public Servant. Durham: Duke University Press, 1960.

"Eugene Clyde Brooks." *North Carolina Education* 26 (March 1960): 23, 44–46.

"North Carolina's Role in the Establishment of the Great Smoky Mountain National Park." *North Carolina Historical Review* 37 (April 1960): 165–84.

"Eugene Clyde Brooks and Negro Education in North Carolina." *North Carolina Historical Review* 38 (July 1961): 362–79.

"Conservation and Politics in the South." *The Georgia Review* 16 (spring 1962): 29–42.

"North Carolina and Federal Aid to Education: Public Reaction to the Blair Bill." *North Carolina Historical Review* 40 (October 1963): 465–88.

"The Evolution Controversy in North Carolina, 1920–27." *Mississippi Quarterly* 17 (fall 1964): 192–207.

"Arkansas Negroes in the 1890s: Documents." *Arkansas Historical Quarterly* 33 (winter 1964): 293–325.

"North Carolina Methodism and the Fundamental Controversy." *Wesleyan Quarterly Review* 2 (May 1965): 67–83.

"North Carolina Methodism and the Fundamentalist Crusade at High Tide." *North Carolina Historical Review* 42 (July 1965), 275–90.

"The Lincoln Penny: Mid-Summer Madness of 1909." *The Lincoln Herald* 67 (fall 1965): 119–23.

"Embattled Scholar: Howard W. Odum and the Fundamentalists, 1925–27." *Journal of Southern History* 21 (November 1965): 373–92.

"The President and the Deacon in the Campaign of 1912." *Ohio History* 74 (winter 1965): 35–54.

"Theodore Roosevelt and the Coinage Controversy." *The American Quarterly* 18 (April 1966): 35–51.

"From McKinley to Kennedy: New Appraisals of Recent America." *South Atlantic Quarterly* 65 (winter 1966): 124–42.

Preachers, Pedagogues, and Politicians: The Evolution Controversy in North Carolina, 1920–1927. Chapel Hill: University of North Carolina Press, 1966.

"Theodore Roosevelt and the 'Kinesctoscope Fakes': An Incident in the Campaign of 1904." *Mid-America* 44 (summer 1967): 190–99.

"Theodore Roosevelt and the Indianola Affair." *Journal of Negro History* 53 (January 1968): 48–69.

"Present Plight of Political Annihilation: The Views of a Southern Negro, 1903." *Research Studies* 36 (September 1968): 244–49.

"William D. Crum: A Negro in Politics." *Journal of Negro History* 53 (October 1968): 301–20.

"Woodrow Wilson: The Formative Years, 1856–1880: An Essay Review." *The Georgia Review* 22 (fall 1968): 305–15.

Controversy in the Twenties: Modernism, Fundamentalism, and Evolution. Nashville: Vanderbilt University Press, 1969.

"Guess Who's Coming to Dinner." *Atlanta Magazine* (June 1969): 15 ff.

"Booker T. Washington and the Ulrich Affair." *Phylon* (fall 1969): 286–302. Reprinted in *Journal of Negro History.*

"Theodore Roosevelt and Southern Republicans: The Case of South Carolina." *South Carolina Historical Magazine* 70 (fall 1969): 251–66.

"Negro Troops in Florida, 1898." *Florida Historical Quarterly* (fall 1970): 1–15.

Theodore Roosevelt and the Art of Controversy. Baton Rouge: Louisiana State University Press, 1970.

"Woodrow Wilson and the University of Arkansas." *Arkansas Historical Quarterly* 30 (summer 1971): 83–94.

"Kansas Negroes and the Spanish-American War." *Kansas Historical Quarterly* 37 (autumn 1971): 300–13.

"North Carolina's Negro Regiment in the Spanish-American War." *North Carolina Historical Review* 48 (October 1971): 370–87.

"Smoked Yankees" and the Struggle for Empire: Letters from Negro Soldiers, 1898–1920. Urbana: University of Illinois Press, 1971. Reprinted in Fayetteville: University of Arkansas Press, 1987.

"A Negro Editor on Imperialism: John Mitchell, 1898–1901." *Journalism Quarterly* 69 (spring 1972): 43–50.

"An Experiment in Color: The Eighth Illinois Volunteers, 1898–99." *Journal of the Illinois State Historical Society* 65 (autumn 1972): 293–312.

"Virginia's Negro Regiment in the Spanish-American War: The Sixth Virginia Volunteers." *Virginia Magazine of History and Biography* 80 (April 1972): 193–217.

"Alabama's Negro Soldier Experiment, 1898–1899." *Journal of Negro History* 57 (October 1972): 333–51.

"Black Americans and the Quest for Empire, 1898–1899." *Journal of Southern History* 37 (November 1972): 545–66.

"Negro Legislators in Arkansas, 1891: A Document." *Arkansas Historical Quarterly* 31 (autumn 1972): 220–33.

"Indiana Negroes and the Spanish-American War." *Indiana Magazine of History* 69 (spring 1973): 115–39.

"Ohio's Negro Battalion in the Spanish-American War." *Northwest Ohio Quarterly* 45 (spring 1973): 55–66.

"Theodore Roosevelt and Arkansas." *Arkansas Historical Quarterly* 33 (winter 1973): 3–24.

"A Black Editor on Imperialism: Edward E. Cooper of the *Colored American,* 1898–1901." *Mid-America* 57 (January 1975): 3–19.

"Black Americans and the Military." *Reviews in American History* 3 (March 1975): 31–36.

Black Americans and the White Man's Burden, 1898–1903. Urbana, Illinois: University of Illinois Press, 1975.

"The Rediscovery of Local History." *Georgia Archive* 3 (1975): 146–60.

"Kate D. Chapman Reports on 'The Yankee Colored People,'" *South Dakota History* 7 (winter 1976): 28–35.

"Edward E. Cooper and the '10 Greatest Negroes' Contest." *Negro History Bulletin* 40 (May–June 1977): 708–10.

"Henry Allen Ironside." *Dictionary of American Biography,* Supplement 5 (1977): 345–47.

"The American Experience: The Southern Variable." *The American Experience.* Fayetteville: University of Arkansas, 1977, 26–42.

"William David Upshaw," *Dictionary of American Biography,* Supplement 5 (1977): 701–2.

"Last Hope, or Hopeful at Last? Recent Views of the American South." *The Georgia Review* 32 (spring 1978): 172–98.

"Edward E. Cooper, Black Journalist." *Journalism Quarterly* 55 (summer 1978): 269–78, 324.

"Francis Burton Harrison." *Dictionary of American Biography,* Supplement 6 (1979): 279–81.

"Henry Plummer Cheatham." *Dictionary of North Carolina Biography,* 359–60 (1979).

"Progressivism: From the Old Style to the New." *Journal of Interdisciplinary History* 10 (summer 1979): 147–53.

"Rendering Striking Historical Service: North Carolina's Historical Publication Program, 1903–1978." In *Public History in North Carolina, 1903–1978,* 147–53. Raleigh, North Carolina, 1979.

Slave and Freeman: The Autobiography of George L. Knox. Lexington: University of Kentucky Press, 1979.

"Southern Progressivism." In *Encyclopedia of Southern History,* 1006–9. Baton Rouge, Louisiana: Louisiana State University Press, 1979.

"Strangers in the Southern Eden: The South and Immigration, 1900–1920." *Proceedings of the Tenth Annual Gulf Coast History and Humanities Conference* (Pensacola, 1979).

"Willis Hodges: Freedom Pioneer." *Negro History Bulletin* 43 (January–March 1979): 12–13, 16.

"Booker T. Washington." In *Encyclopedia of Black America,* 839–45. New York: McGraw-Hill, 1981.

"Frederick Douglass and the Building of a 'Wall of Anti-Slavery Fire,' 1845–1846." *Florida Historical Quarterly* (January 1981): 340–44.

The Governors of Arkansas. Co-edited with Timothy P. Donovan. Fayetteville: University of Arkansas Press, 1981.

"John Hanks Alexander of Arkansas: Second Black Graduate of West Point." *Arkansas Historical Quarterly* 41 (summer 1982), 103–28.

"Frederick Douglass in Arkansas." *Arkansas Historical Quarterly* 41 (winter 1982): 303–15.

"The Agrarians From the Perspective of Fifty Years: An Essay Review." *Florida Historical Quarterly* (January 1983): 313–21.

"The Great Smoky Mountains National Park." In *Encyclopedia of American Forest and Conservation History,* ed. Richard C. Davis, 1:281–82. New York: MacMillan, 1983.

"'To Be Truly Free': Louis Sheridan and the Colonization of Liberia." *Civil War History* 29 (December 1983): 332–48.

"A Republican President and Democratic State Politics: Theodore Roosevelt in the Mississippi Primary of 1902." *Presidential Studies Quarterly* (summer 1984): 428–36.

"From Scopes to Creation Science: Decline and Revival of the Evolution Controversy." *South Atlantic Quarterly* 83 (autumn 1984): 363–83.

Free Man of Color: Autobiography of Willis Augustus Hodges. Knoxville: University of Tennessee Press, 1982.

"Professors, Fundamentalists and the Legislature." In *The North Carolina Experience,* ed. Lindley Butler and Alan Watson, 355–79. Chapel Hill: University of North Carolina Press, 1984.

"William Grant Still's Little Rock." In *William Grant Still Studies,* 10–12. Fayetteville, Arkansas: University of Arkansas Press, 1985.

"After Scopes: Evolution in the South." In *The South Is Another Land: Essays on the Twentieth Century South,* ed. Bruce Clayton and John A. Salmond, 124–49. New York: Greenwood Press, 1987.

"From Scopes to Creation Science: The Decline and Revival of the Evolution Controversy." Reprinted in *American Vistas: 1877 to Present,* ed. Leonard Dinnerstein and Kenneth T. Jackson, 143–64. New York: Oxford University Press, 1987.

"'White Primary' System Completes Removal of Blacks From Politics." *The Arkansas News* (spring 1987): 3.

"Alonzo Clifton McClellan: Black Midshipman From South Carolina, 1873–1874." *South Carolina Historical Magazine* 89 (January 1988): 24–39.

"Aristocrats of Color: South and North, The Black Elite, 1880–1920." *Journal of Southern History* 54 (February 1988): 3–20.

"John Francis Cook: Antebellum Black Presbyterian." *American Presbyterians: Journal of Presbyterian History* 67 (fall 1989): 221–30.

Aristocrats of Color: The Black Elite, 1880–1920. Bloomington: Indiana University Press, 1990.

"Gifts and Trials." In *The Arkansas Delta: Landscape of Change,* 1–13. Little Rock, Arkansas: Department of Arkansas Heritage, 1990.

"The Perils of Passing: The McCarys of Omaho," *Nebraska History* 71 (summer 1990): 64–70.

"Sunnyside: The Evolution of an Arkansas Plantation, 1848–1945." *Arkansas Historical Quarterly* 50 (spring 1991): 5–29.

"The Remarkable Misses Rollin: Black Women in Reconstruction South Carolina." *South Carolina Historical Magazine* 92 (June 1991): 172–88.

"An 'African Prince, Majestic in His Wrath': William S. McFeely's Biography of Frederick Douglass." *Florida Historical Quarterly* 70 (October 1991): 192–202.

"Richard Brevard Russell: The 'Georgia Giant.'" *Georgia Historical Quarterly* 76 (spring 1992): 46–57.

"Theodore Roosevelt and the Shaping of the Modern Presidency." *Reviews in American History* 20 (1992): 512–17.

"Josephine B. Willson Bruce." In *Black Women in America: An Historical Encyclopedia,* ed. Darline C. Hines, 1:187–88. Brooklyn, New York: Carlson Publishing Company, 1993.

"Sunnyside: The Evolution of an Arkansas Plantation, 1840–1945." In *Shadows Over Sunnyside: An Arkansas Plantation in Transition, 1840–1945,* 3–24. Fayetteville, Arkansas: University of Arkansas Press, 1993.

The Arkansas Delta: Land of Paradox. Co-edited with Jeannie Whayne. Fayetteville: University of Arkansas Press, 1993.

"School Desegregation in Fayetteville: A Forty Years Perspective." In *Civil Disobedience: An Oral History of School Desegregation in Fayetteville, Arkansas 1954–1965,* 1–28. Fayetteville: University of Arkansas Press, 1994.

"W. E. B. Du Bois: Elitist as Racial Radical." *Georgia Historical Quarterly* 67 (summer 1994): 306–25.

"Significance of Skin Color." In *Encyclopedia of African American Culture and History.* New York: MacMillan and Company, 1995.

"Introduction." In *The New Man: Twenty-Nine Years a Slave, Twenty-Nine Years a Free Man,* vii-xviii. Lincoln: University of Nebraska Press, 1996.

In the Shadow of the Revolution: Savannah's First Generation of Free African American Elite in the New Republic, 1790–1830

Whittington B. Johnson

Throughout early American history, a few individuals in new communities have risen to the apex of society by achieving more than the other inhabitants and eventually amassing a larger share of the communities' wealth, enabling them to enjoy a higher standard of living than most. The seventeenth-century Puritan town of Dedham, Massachusetts, and the nineteenth-century prairie community of Sugar Creek, Illinois, are two examples of such upward mobility that historians have studied.[1] Similarly, this phenomenon also occurred in African American communities, though understandably on a more limited basis. This study focuses on such a group of individuals in Savannah, Georgia. In addition to focusing on a sector of free African Americans that historians have tended to ignore, this study examines that group in a broader context than previous studies of the African American experience by including free blacks and coloreds in the Bahama Islands. In a sense then, the experience of Savannah's free African Americans is viewed through a wider lens than usual, encompassing English-speaking slave communities in the American South and in a British Caribbean colony, as well as free African Americans in northern communities. This study will show that a small group of free African Americans in Savannah, mainly males, exploited the limited opportunities available to blacks and carved niches in the economy and the church that profoundly altered the lives of African Americans in Georgia's principal city.

The free African Americans who resided in Savannah in 1790 lived in a republic rather than in a colony of Great Britain and witnessed the ratification of the Bill of Rights (1791), which guaranteed Americans protection against the federal government's abuse of power. Thus, they were the first free African Americans to live in a free country, but the term *free* was illusory for nonwhites. The *free* preceding the term *African American* alluded to freedom from bondage, not freedom to enjoy the Bill of Rights. So in this regard, Gordon S. Wood's assumption that the American Revolution was "the most radical and most far-reaching event in American history"[2] is an overstatement. To remove any doubt of the intent of the Founding Fathers, Chief Justice Roger B. Taney excluded free blacks from the protection of the Bill of Rights quite clearly in *Dred Scott v. Sandford* (1857), declaring that they were ineligible for citizenship in the republic.

Any discussion of the free African American elite must therefore take into consideration the civil and economic disabilities imposed upon them, first by the Founding Fathers, and next by the political leaders of Georgia, a slave society. From the founding of the republic, African Americans in Savannah could not vote, hold public office, sit on juries, testify against whites in court, own firearms, or pursue careers in law, medicine, or education. Furthermore, they were prohibited from engaging in certain types of businesses, including drug stores, and they even had to register annually,[3] a restriction unique to African Americans. Since these prohibitions were placed on all African Americans, free and slave, the African American elite of Savannah did not fare any better than slaves and propertyless free African Americans in certain respects. The fact that a small group of free African Americans prevailed against such obstacles merits emphasizing these persons collectively and individually.

According to the first official census of Savannah (1809), there were 329 free African Americans, 3,211 slaves, and 2,702 whites.[4] These numbers had changed significantly by 1830 when there were 404 free African Americans, 9,481 slaves, and 3,620 whites.[5] In spite of the civil and economic disabilities, a small group of free African Americans, the elite of the black community, made "large sums of money," as William Harden, a white Savannahian, recalled in his memoirs.[6] Some of their children even attended school,[7] although its illegality mandated secrecy. In 1810, there were 108 African Americans listed in the city's tax digest, 30 of whom owned property assessed at a minimum of two hundred dollars and 5 of those owned property valued at a minimum of one thousand dollars: William "Billy" Goldsmith (butcher), Richard Houstoun (tailor), Simon Jackson (tailor), Saunders Motta (barber), and Leah Simpson (seamstress).[8] Ten years later the number of free African Americans on the tax digest had increased to 207, including 45 who owned property assessed at a minimum of two hundred dollars, and nine of those persons' property was assessed at a minimum of one thousand dollars.[9] The number of women among the largest property owners had increased from 1 to 4 from 1810 to 1820. Moreover, there were 19 free African American slaveholders in 1820 and 22 in 1823, but only 1, Anthony Odingsell, owned slaves in double-digit numbers; he owned 10.[10]

All free African Americans were restricted to the same occupations, but the elite successfully overcame this obstacle and consequently amassed small fortunes and owned valuable property, including slaves. Free African Americans owned slaves primarily for economic reasons, but unlike their counterparts in Charleston, it was not a situation where the slaves were black and the slaveholders were mulatto.[11] Although most of Savannah's African American slaveholders were mulatto and most of their slaves were black, some slaveholders were black and some slaves were mulatto.

There were also differences between free African American slaveholders in Savannah and their counterparts in the Bahama Islands. The few available records concerning manumission indicate that free African Americans were far less inclined to free their slaves than their counterparts in the Bahama Islands, where in some years 25 percent of all the slaves manumitted belonged to nonwhites.[12] Usually when African Americans in Savannah were involved in a manumission it was to purchase their own freedom or that of close relatives. Savannah's free African American slaveholders generally did not own slaves who were their wives, children, grandchildren, or other relatives, as did their counterparts in the Bahamas.[13] Another difference between free African American slaveholders in Savannah and free black and colored slaveholders in the Bahamas was that religious leaders in the latter were not slaveholders,[14] but those in Savannah were. Part of the reason for this difference may have been economic. Free African American preachers in Savannah were more affluent than nonwhite preachers in the Bahamas.

The free African American elite in Savannah gained recognition through achieved status: accumulation of real estate, ownership of slaves, operation of successful businesses, or leadership of religious and educational institutions. None at this time were the beneficiaries of ascribed status. Teachers relied upon their position to gain status. They were not as highly esteemed as preachers, however, who were the most powerful persons in the community. The two independent black churches, First African Baptist Church and

Second African Baptist Church, were permitted to operate publicly and had large congregations, whereas the schools were operated clandestinely and outside the law.

The elite came from diverse cultures and were of different colors, but they were mainly American-born and mulatto. The majority were born in Georgia, mainly in Savannah, but a few were from surrounding areas and other states. A small minority came from Saint Domingue (Haiti), from which they fled after the revolution turned bloody. Jean Baptiste du Bergier (tailor), Louis Mirault (tailor), Andrew Morel (tailor), Clemente Sabbatte (barber), Julien Fromantin (carpenter/teacher), Manette Tardieu (shopkeeper), and Phillis Savage (seamstress) were from Saint Domingue. Ragist Jackson (baker) was from Martinique and Catherine Deveaux (seamstress/teacher) from Antigua, two other Caribbean cultures.[15] Although the French-speaking elite tended to interact with each other, there was no apparent tension or conflict between the cultural groups despite their preference for endogamous marriages. Haitians married each other, and the American-born married fellow native-born residents. Moreover, blacks and mulattoes within each group tended to marry persons of the same color.[16]

There was a definite West Indian presence among the elite, but this was less pronounced than their mulatto color. Since the United States did not list colors other than white and black (Negro) until 1860, complete information on the complexion of the elite is non-existent. But records, especially those of the Catholic and Episcopal churches, occasionally identified mulattoes; and wills, newspapers, and accounts of white contemporaries often described the complexion of African Americans. These sources reveal that most of the elite were mulattoes. For instance, in 1810 four of the persons who owned property assessed at a minimum of one thousand dollars were mulattoes, the lone exception being Saunders Motta who married Eve Dolly, a black woman, leading to a conclusion that he, too, was black.[17]

Although mulattoes owned more real estate and slaves than blacks did, they were not entitled to any special privileges and suffered under the same civil and economic disabilities as blacks. There were far fewer free mulattoes in Savannah than in Charleston, New Orleans, Pensacola, and Mobile.[18] In fact, in the English-speaking Western Hemisphere, only the Bahamas had a smaller percentage of free mulattoes than Savannah, due to those islands' high manumission rates.[19] Similarly, Savannah's mulattoes were less affluent than most of those in other lower South communities as well as those in the British West Indies. The wealth of mulattoes in Charleston and New Orleans is generally well known, but little is known about the situation in the Bahamas, the British West Indies colony nearest the American South, other than that it was not a sugar producer and was therefore not wealthy. One of the wealthiest mulattoes in the Bahamas, Margaret Clarke of Exuma Island, owned over twenty-five hundred acres of land and fifty-eight slaves when the legislature passed the Manumission Act (1834).[20] No mulatto in Savannah could approach these numbers.

Savannah's elite differed from its counterparts in other urban areas of the lower South and in the Bahamas in another regard: ministers were at the top of the social hierarchy. Charleston and New Orleans had weak black religious communities and did not produce strong religious leaders,[21] at any rate not any who were permitted to remain there. The Baptist Church in the Bahamas was all black, but it was perceived as a pariah by the Anglican Church and hence its leaders were ostracized. On the other hand, the first generation elite in Savannah produced strong African American religious leaders and continued to do this well into the twentieth century. Andrew Bryan, Andrew C. Marshall, and Henry Cunningham established a tradition of strong leadership in the Baptist Church in Savannah and subsequent generations continued this practice. For instance, during Reconstruction the pastor of First Bryan Baptist Church, Ulysses Houstoun, was elected to the Georgia legislature.[22]

In addition to ministers, the male elite included tailors, tradesmen, barbers, and a planter; females were seamstresses, washerwomen, pastry cooks, and shopkeepers. The elite often served white customers. In fact, the elite was not segregated from whites; they lived in the same wards, attended some of the same churches, and shopped in the city market. Black Baptist churches belonged to the same association as white denominations. The elite, however, subscribed to the ban on commingling among the races and may have attempted to emulate whites by participating in duels.[23]

Because of the type of society in which they lived—a small urban slave society—the free African American elite were limited in their vocational options. For example, they were prohibited by statute from owning a fleet of ships as Paul Cuffe did in Massachusetts. Cuffe, a transporter of products and produce from American markets to Europe and the Caribbean, once stopped in Savannah to load cargo bound for Gottenburg, Sweden.[24]

Similarly, the elite could not own and operate a sail loft with an interracial work force as the free African American James Forten did in Philadelphia[25] because social convention did not allow it. The elite, moreover, could not tap into the wealth that pervaded prosperous larger southern towns such as Charleston and New Orleans because such wealth did not exist in Savannah. This hampered the accumulation of huge fortunes.

Furthermore, the elite did not have the caliber of schools that existed in some other places. Thomas Bonneau and Daniel Payne, two highly regarded Charleston educators, did not have counterparts in Savannah. In fact, James Porter, one of the leading schoolmasters in antebellum Savannah, received his training in Charleston.[26] The Bahamas had a free black schoolmaster, Joseph Gould Watkins, who received compensation from the government to operate a schoo1[27] at a time when governmental officials in Savannah proscribed teaching African Americans to read and write.[28] Nevertheless, Savannah African American schools operated, even if they were inferior. In 1819 Julien Fromantin, a Haitian emigre, opened a school that continued operating well beyond 1830, notwithstanding the statute forbidding it; Catherine Deveaux of Antigua also operated one about the same time.[29]

Since the first black schools were not established until early in the nineteenth century, when the first elite were adults, one could assume that the early elite who learned to read and write were self-taught. Surprisingly, a larger number could read than would have been expected, and a small group could both read and write. Andrew Bryan and Andrew C. Marshall could read but they could not write.[30] The other preacher in the community, Henry Cunningham, could read and write. Richard Houstoun and Simon Jackson, both tailors, were also literate.[31] Many of the emigres from Haiti and other Caribbean islands probably were literate, but the absence of written documents requiring their signature prevents scholars from identifying these persons.[32] Even though the Savannah elite generally lagged behind its counterparts in education in other urban areas, it nonetheless contained the best-educated African Americans in the community and was responsible for introducing black schools to Savannah.

Many free African Americans were churchgoers, and the elite were no exception. The largest number of free African Americans worshiped in the independent black Baptist church instead of in other Protestant churches or in the Catholic Church. The strength of the black church in Savannah rested upon its support from free African Americans. The church membership of Second African Baptist read like a who's who in the black community. Richard Houstoun, Leah Simpson, and Simon Jackson were charter members.[33] They probably belonged to First African Baptist before being dismissed to join its newly formed sister church, but the mere fact that they went with Andrew Bryan's blessings suggests that First African Baptist Church was not drained of elite.

Here once again the elite deviated from practices of their counterparts in other urban areas. In Charleston and New Orleans, the Episcopal and Catholic Churches attracted most of the elite. Similarly, the Bahamian elite mostly congregated as Anglicans. Haiti did not have a Baptist church at the time that the emigres left, so they were not familiar with that faith. Most were Catholics in Haiti and became Catholics in Savannah; Jean Baptist du Bergier, Louis Mirault, and Andrew Morel joined Saint John The Baptist Catholic Church.[34] Clemente Sabatte, Phillis Savage and a small minority of elite from Haiti joined the Independent Presbyterian Church where they worshiped with Juno Guard from Savannah.[35] Furthermore, Maria Cohen of Jacksonville joined Christ Episcopal Church.[36]

Although free African Americans worshiped in biracial Catholic, Presbyterian, and Episcopalian churches, they probably were segregated during the worship service. This was similar to the housing situation where African Americans and whites lived in the same wards but probably did not entertain each other in their homes. By belonging to those churches, the elite acquiesced to the practices of the day that prohibited nonwhites from joining the ordained ministry. Baptists practiced a different kind of segregation; African Americans and whites attended different churches. Unlike the other denominations, however, the Baptist church ordained African Americans to the ministry, albeit in a segregated setting. Moreover, African Americans organized the First African Baptist Church in Savannah fully a decade before white Baptists established their church.[37]

It appears as if the free African American elite may have been more serious about avoiding social commingling with whites than other free African Americans. This is ironic since most of these elite mulattoes were the result of commingling of the races. Whites, furthermore, catered to mulatto-owned businesses more than to black-owned ones. Nevertheless, biological ties and business dealings did not foster interracial liaisons. This was undoubtedly because such behavior came with a high price tag for those caught in interracial affairs. Since the elite had more to lose, it was probably very careful about crossing the line of acceptable behavior. The few instances when interracial affairs may have occurred were aberrations.

The occupations in which the elite worked were not ones that lent themselves to a life of leisure, and the businesses were usually small, suggesting that the elite followed a different lifestyle from the upper crust of Savannah's white society. These occupations also differed from those of the white affluent class, who generally were in the professions and business and through these—or through marriages or inheritance—acquired considerable wealth and extensive property.

The names of the free African American elite were different from those given to slaves. Names of days of the week, months, British cities, and Roman and Greek heroes were often given to slaves, and when allowed to have African names those most frequently selected were Cuffe, Sukey, Juba, and Quash. None of the property holders matched the Dolly family's penchant for slave names; London, Quash, and Quamina[38] were all names frequently found among slaves and retained in the Dolly family, but none of the Dollys with these names was born in Africa. Furthermore, names associated with American independence, such as Freedom, Liberty, and names of the Founding Fathers were not common among the elite. One could conclude from this that the absence of African and slave names among the elite is the result of their being born free, but the fact that Andrew Bryan, Andrew Marshall, and Henry Cunningham were born slaves suggests otherwise.

In addition to shunning African names, the African American elite appear to have had a low retention of Africanisms. In the Bahamas, for instance, *asue* (a West African practice of pooling money), *Jukanoo* (a West African dance festival), and the shout were some of the Africanisms retained,[39] but none of these survived in Savannah, at least not among the elite. Moreover, if *obeah* (witchcraft or sorcery) was practiced, it happened among the lower classes, not the elite.

Only a tiny minority of the elite appear to have been able to afford the same kind of medical care that affluent whites received. Henry Bourquin Jr., a white physician, was one of the best doctors in Savannah, and several of his patients were free African Americans. Simon Jackson secured the doctor's service more than any other African American. He used the doctor for his wife's illness, a "negro" boy, a girl, an apprentice, and himself. The boy and girl were doubtless his slaves. Other free African Americans whom the doctor treated were Thomas Lloyd, a mulatto carpenter, his children, Jack Gibbons, and Andrew Morel. Bourquin always referred to the African Americans by their surnames without attaching a title like Mr. or Mrs., except for one occasion when he called Jackson "Mr.," but he always used a title when referring to whites.[40] The difference in treatment probably stopped there.

The elite was an achieving group of free African Americans who labored under onerous civil and economic disabilities, but each was also an individual who by his or her perseverance achieved success in the limited socioeconomic space allotted. The elite included Andrew Bryan, Andrew Marshall, and Henry Cunningham, charismatic preachers; Jean Baptist du Bergier, Louis Mirault, Andrew Morel, Richard Houstoun, and Simon Jackson highly regarded tailors; John "Jack" Gibbons, a carpenter; and Anthony Odingsell, fisherman, farmer, and planter. These individuals epitomized the first generation of free African American elite.

Bryan was the preeminent black preacher in Georgia. This former slave was born in Goose Creek, South Carolina, in 1737 [41] and, prior to the American Revolution, was brought to the Savannah area, where he became a valuable slave on Jonathan Bryan's Brampton Plantation about nine miles outside of Savannah. George Liele, a slave evangelist, converted Bryan to Christianity, and in 1782 when Liele, who subsequently was manumitted, left for Jamaica with the British, Bryan filled the void that Liele's departure created.[42] On January 20, 1788, Bryan's congregation was organized into the church that eventually became known as First African Baptist Church.[43] Six months later, the small group had grown to 575 members, mostly slaves, and on May 5, 1789, Bryan was permitted to purchase his freedom for fifty pounds sterling.[44]

Although Bryan ultimately had a large congregation, reaching over one thousand members, he supported "himself by his own labour."[45] In a letter written in his behalf in 1800, Bryan stated that "by a kind Providence, I am well provided for . . . having a house and lot in this city [Savannah], besides land on which several buildings stand, for which I receive a small rent, and a fifty-six acre tract of land with all necessary buildings, four miles in the country, and eight slaves . . ."[46]

Even if Byran had not been successful in his religious ministry, he would have ranked among the elite because of his financial situation. Bryan was well past his prime years when he was manumitted, yet he managed to acquire more property than many whites who did not carry the same cultural baggage. As a landlord and slaveholder,[47] Bryan lived very well without financial assistance from his congregation, qualifying him to join the community elite.

Bryan believed, however, that he was a preacher first and foremost. He was described as stout, black, and graceful with "white fleecy and well-set locks."[48] A strict disciplinarian, he visited church members frequently and sternly admonished them for sinking into sinful behavior. In the latter days of his ministry, white slaveholders often asked him to intercede in punishing their slaves because these masters realized that their slaves were more fearful of Bryan's wrath and probable expulsion from the Christian fellowship of First African Baptist Church than of their own whippings. Bryan thus saved many slaves from whippings and slave families from separations.[49] The slave masters seeking out Bryan for help enhanced Bryan's image in the community and ensured that his church would not be closed. So, while gaining financial security from his business dealings, Bryan simultaneously gained power through his ministry, thereby paving the way for a highly visible black church in Savannah and a high regard for black preachers. He died on October 12, 1812, leaving a congregation that was the largest Baptist church in Georgia and an estate worth well over $3,000,[50] a very large sum in a day when only a relatively few free black workers earned annual wages in excess of $150. The estate was willed to Dolly Bryan, his wife.

Andrew C. Marshall, nephew of Andrew Bryan and his eventual successor as pastor of Savannah's oldest Baptist church, built upon the solid foundation created by his uncle. By the time Marshall assumed the pastorate he owned the largest dray business in Savannah. In 1820 his property was assessed at sixty-five hundred dollars, but Marshall's wife, Rachel, appears on the tax digest because he was still a slave and technically could not own property. He had been manumitted, however, by the time the call came from First African Baptist Church. During the early years of his ministry, Marshall was probably perceived more as a successful businessman than as a preacher, but this had changed by the mid-1830s. At the time of his death in 1855, he was one hundred years old and considered Georgia's leading African American.[51]

Marshall was a member of Second African Baptist Church when he was called to lead First African Baptist Church. The pastor of Marshall's former church was Henry Cunningham, a protégé of Andrew Marshall at First African Baptist Church. Cunningham was born in nearby McIntosh County (ca. 1764),[52] but little is known about the time he spent there or when he came to Savannah. In 1802 Bryan tapped him to become pastor of the new church—named Second African Baptist Church—that was being formed on the east to relieve crowding at First African Baptist Church.[53] According to Henry C. Holcombe, former pastor of First Baptist Church (a white church), Bryan and Cunningham were charter members of the Savannah River Association, a group of Baptist churches.[54] Over time Cunningham, of whom Holcombe spoke highly, came to exercise the same influence on the east side that Bryan and later Marshall exercised on the west.

In addition to being a successful preacher, Cunningham, who also received only meager support from his church, made profitable investments in property and bought a few slaves. His slave holding probably began on June 11, 1811, when he bought a slave for four hundred dollars, and by 1830 he owned five.[55] Cunningham owned and rented real estate in Greene and Columbia Wards; additional income probably came into the household from earnings of his wife, Elizabeth "Betsey" Cunningham, who was an excellent seamstress. Cunningham always listed his vocation as preacher, so the money to buy slaves and real estate did not come from an outside occupation. Although his real estate was never assessed at more than five hundred dollars,[56] his possessions still placed him in the upper tier of free African Americans who owned real estate and slaves. Cunningham was thus a heavyweight in the community because of his status and accumulated wealth.

The three preachers mentioned above had no peers in the black community, but there were five tailors who were also highly respected; two of these were members of Cunningham's church and the others were from Saint Domingue, Haiti. Whereas the preachers' prestige came primarily from their position as head of large and influential religious institutions, the tailors' status stemmed from the wealth that they acquired and their demonstrated community leadership. All five were literate, which was not true of most preachers, and their signatures appear on extant wills and church registers. These five men—Jean Baptist du Bergier, Louis Mirault, Andrew Morel, Richard Houstoun, and Simon Jackson—were the most successful tradesmen of their day.

Du Bergier was probably the patriarch of the Haitian emigres, some of whom may not have fled that island empty-handed when they began to leave in the 1790s. In 1806, he owned the most valuable property of any nonwhite in Chatham County. To give an idea of the value of this property, its taxes were triple those of the next person on the list, Andrew Bryan's, whose taxes were 50 percent higher than the third person on the list, William "Billy" Goldsmith,[57] whose property was assessed at $2,200. Du Bergier was active in the Catholic Church where his signature appears on the register either as godfather or as witness. On July 18, 1803, a mulatto couple was married at Saint John The Baptist Catholic Church in Savannah, and the following entry appears in the register: "present to the celebration of their marriage were John [Jean] Baptiste du Bergier, Louis Mirault, and Simon Hyacinthe, all three mulattoes, who have signed with me . . ." Another entry reads, "Jean [Julien] Fromantin a 23 year old mulatto man born in St. Domingue and Mari Charlotte 14 years old, also mulatto and native of St. Domingue were married. Present were . . . M. Jean Baptiste du bergier."[58] Fromantin started the first school for African Americans in Savannah about fourteen years later.

Louis Mirault appears in the church register almost as often as du Bergier. An entry states that a mulatto Haitian slaveholder baptized the son of one of her slaves and she asked Mirault to stand as godfather of the infant while she stood as its godmother. The slaveholder, Sophia, also asked Mirault to be the godfather of her daughter, Mary Joseph.[59] Although Mirault interacted very closely with fellow Haitian emigres, many of the customers in his tailoring business were white businessmen and professionals.[60] Mirault, owner of nine slaves in 1820,[61] could have brought slaves with him from Haiti because at that time their importation was not illegal. Similarly, Morel, the remaining tailor of the Haitian trio, was a slaveholder and owner of real estate assessed at one thousand dollars.[62]

Richard Houstoun was one of two very successful American-born tailors. In 1810 Houstoun's property was assessed at $1,125, ranking third among free African American property owners.[63] Prior to his death in 1814, he owned two parcels of land, assessed at a total of $1,532, and three slaves.[64] Houstoun left the bulk of his estate to his pregnant wife, Nancy, and their children, Sarah and Richard Ann, and the remainder to his mother, Dolly, who received a small house. Houstoun also left $50 cash to each of his two nephews and $450 cash to his wife.[65] The total of $450 in cash was a large sum and reveals Houstoun's financial security. The appearance of extended family members in his will perhaps represents a desire to continue in death the support that he had provided while alive.

Simon Jackson, the other very successful American-born tailor, was a close friend of Houstoun. Between 1810 and 1820 his property's assessed value increased from $1,200 to $5,000,[66] the latter being second only to Rachel Marshall's. Jackson was also a slaveholder. Among the leaders in real estate ownership, he placed near the bottom, however, in slave ownership. Jackson left more records than any other member of the elite partly because of his dealings with Richard M. Stites, a prominent white lawyer. These records disclose Jackson as an astute, well-connected individual who developed a reputation for handling business matters efficiently and honestly. He could also, when necessary, be a friend to the friendless. In 1807 Jackson sold Stites, a thirty-year-old slave, for $200, and in 1809 he purchased a male slave from a South Carolina resident.[67] On several occasions Stites supported Jackson's business ventures. Jackson's account with Stites shows that in September 1810, he purchased $29.75 worth of goods from New York, and the next June, 1811, he sold clothing worth $145.50 to William H. Nicoll. Moreover, that year Stites wrote a letter of recommendation on behalf of Jackson and loaned him $1,500 to buy property in Reynolds Ward from a white family in Charleston.[68] The text of the following will of Daniel Huguein, the Irish owner of a confectionery, shows Jackson's compassion: "Having no relations in this country and having received many acts of kindness from Simon Jackson of Savannah a free man of color, I do hereby give and bequeath any of my possession of whatever kind, it may be to John Lawson of Savannah Esquire in trust for Simon Jackson, his heirs and assigns forever."[69] The value of the items inventoried was $175.50.[70] Jackson also was appointed executor of wills, two of which belonged to sailors on an American warship.[71] The exact year of Jackson's death is unknown, but the 1823 register lists Susan Jackson, a pastry cook and his wife, as the owner of the property.

Obtaining information on the elite barbers, butchers, carpenters, and coopers is difficult because they generally did not leave wills or any other records. The lone exception to this was John "Jack" Gibbons. Gibbons was probably formerly owned by Thomas Gibbons, from whom he gained his freedom. He then committed himself to securing the freedom of his wife, Chloe, and his sons, Billy and Joseph. After paying the $400 purchase price for Chloe in four installments, Gibbons gained his wife's freedom on December 27, 1799. It took a little over another year to earn the $275 purchase price of his sons, but on January 12, 1801, Thomas Gibbons manumitted the last of Jack Gibbons' family who were still in bondage.[72] Once that goal was achieved, Gibbons devoted his funds toward buying real estate and slaves. In 1813, Gibbons owned $1,050 in real estate and one slave. The next ten years he acquired four more slaves.[73]

Anthony Odingsell, the only planter-elite, was born a slave, like many others of the elite, but his experience was quite different from many other slaves because his former owner, probably his father, made generous provisions for him in his will. This former master, Charles Odingsell, provided Anthony, who was nine years old when the will was made, with freedom, land (a whole island), nine slaves, and funding for an education.[74] Anthony Odingsell listed his vocation at various times as fisherman, farmer, and planter and his residence as Wilmington Island, Skidaway Island, and Little Wassaw Island, the latter an inheritance from Charles Odingsell.[75] Anthony Odingsell owned more slaves and land than any other elite, but he may not have been as influential as many who owned less land and significantly fewer slaves because he does not appear to have spent much time in Savannah and did not affiliate with churches there. Since he did not move among the people of Savannah, they did not embrace him. Nevertheless, Odingsell was an elite.

Unlike successful whites, the black elite played by rules that were not of their making, a situation that successful whites did not have to endure. White leaders enacted the statutes and ordinances under which African Americans had to live, and by 1830 the boundaries had been well defined. The laws were very confining, but some avenues to advancement remained open and the free African American elite, exhibiting traits characteristic of successful persons regardless of race or color, used these open avenues to improve themselves by pursuing profitable vocations and accumulating property. Furthermore, they collectively established the largest independent black church in the South and that institution became the pride of the black community. This group thus practiced self-help almost a century before Booker T. Washington popularized the concept.

The cultural diversity that pervaded Savannah's African American community in 1790 had disappeared by 1830 when African American culture became much more homogenized. Many of the first generation of elite had died by 1830, but they often left estates that allowed their heirs to live comfortably and become antebellum success stories. Because of the successes of the free African American elite, African Americans in all socioeconomic groups were assured that the disfranchised need not become hopeless, that the powerless need not become paupers, and that an African American minority could succeed in a white-dominated society. Finally, in accomplishing much, in spite of great obstacles, the free African American elite refuted by deed white-held stereotypes about African Americans, even if whites refused to admit their misconceptions.

"A Model Man of Chicot County": Lycurgus Johnson and Social Change

Thomas A. DeBlack

For antebellum planters in the Arkansas Delta, change was one of life's few constants, and the ability to adapt to change was necessary for survival. In a little more than a single generation they transformed large tracts of Delta wilderness into one of the most productive cotton growing regions on earth, survived frequent fluctuations in the international cotton market, and immersed themselves in the ever-changing currents of Jacksonian politics. In doing so, they established a social, economic, and political hegemony that lasted throughout the antebellum era. In the quarter century since Arkansas entered the Union in 1836, the planter-elite withstood numerous challenges to that hegemony. But the Civil War, emancipation, and Reconstruction posed a far greater threat to their elite status than anything that they had previously encountered. The experiences of Lycurgus Johnson of Chicot County, Arkansas, were in many ways typical of the dramatic changes faced by Arkansas Delta planters in this period.

The Johnsons first established themselves in the Arkansas Delta in 1831. In that year forty-year-old Joel Johnson sold his house and gristmill in Scott County, Kentucky, and, leaving behind a wife and five children, set off for Chicot County in the southeasternmost part of the Arkansas Territory. The Johnsons were Kentucky aristocrats. Joel's father, Robert Johnson, was active in Democratic-Republican politics and a longtime member of the Kentucky legislature. He had been instrumental in the founding of the Transylvania Seminary (later Transylvania University) in Lexington, the Rittenhouse Academy in Scott County, and the Kentucky Society for Promoting Useful Knowledge. Joel's mother, Jemima Suggett Johnson, was a hero of the 1782 battle of Bryant's Station, Kentucky, in which ninety settlers held off an attack by five hundred Indians.[1]

Five of Joel's brothers served with distinction in the War of 1812, and one, Richard Mentor Johnson, was credited with firing the shot that killed the great Shawnee leader Tecumseh at the Battle of the Thames in October

1813. Three of the brothers later served in the U. S. Congress, and Richard Johnson was elected to the U. S. Senate and later served as vice president of the United States under Martin Van Buren. Two other brothers attained prominence in the Old Southwest. Henry Johnson established a prosperous plantation in the Mississippi Delta, and Benjamin Johnson left a position as a circuit judge in the Lexington area to go to Arkansas, where he served as a territorial judge and, later, a federal district judge. Joel's two sisters married prominent Kentucky men and raised large families.[2]

It is not clear what considerations prompted Joel Johnson to move to the Arkansas Delta. It may have been that he felt he could never match the achievements of his older brothers in Kentucky; he may have been inspired by the success that Henry and Benjamin had experienced; or he may simply have felt the same desire that had prompted his father and thousands of other young men to move to a new region where opportunity and adventure abounded for a young man on the make.

The southern expanse of the Arkansas Delta that Joel Johnson entered in 1831 was a foreboding frontier wilderness. Bordered by Louisiana on the south and by the Mississippi River on the east, the county's name may have originated with French riverboatmen of an earlier era who referred to the snags that threatened their boats as "chicots," the teeth of the river. Nourished by the Mississippi and other streams, the incredibly fertile soil would make the Delta one of the most productive agricultural regions in the world.[3] But, as historian Willard Gatewood has pointed out, "The same rivers and bottomlands that nourished the Delta's economy also jeopardized public health. Mosquito-borne malaria was a constant threat to inhabitants; contaminated water spread cholera and dysentery; and the damp climate contributed to a host of respiratory ailments that were a principal cause of death."[4] Frequent flooding menaced those living along the river.[5]

The paradox in the nature of the land was reflected in the people of the region. "In this solitude," an early resident noted, "were found very worthy cultivated people, as well as some very bad characters."[6] The territory quickly developed a reputation for violence and lawlessness. Missionaries who traversed the region in the early nineteenth century were appalled at the conditions they found. A Congregational minister noted, "It is painful to witness the deplorable state of morals in this place. The Sabbath is awfully profaned; idleness, drinking, swearing, and gambling almost universally prevail."[7]

The early white settlers of the region exploited what the historian Walter

Prescott Webb called the "primary windfalls," the wild game, fur-bearing animals, and fish that abounded in the area. But the second generation of white settlers, of which Joel Johnson was a part, was concerned with the "secondary windfalls," the abundant timber and rich land. Their arrival dramatically altered the natural and social landscape of the Delta.[8]

Many of those who came to the Trans-Mississippi frontier envisioned establishing plantations like those in the more settled southeastern states. But settlers arriving in the Delta expecting to find vast open fields ready for the plow would be disappointed. Chicot County's 850-square miles were heavily forested with cane from four- to sixteen-feet-tall growing among the hardwood. Before the fertile soil could produce a crop, it had to be "cleared" of trees and underbrush. Even after the clearing was accomplished, it took years of additional "grubbing" away bushes, clearing stumps, and leveling to make a field smooth.[9]

The first generation of planters was often able to clear only enough land to raise a small crop. The more land that they could clear, the larger the crop that they could plant, and the greater their potential profits. In the years to come, those profits, and the power and prestige that accompanied them, would be derived from three major sources—ownership of large tracts of rich Delta land, ownership of black slaves to provide a reliable source of cheap labor, and the production of a cash crop. In this part of the Delta, that crop was cotton.[10]

In 1830 Chicot County's population stood at only 1,165. Of that number, 888 (76.2 percent) were free whites, 270 (23.2 percent) were black slaves, and 7 (.6 percent) were free persons of color. The percentage of slaves was considerably higher than it was in the state as a whole but significantly lower than in the neighboring slave states of Mississippi and Louisiana. Slaveowners were only a small minority of the county's population, and those who did own slaves owned only a few. Census records indicate that only two men in the county owned twenty slaves, the generally accepted minimum number to be considered a "planter." When Joel Johnson arrived in the county in 1831, his twenty-three slaves made him the largest slaveowner in the county.[11]

Johnson purchased a tract of land southeast of Old River Lake (present-day Lake Chicot) just above a large oxbow curve in the river called American Bend. The plantation that he developed there was named Lakeport after a nearby steamboat landing. By 1840 Johnson owned 1,970 acres of Chicot

County land with an assessed value, including improvements, of $16,250. In addition he owned fifty-five slaves with an assessed value of $27,500, eleven horses and mares, twelve mules, and fifty head of cattle. The total taxable value of his property was $45,870.[12]

In addition to his growing holdings in land and slaves, Joel had powerful political connections. The Johnsons became an integral part of the state's Jacksonian Democratic machine, which also included the Conway and Sevier families. This group, known as "the Family" or "the Dynasty," dominated Arkansas politics until the Civil War. In 1840 one of Joel's brothers (Richard Mentor) was vice president of the United States, and another (Benjamin) was a federal judge for the district of Arkansas. His niece's husband, Ambrose Sevier, was a U. S. senator, and Sevier's first cousin, James Conway, was the governor of the state. By 1845 the state Democratic Central Committee included two Conways and two Johnsons.[13]

At the time of his death in June 1846, Joel Johnson owned over 3,700 acres of delta land and ninety-five slaves. His estate was divided among his six surviving children, with his eldest son, Lycurgus Leonidas Johnson, receiving the largest share. Lycurgus was twenty-eight years old when his father died. Born in March 1818 in Scott County, Kentucky, he joined his father in the Arkansas Delta in the mid-1830s and acquired land just south of his father's Lakeport holdings. In January 1842 Lycurgus married Lydia Taylor. The union produced twelve children, four of whom died before reaching age three.[14]

To the casual observer, Chicot County at the time of Joel Johnson's death might have seemed little different from the wilderness frontier he had found there fifteen years before. Crude roads had begun to replace the "bridle paths" that linked the county's settlements, and as early as 1835 a contract had been let to clear a road all the way to the territorial capital in Little Rock. But dense forests and thick undergrowth still covered much of the county, making travel difficult. An early resident recalled that, as late as 1847, it was common to see men and women traveling by horseback through the forests, the young ladies riding side-saddle, accompanied by an attendant and carrying their wardrobes in a "carpet-bag" suspended from the saddle's right horn.[15] When it rained, overland travel became virtually impossible. After one downpour in February 1849, a resident noted in his journal, "[T]his afternoon I have been to town with Richard[.] [W]e had to ride as much as a mile in water from six inches to four feet deep."[16]

The county seat, Columbia, was still a crude village. "It has some four or five stores[,] a tavern or two and some thirty or forty houses," a citizen of the county wrote in December 1848. "It has no Church and no Court house if we except an old dilapidated building which is used for one."[17] Malaria and cholera were still common, especially in the "fever season" of summer and early fall. Steamboats remained the county's principal link to the outside world.[18]

Despite these primitive conditions, slavery continued to grow in the county. Between 1840 and 1850, the white population increased by a net total of only 7 people, while the slave population increased by 1,286. Blacks outnumbered whites in the county by almost 4 to 1, and Chicot surpassed every other county in the state in proportion of slaves to total population. Sixty men now owned 20 or more slaves, and eight owned over a 100.[19]

In 1850 Chicot County planters produced 12,192 bales of cotton, almost one-fifth of the state total, and the cash value of county farms reached $1,324,607. While a legal challenge kept Joel's estate tied up in litigation for several years, the 1850 census still showed Lycurgus with 2,850 acres and 95 slaves. Those holdings and his father's estate, which Lycurgus administered, combined to produce 742 bales of cotton, 7,000 bushels of corn, and 400 bushels of sweet potatoes, in addition to Irish potatoes, peas, beans, wool, and honey.[20]

Lycurgus was also active in politics and retained his family's powerful political alliances. In 1851 he joined several other prominent Chicot County planters as the county's representatives to the Democratic party's state convention in Little Rock. The delegation chose Lycurgus to be its secretary, and his nearest neighbor, Elisha Worthington, was elected chairman.[21]

The group affirmed the party's commitment to the principles of strict construction of the Constitution and its opposition to rechartering the Bank of the United States, protective tariffs, and internal improvements that were not "clearly national and necessary to the exercise of some expressly delegated power." It also reaffirmed its opposition to any attempt by Congress to interfere with slavery in the territories.[22]

Lycurgus's first cousin, Robert Ward Johnson, was elected to Congress in 1846 and remained there until 1853 when he became a U. S. senator. In Congress, Robert Johnson became an ardent supporter of John C. Calhoun and an outspoken proponent of southern rights. It is unclear whether

Lycurgus Johnson shared his cousin's extreme opinions, although the Johnsons were known to be associated with the secession wing of the Democratic Party.[23]

But while politics was the main concern for many of the Johnsons, Lycurgus Johnson was more interested in developing his plantation. The fortunes of Chicot County planters rose and fell with the price of cotton. In the mid-1840s, cotton prices declined and remained low through the mid-1850s. Lycurgus Johnson's holdings in land and slaves increased only marginally during the years from 1850 to 1856, but events of the following four years vaulted him to the very pinnacle of wealth and power in the Delta. In 1856 the price of cotton rose by over 3¢ per pound to 12.4¢, the highest level since 1838. Prices for the years 1856–1860 averaged 11.4¢ per pound.[24] "If cotton will only hold present prices for five years," one state newspaper proclaimed in May 1857, "Arkansas planters will be as rich as cream a foot thick."[25]

For Lycurgus Johnson, that prediction was coming true. Improvements to the levee system lessened the threat of overflows and dramatically increased the value of plantations near the river. In May 1857 a favorable legal settlement enabled Joel's widow and his children to gain complete control of his estate. Lycurgus was able to add the Lakeport portion of the estate to his holdings. In December 1858 Lycurgus capped off a very profitable year by purchasing 40 acres of land from the widow of former U.S. senator Chester Ashley for a thousand dollars. In May 1859 he purchased an additional 80 acres of land, and in October he bought out his brother John's rights and title to 1,680 acres of land allotted to him in the partition of the previous year.[26]

The large-scale transactions involving ownership of the land were accompanied by dramatic changes in the physical appearance of the Lakeport area. These changes were the result of both natural and man-made occurrences. In the quarter of a century following Joel's arrival in the Delta, the narrow neck of land at American Bend in the river directly east of Lakeport had dwindled from three miles in width to less than one mile. Timber no longer grew there, and during periods of high water, the river flowed over this narrow stretch almost unimpeded.[27]

During a severe flood in 1858, the Mississippi abandoned its previous path and swept across the bend, creating a new channel. The current, which had previously flowed through the bend at a leisurely rate, dramatically increased in speed as it passed through the cut-off, slicing away acres of land on both sides. Steamboats attempting to move upstream in the new channel were often unable to do so.[28]

Lycurgus Johnson was transforming the Delta landscape in other ways. In 1858 he began the construction of a large plantation house at Lakeport. The house, built in a modified Greek Revival style, was an imposing two-story, L-shaped structure containing seventeen rooms and measuring sixty-six feet long and forty-four feet wide. Constructed largely of cypress and situated amid the surrounding cotton fields, the mansion faced east toward the river. A two-story portico with a triangular pediment gable and centered rose windows graced the front of the structure along the base of the "L." Tapered white columns supported both levels of the portico.[29]

The house was built on a slight elevation in the terrain, and the first floor was set four feet above the grade for protection against flooding. Entry was gained through eleven-foot-high wood paneled doors flanked by glass side-lights into a large central entry hall measuring over twenty-six feet long and almost sixteen feet wide. An elaborate ceiling rosette, from which a chandelier hung, adorned the fourteen-foot high ceiling, and a decorative painted cloth covered the floor. The hallway was large enough to accommodate parties and dancing. The interior of the house was adorned with large portraits of Lycurgus and Lydia Johnson encased in elaborate plaster frames.[30]

The Lakeport plantation house was a showplace of the state's "cotton aristocracy," and Lycurgus Johnson staffed it accordingly. He purchased house servants to attend to the family's personal needs and hired a tutor for his children. The tutor, Nancy Sherrard from Steubenville, Ohio, later recalled:

> That summer of 1860 Mr. Sayre, of Lexington, finding that I was not engaged in any school duties, recommended me to Mr. Lycurgus Johnson, a wealthy planter of Lake Port, Arkansas, who wished a private instructor for his children. Miss Martha Torrance, of New Alexandria, Pa., went with me, and she taught two children in the family of Mrs. Governor [Julia] Johnson, one mile distant. I taught four children, three girls and one boy.

Sherrard also noted, "In the family of Mr. Johnson there were seven or eight house servants. He had a well-trained dining room servant, whom he had bought a year before, who was valued at $1,700. Mr. Johnson had bought him, his wife, and a child three years old, for the sum of $3,000."[31]

By 1860 Lycurgus Johnson was one of the wealthiest men in the Delta.

The exact extent of his land holdings is difficult to determine. The federal agriculture census for 1860 lists him with 1,300 improved acres of land and 1,400 unimproved acres. Nancy Sherrard estimated that the plantation consisted of 2,000 acres, but Chicot County tax records for 1860 list Johnson's acreage at 4,475, a figure that is more easily reconciled with his acquisitions of the last years of the decade. County tax records for the years 1861 through 1863 consistently place his acreage at between 4,493 and 4,633.[32]

Sherrard noted that Johnson owned 150 slaves. This is very close to the federal slave census figure for 1860, which listed him with 155 slaves. The total made Lycurgus Johnson the fifth largest slaveholder in Chicot County and one of only sixty-six in the state who owned one hundred or more slaves. In fact, less than 3 percent of southern slaveowners in 1860 owned fifty or more slaves, and only about three thousand families in the entire South owned over one hundred slaves.[33]

Sherrard further noted, "That summer of 1860 they had raised twelve hundred acres of cotton and three hundred acres of corn."[34] Agricultural census records credit Johnson with producing over thirteen hundred bales of cotton and ten thousand bushels of corn in that year. Only five planters in the county produced more cotton, and only two produced more corn. The Lakeport plantation also produced two hundred bushels of sweet potatoes and five hundred pounds of butter. The farm contained thirty horses, fifty-five asses and mules, sixteen milk cows, thirty working oxen, thirty-five other cattle, forty sheep, and fifty swine. The value of animals slaughtered was $1,000. Farm implements were valued at $5,000, and the total cash value of the farm was placed at $72,686. Chicot County tax records placed the total value of Lycurgus Johnson's taxable property at $204,850.[35]

Johnson's prosperity reflected that of the county. Between 1850 and 1860 the number of improved acres had risen from 29,886 to 66,423. The yield of corn was 329,941 bushels, an increase of over a hundred thousand bushels from a decade earlier. Cotton production had more than tripled to a total of 40,948 bales, and the county's nine thousand bushels of rice was the highest in the state. The value of livestock and farm implements had also tripled, and the total cash value of farms had increased to over $4.3 million.

Agricultural production was up dramatically statewide, and signs of economic development were also beginning to appear in other areas. By 1860 manufactured items were valued at almost three million dollars. After a slow and clumsy beginning, Arkansas seemed to be on the verge of a promising economic future.[36]

If the state's future was bright, Lycurgus Johnson's was brilliant. A planter living near Old River Lake had written in 1854 that "after the heavy masses of vegetation are once removed from the surface, and the population comfortably quartered in good houses, and bring to their enjoyment and use the means that nature so lavishly furnishes from a rich soil," Chicot County residents would experience "[what] may be termed *good generous living*."[37]

By 1860 that prediction seemed to have come to pass. Looking back on the period in later years, a northern traveler recalled:

> Chicot County in ante-bellum times was the richest, fairest and most productive county in the state. Old River lake, a beautiful sheet of water in the shape of a horse-shoe, eighteen miles in length and about a mile in width, is lined on either side with plantations entirely above overflow, which . . . were like a continuous garden all under cultivation, raising a bale of cotton to the acre, with elegant houses, negro quarters, stables, etc. Lake Village, the county seat, was a prosperous village on the bank of the lake, at its head or toe of the horse-shoe, and from this point you could see eight or ten miles down on either side of the lake, take in at a glance twenty or thirty large plantations, and in the distance the river and steamboats. It was indeed the most beautiful spot for a home I have ever seen in any country, and as rich as beautiful. Corn, cotton, and fruit of every variety grew in luxuriance.[38]

In this firmament, Lycurgus Johnson's star shone brightly. At age forty-two, he was one of the wealthiest men in the state, owning thousands of acres of some of the best farm land in the world and over 150 slaves to make that land produce abundantly. His family was in good health and enjoyed as luxurious a lifestyle as the frontier state could offer. His magnificent new house was the envy of the Arkansas Delta. He was truly able to enjoy "good generous living." But lying at the very core of that good life, at the heart of his wealth and power, were the seeds of its dissolution. Black slavery, which formed the foundation upon which the region's economic and social systems were built, brought on the great war which transformed both forever.

In February 1860 the editor of the *Arkansas State Gazette* opined, "[I]t is our belief that the American Union stands on a firmer foundation than ever before . . . The union of States is cemented by a community of interests, which will forever operate as a natural check to secession and dissolution . . . Therefore, we may assure ourselves that the Union is not in danger."[39] At the time the editor made that statement, Lycurgus Johnson might well have been reflecting on the good fortune that the preceding decade had brought him and pondering an even brighter future. Cotton prices were high and the previous year's harvest had been abundant. As Johnson's economic status continued to grow, so did the size of his family. In July of the new year, a tenth child was born to Lycurgus and Lydia, a girl named after Lycurgus's eldest sister. But by the time Julia Johnson arrived in Chicot County, events and forces were already in motion that would undermine the editor's optimism and dramatically alter the future of Lakeport plantation, Chicot County, and the nation.[40]

At the same time that Lycurgus Johnson's personal family was growing, his political "Family" was entering a period of crisis. Two of the dynasty's patriarchs, Gov. Elias Conway and U. S. senator Robert W. Johnson, were leaving office. Robert Johnson had chosen not to seek another term in the U. S. Senate, and Conway was prevented by the state constitution from running for a third four-year term as governor. The Family managed to secure the gubernatorial nomination for Lycurgus' first cousin (and Robert Ward's younger brother), Richard H. Johnson, the editor of the Family organ, the *Little Rock True Democrat.* But an insurgent group of Democrats led by the fiery Thomas Hindman broke away and nominated a rival candidate, Henry Rector, for governor. The insurgents drew strength from other disgruntled Democrats and former Whigs who had long chafed under the Dynasty's domination.[41]

When the election was held on August 6, the Family suffered a devastating defeat. Rector defeated Johnson by almost three thousand votes, and both Hindman and fellow insurgent Edward W. Gantt were elected to Congress. The shock wave from the election shook the state's political establishment to its core. But before the significance of the state election could be fully realized, national political developments took center stage.[42]

The national Democratic party was also rent by dissension in 1860. When two separate national party conventions failed to adopt a platform guaranteeing the protection of slavery, the party splintered into northern and southern wings. In June northern Democrats nominated Stephen A. Douglas of Illinois for president, while southern Democrats, meeting separately, chose

Kentuckian John C. Breckenridge. Like many southern states, Arkansas sent no delegates to the Republican convention in Chicago, and its candidate, Abraham Lincoln of Illinois, was not a factor in the state election.[43]

The presidential contest in the state was, therefore, a three-way race between Democrats Breckenridge and Douglas, and John Bell, the candidate of the new Constitutional Union Party whose only principal was unconditional support for the Union. Both the Family and the Hindman-Rector insurgents united behind Breckenridge.[44]

In the November election Lincoln carried all eighteen free states and with them a clear majority of the electoral votes, though his popular vote total amounted to only slightly over 39 percent. In Arkansas Breckenridge garnered 27,732 votes, but the two Unionists candidates captured almost as many. Bell won 20,094 votes, and Douglas received 5,227. Ironically, many counties that were considered strongly Unionist gave majorities to Breckenridge, while four of the southeast cotton counties, including Lycurgus Johnson's Chicot County, gave sizable margins to Bell.[45]

Lincoln's election deeply alarmed several deep South states, but most Arkansans adopted a "wait-and-see" approach. On November 24 the moderate *Arkansas State Gazette* reminded its readers that Lincoln was "elected to the Presidency by the majority, and in the manner prescribed by the Constitution," and urged that "[n]o precipitate action be taken."[46]

Arkansas did not rush to join the seven southern states that seceded following Lincoln's election. The most Arkansas secessionists were able to accomplish was the calling of a convention in early March 1861 to *consider* secession. Despite the best efforts of the radical leaders, including a strong speech in favor of secession by Robert W. Johnson, the results were disappointing to southern radicals. The convention voted against secession by a margin of thirty-nine to thirty-five.[47]

The delegates did consent to a popular vote on August 5 to determine whether the majority of Arkansans favored continued cooperation with the Union or secession,[48] and they agreed that the coercion of a seceding state by armed force would "be resisted by Arkansas to the last extremity."[49] This was the Achilles' heel of the Unionists' position. As the delegates left Little Rock for their respective homes, events some eight hundred miles away were beginning to destroy the bonds that bound Arkansas to the federal Union.

The Confederate attack on Fort Sumter in Charleston Harbor on April

12, 1861, and President Lincoln's call for seventy-five thousand troops to suppress the rebellious elements in the seceded states drove most of the remaining Arkansas Unionists into the secessionist camp. On May 6 the state convention reassembled in Little Rock and voted overwhelmingly for secession. The delegates also chose Robert W. Johnson as one of the state's five delegates to the Confederate Congress. He would later represent Arkansas in the Confederate Senate.[50]

In the early stages of the Civil War, Chicot County remained remote from the fighting, and for many life went on much as before. There is no evidence to indicate that Lycurgus Johnson ever served in the armed forces of the Confederacy. Forty-three years old when the war began with a wife and seven children to take care of, he was not subject to the first conscription act of April 1862, which made all white males between eighteen and thirty-five subject to the draft.[51] Though later draft laws extended the age limits, Lycurgus may have been exempted because of the service he rendered to the Confederate war effort. A memorandum on file with the Federal Commissioners of Claims noted that "L. L. Johnson . . . acted as a kind of agent for the C[onfederate] S[tates] Govt. in procuring clothing and supplies for the army." The memorandum further stated that a request had been made "for permission to remove [Confederate] Govt. cotton to his plantation for safety."[52]

Throughout the first two years of the war, Lycurgus managed to hold on to and even increase his property holdings. County tax records for 1861 indicate that his acreage increased slightly as did his number of slaves, though the assessed value of both declined. He also increased his holdings in horses and mules. The same was true of the following year. In 1862 he even purchased 480 additional acres of land from Elisha Worthington for $6,000. His holdings in slaves stood at 120, and his total taxable property remained over $168,000.[53]

But it is highly unlikely that these two years proved profitable for the master of Lakeport. Great pressure was placed on cotton planters to embargo exports of cotton in order to put diplomatic pressure on England and France. In 1862 the Arkansas legislature levied a thirty-dollars-per-bale tax on cotton and limited the amount of land that could be planted in cotton to two acres per hand. Violators risked penalties ranging from five hundred to one thousand dollars. Trading with the enemy was punishable by fines of from one thousand to ten thousand dollars.[54] In the spring of 1862 Confederate authorities in Arkansas, concluding "that all cotton in Arkansas and North Louisiana was in imminent danger of falling into the hands of the enemy," issued an order directing "that all cotton adjacent to the enemy's lines should be burned immediately."[55]

It is unclear whether Lycurgus Johnson observed the embargo, reduced his cotton acreage, or had his cotton seized and burned. A handwritten statement signed by the sheriff and collector of Chicot County indicates that some of Johnson's neighbors were affected by the order. The statement, dated June 28, 1862, reads, "I do hereby certify that I have this day destroyed (by burning) Six (6) Bales cotton weighing Twenty four Hundred (2400.) pounds, the property of Wm H Davies of this county, by order of Major Genl Hindman."[56]

Whether Lycurgus Johnson was directly affected or not, the fears that had given rise to such an order were real. The river that had been the county's lifeblood now became the highway of invasion, and Chicot County's strategic location and its agricultural abundance soon brought the war to Johnson's doorstep. By the end of 1862 Federal gunboats and supply ships were a common sight on the Mississippi River near Lakeport. Both armies foraged in the county, and partisan bands roamed the countryside, taking what they needed from area residents.[57]

In later years Lycurgus Johnson's son, Victor Johnson, recalled his father telling him that in "about 1863 or [186]4" Federal troops came to Lakeport and "confiscated all of the mules, horses, and cattle that were on the property at that time. The officer in charge wanted my father to take a receipt for them but he either lost it or did not take it . . . They left one mule at Mrs. Lydia Johnson's request to haul wood for the children."[58]

Lycurgus Johnson did not resist. Victor noted, "He had . . . a house full of children to look after and to provide for."[59] Records of the Southern Claims Commission reveal that Lycurgus Johnson later filed a claim with the federal government for two hundred head of cattle valued at five thousand dollars, eight mules valued at twelve hundred dollars, and two horses valued at three hundred dollars confiscated by northern troops.[60]

Victor does not say what fate befell Lycurgus Johnson's slaves, but it is clear that Chicot County planters feared the loss of their bondsmen. In late 1862 Elisha Worthington of Sunnyside plantation, the largest slaveowner in the county in 1860, took the majority of his slaves and livestock to Texas. Other county residents sent their slaves to the "interior" at Little Rock or Arkadelphia, sometimes hiring them out to residents of those towns. But these towns proved not to be safe havens either. President Lincoln's Emancipation Proclamation went into effect on January 1, 1863, but it was the presence of Federal soldiers that set the slaves at liberty.[61]

Blacks began to flee the county in large numbers. A resident wrote that "a good many of the negroes have left and are still leaving the County."[62] It is impossible to say with any certainty whether Lycurgus's slaves were freed by Federal troops, sent to safety in the "interior," or simply ran away. But it is clear that there was a dramatic upheaval in the slave community at Lakeport. County tax records for 1863 list Lycurgus with only twenty-four slaves between the ages of five and sixty, a decrease of almost a hundred from the previous year.[63]

Though outnumbered and out-gunned, the Confederates did not concede the county to Union forces. Small Rebel units continued to stage hit-and-run raids on detached Federal units and harassed Union shipping on the Mississippi River. Union forces retaliated, and Chicot County residents were caught in the middle.[64] "We are here worse than 'between the Hawk and Buzzard,'" one county resident remarked in March 1864. "We have federals on the river and out in the country occasionally, then our own soldiers . . . stealing from folks who did not move to Texas . . . and consequently they must be Yanks or Union men. We also have some partisan Rangers who do as they please generally."[65]

The combination of regular military operations, raids, and guerrilla activity seriously depleted the county's reserves of food and supplies. Faced with such shortages, many Delta residents turned to trading with the enemy. As early as March 1863, Gen. Edmund Kirby Smith, Confederate commander in the Trans-Mississippi, was authorizing civilian agents to negotiate the exchange of cotton for supplies. In August Smith attempted to systemize this commerce by establishing the Cotton Bureau.[66]

Lycurgus Johnson was apparently an active participant in this trade. A memorandum in the files of the Southern Claims Commission stated that on February 14, 1864, Johnson sold "rope and bagging to the amount of $1,164.15 for which he received . . . 4656 lbs. of cotton. . ." On March 1, 1864, Johnson traded "12000 pounds of cotton . . . for $3,000 of Federal currency ('Greenbacks') procured for him," and shortly thereafter, the memorandum continued, "L. L. Johnson, Chicot Co. Ark, sold to Maj. Jas. T. Robinson, acting for the Cotton Bureau . . . 424 lbs rope for $63.60 for which he received . . . 252 lbs. of cotton."[67]

Such desperate measures could not rescue the Confederate cause nor could it ameliorate the war's destruction. By the time of the Confederacy's final surrender in the spring of 1865, Chicot county was thoroughly devastated. Returning soldiers found homes and barns destroyed, livestock gone, and fields overgrown with weeds.

Beyond the physical devastation, the Confederacy's defeat meant the end of a way of life for residents of Chicot County. The former slaves rejoiced at their newfound freedom, but for many white residents of the county, the legacy of the war was financial ruin, bitterness, and despair. For both black and white, the end of the war brought a lingering sense of uncertainty about the future. The old forms and relationships had been destroyed by the war, but exactly what new forms would replace them was unclear.

Wealthy planters like Lycurgus Johnson were profoundly affected by the war. Johnson's loss in slaves alone was well over a hundred thousand dollars, to say nothing of the his losses in crops and livestock. County tax records for 1865 make no mention of the pleasure carriage, jewelry, or expensive household furniture that had graced Lakeport before the war.[68]

But while the lives of most planters were radically altered by the war, the planter-elite as a whole survived the war better than their poorer neighbors. For all of their losses, the planters still controlled the land. Chicot County freedmen controlled the other major part of the economic equation—labor—and to secure that labor, Chicot County planters now had to negotiate contracts. Many freedmen, devoid of money or property, had to negotiate contracts with their former masters or other area planters. A federal agency, the Freedmen's Bureau, was given the task of supervising the letting and carrying out of these contracts.[69]

In the months following the end of the war, a wide variety of arrangements between planters and laborers emerged. Some planters paid their workers cash wages, others a share of the crop. At Lakeport, Lycurgus Johnson utilized both systems.[70]

Cotton prices were high in 1866, and good weather and a bountiful harvest might have gone a long way toward rescuing the planters from their economic distress. Similarly, with demand for labor great, Delta freedmen might have established an economic foothold that would have put them on a path to some degree of economic independence. But it was not to be. All the vicissitudes of nature seemed to conspire against Chicot County planters and freedmen in 1866 and 1867. Floods, drought, and an infestation of army worms caused crops to fall far short of expectations. High interest rates, a chronic shortage of cash, and declining cotton prices further compounded the problem. The local Freedmen's Bureau agent received numerous complaints that planters were defaulting on their contracts.[71]

While the agricultural crisis threatened the planters' economic survival, the advent of Congressional Reconstruction threatened their political hegemony. Many whites who had served the Confederacy were barred from voting, while Chicot County freedmen were given the vote. In this heavily black majority county, the political implications of this development alarmed area whites. When a well-educated, charismatic mulatto was elected county judge, those fears grew and racial tensions increased. There were scattered instances of violence against the freedmen, but the county avoided much of the political and racial violence that swept the state in 1868.[72]

In December 1871, however, the murder of a prominent black man by a local planter in a Lake Village store touched off a race riot. A detachment of the Governor's Guard and 250 Federal troops were dispatched to Chicot County to restore the peace, but the riot further imperiled the county's fragile economy.[73]

A visitor traveling through the region at the time of the disturbance described the county as a "gloomy place" and noted, "Homes are desolated, buildings going to decay, stock all gone, land grown up in weeds, . . . white men afraid for their lives and getting away as fast as possible, every plantation for sale at a fraction of its former worth, a large portion of the cotton crop still in the field wasting in the wind."[74]

But while many of his neighbors were sinking into economic ruin and despair, Lycurgus Johnson was moving ahead. A new federal bankruptcy law of 1867 made it possible for Johnson and other large planters to gain some relief from their debts. Johnson was also able to successfully negotiate for the services of many of the freedmen who had been his slaves before the war, and he quickly developed a reputation as a fair and honest employer.[75]

Unlike many Chicot County planters, Johnson also developed a good working relationship with the Freedmen's Bureau. The bureau agent in the county was constantly in conflict with planters who were unable or unwilling to adapt to the new labor arrangements. He noted in his records that one was a "[h]ard master during slavery, still the same, one of the old slave holding aristocracy with all their failings, requires the attention of this office." Another was a "[b]ad man and requires watching," a third "a whiskey drinking loafer," a fourth "requires strict watching as he failed to pay his hands last year."[76]

But extant records indicate that as early as 1868, Lycurgus Johnson was corresponding with and acting on requests from the local bureau agent. That agent noted that Lycurgus Johnson "works one hundred hands & does them the fullest justice." He was, the agent concluded, a "*model man* of *Chicot County*."[77] This reputation and the fact that his plantation was ten miles away from the turmoil in Lake Village enabled Lakeport to avoid the racial strife that plagued much of the county in the postwar years.

By 1870 the presence of an experienced work force familiar with the operations at Lakeport helped Johnson establish himself as the leading planter in the county. A gold watch and a pleasure carriage reappeared on his 1870 tax records, and to these was added a piano. Still, Lycurgus Johnson ruled over a greatly reduced realm. In 1860 the thirteen hundred bales of cotton produced at Lakeport had ranked him no higher than fifth among county growers. In 1870 his six hundred bales made him the largest cotton producer in Chicot County.[78]

A chronicler of the county in the postwar period referred to Johnson as "a good citizen and able business man," and "a gentleman of superior education, . . . noted for hospitality, dignity, and social culture." Aside from serving as a local justice of the peace and a brief stint in the Arkansas House of Representatives in 1874, Johnson "passed the latter portion of his life surrounded by the peaceful and beautiful charms of rural life, free from the busy din of city life, and where, surrounded by all the comforts that wealth can provide, he lived happily and contently until he reached his fifty-eighth year."[79]

On the occasion of his death on August 1, 1876, an anonymous newspaper writer noted:

> In the death of this good man the county and the state have suffered an irreparable loss. His greatest worth was in his noble example. He was a

> quiet, modest and unobtrusive gentleman; always consulted with marked respect, knowing that his counsels were pure and honest and of the most unselfish character. It will not be an exaggeration to say that a better man never resided in the state. His whole aim in life seemed to be to perfect the happiness of his family, and promote the best interests of his friends. His kindness, hospitality and social virtues will long be remembered. He was a most exemplary father and husband, and as a citizen admired by all who knew him. He bore his sufferings with patience—being resigned to the will of God and in the full faith of the gospel, calmly resigned his spirit to his Maker.[80]

When Lycurgus Leonidas Johnson first came to Chicot County to join his father in the 1830s, the Delta was still a frontier wilderness. During the course of his life, he watched it develop into a burgeoning empire of cotton and slavery and saw that empire crushed by an invading army that marched under the same flag his forebears had served with honor and distinction. He amassed great wealth and saw it greatly depreciated by war and emancipation. He rejoiced at the births of his twelve children and grieved at the early death of five. Evidence indicates that he treated his black workers, both as slaves and later as free men, with a fairness that impressed those around him, even a skeptical Freedmen's Bureau agent who was not otherwise inclined to praise Delta planters.

What separated Johnson from many of his peers was his ability to accept his defeats, to adjust his worldview and adapt his practices to conform to new realities, to maintain his dignity and basic decency, and to move on. His greatest accomplishment may have been that he did not remain, in the words of the local Freedmen's Bureau agent, "still the same, one of the old slave holding aristocracy with all their failings."

Today Lycurgus Johnson's magnificent plantation house, though empty and in decline, still stands at the center of a large agricultural operation, towering over the surrounding fields. And the plantation that he and his father created still produces cotton, as it has every year for over 150 years. In his Nobel Prize address, William Faulkner stated his belief "that man will not merely endure: he will prevail."[81] Lycurgus Leonidas Johnson prevailed, not merely by enduring the far-reaching changes in the Arkansas Delta, but by accepting and adapting to them. For him, Faulkner's words were a fitting epitaph.

"I Go To Set the Captives Free": The Activism of Richard Harvey Cain, Nationalist Churchman and Reconstruction-Era Leader

Bernard E. Powers Jr.

Richard Harvey Cain was an unusually skillful, energetic, and accomplished African American leader in antebellum and post–Civil War America. During his lifetime he was active in the North and South and was primarily known through his labors as a preacher and later bishop in the African Methodist Episcopal Church. Cain was also an abolitionist and further distinguished himself in the postwar years as a newspaper editor, state legislator, and congressman from South Carolina. In 1864 even before he reached the most productive phase of his activist career, one observer concluded that "this eloquent Divine is a worthy representative of our race . . . upon the shoulders of such men rests the redemption of our people." In another testament to his great influence, Cain's friend, the far more well-known activist Rev. Henry Highland Garnet, described him as a "distinguished" man whose forceful name "is as a hundred-pound parrot gun in the Church." Because much of what he wrote has been lost, Cain has fallen into relative obscurity compared to more famous contemporaries such as Garnet and Martin R. Delany with whom he shared organizational affiliations and a common black nationalist ideology.[1] In general little is known about the antebellum activities of black Reconstruction leaders who were formerly free. Richard Cain is a rare exception. His life affords a unique opportunity to examine the way his antebellum philosophy and activism shaped his political and community leadership in the Civil War and early Reconstruction South.

Richard Harvey Cain was born a free black in Greenbrier County, Virginia, on April 12, 1825, and he grew to maturity in Ohio after his parents relocated to Portsmouth, Gallipolis, and Cincinnati in the early 1830s. As a young man he worked on Ohio River steamboats. While living in

Hannibal, Missouri, he was licensed to preach in the Methodist church in 1844, but disenchantment with that denomination led Cain to join the African Methodist Episcopal (AME) Church. It was somewhere in "the northwest" that Cain caught the attention of AME Bishop Daniel Payne who described him as "a young man of great uncultivated talents, but rude and unpolished." In 1857 or 1858 Payne appointed him to begin a course of study in the Indiana conference of the church. His first pastoral appointment was to a congregation in Muscatine, Iowa. After the death of his wife in late 1859 or 1860, Bishop Payne sent Cain to Wilberforce University to further his studies, and he remained there until 1861 when he became pastor of Bridge Street Church in Brooklyn, New York. In May 1863 he established the Fleet Street AME church also in Brooklyn, where he remained pastor through the Civil War.[2]

Richard Cain defined his ministerial charge broadly and became involved in some of the most important and even controversial social uplift and antislavery efforts of the 1850s. In 1853 the Rochester National Negro Convention endorsed proposals made by Frederick Douglass and James McCune Smith calling for the creation of the National Council to promote African American interests. As initially planned the council was to be a constituent body with representation from ten states. Its purpose was to reduce African American dependence on whites by promoting the institutional development of the black community. Specific national committees were created to establish a manual labor school, coordinate business affairs, develop a black newspaper, and circumvent the white criminal justice system by the establishment of dispute-resolution commissions.[3]

While ambitious, the Rochester plans were met by an initial enthusiasm as auxiliary councils were established in several cities, primarily in New York and Massachusetts but as far west as Illinois.[4] Richard Cain was involved in the organization of the Illinois State Council; at its January 1854 meeting he served as secretary and also on the rules and constitution committees. At the completion of the meeting, a constitution was written and approved, and two representatives were chosen for the National Council. Impressed with the steps taken to implement the Rochester plans, Cain enthusiastically communicated the progress made in Illinois to the *Frederick Douglass Paper* for publication. The subsequent history of the Illinois Council is unknown, but generally these local efforts proved unsuccessful, plagued as they were by poor attendance and internal disputes. As a form of organization, the National Council idea was defunct by 1855.[5]

Cain's affiliation with the African Civilization Society yielded more concrete results but immersed him in one of the most controversial issues of the 1850s, the debate over emigration to Africa. African emigration never won more than minority support among African Americans, and it was especially stigmatized after the 1816 appearance of the American Colonization Society. This organization of whites argued for the colonization of free blacks in Africa because it was impossible to assimilate them into American society or to ameliorate the degraded conditions that allegedly existed in their communities. Colonization would bring the additional benefit of promoting Christianity in Africa. Most black leaders rejected this organization and its appeal, predicated as it was on such unflattering stereotypes of black people.[6]

Despite the traditional stigma associated with African emigration, interest in the subject increased during the 1850s as free black life deteriorated in the face of the Fugitive Slave Act and the Dred Scott decision. Beginning in 1854 the famous black nationalist ethnographer Martin R. Delany organized a series of emigration conventions, and in 1858 he arranged the Niger Valley Exploring Party to journey to this part of Africa. Simultaneously the African Civilization Society was organized in 1858 with a primarily white constituency and Rev. Henry H. Garnet as president. Both organizations desired the westernization and commercial development of Africa and hoped the production of cotton there would drive slave-grown cotton from the market and force American emancipation. As black nationalists, their ultimate goal was the creation of powerful independent nations in Africa.[7] In 1859 and 1860 Robert Campbell, a Philadelphia teacher with ties to the African Civilization Society, joined Martin Delany's Niger Valley Exploring Party and journeyed to Yorubaland, West Africa, where treaties were signed with local leaders providing for the emigration and settlement of African Americans.[8]

By 1861 Delany desired a closer relationship with the African Civilization Society, and the organization was interested in working with a man of his prestige. But Delany's black nationalist principles made him apprehensive of an organization controlled by whites, some of whom had ties to the American Colonization Society. Cognizant of these issues, African Civilization Society leaders met with Delany and other blacks to harmonize their interests.[9] Richard Cain was one of the main participants at the November meeting.

Reverend Cain's interest in Africa and the diaspora equaled that of Delany and Garnet. In a lecture entitled "Manifest Destiny of the African Race," Cain observed that in antiquity "Africa's sons could vie with the most renowned of mortals," and that only in the modern era had they been so oppressed by Europeans and Americans that they were now "without a name, [and] without nationality." The adversities of the modern era were God's way of preparing the race "for the more arduous duties of self-government and self-reliance—qualifications which every nation must have." Cain contended that for Africans to fulfill their manifest destiny, "They must have a country and be the masters of the soil." The race also required a government in which the people "have access to all its functions and enjoy all of its immunities," a government in which the people are safe and free, regardless of race. Finally, Cain argued that African people needed facilities equal to those of all others for "developing the powers of mind which they possess," so that they could become "educators in law, morals, science and art."[10] These black nationalist sentiments—the assumptions upon which they were based and the destiny that they projected for African people—were indistinguishable from those articulated at various times by both Martin Delany and Henry H. Garnet.

At the special November 1861 meeting of the African Civilization Society, Richard Cain was chosen chairman of a committee to reexamine and clarify goals and principles of the society. Other committee members included Martin Delany, the famous abolitionist Rev. James W. C. Pennington, and Robert Hamilton, the editor of the *Weekly Anglo African* newspaper.[11] The committee proposed two major additions to the original constitution. They were designed to more clearly distinguish the African Civilization Society from the American Colonization Society and to identify the empowerment of African people as an unequivocal objective. The first article rejected en masse emigration and encouraged only those with the good character and skills to benefit the African continent. The second article stated that emigration's political objective was to promote "Self-Reliance and Self-Government, on the principle of an African Nationality, the African race being the ruling element of the nation, controlling and directing their affairs." Both additions were adopted.[12]

The modifications to the African Civilization Society constitution brought new support from a group of black clergymen, and Martin Delany joined as one of its vice presidents. Emigration and the Pan-African strategy remained unpalatable for most African Americans. Rev. Richard Cain was undeterred by public sentiment, and his willingness to advocate an unpopular cause demonstrated an independence that characterized his leadership throughout his activist career. When once speaking for the society, he observed "that in presenting the claims of Africa, he would be advocating what was, generally, distasteful to colored people" and that "any other subject would find admirers among his race, but the one, which should, of all others, interest them." He could not understand "why the descendants of African ancestors should despise their father-land, when the Irishman from Cork, the Scotchman, Englishman, and German, all look back to their country with pride." After Cain's presentation, no less a personage than Frederick Douglass, a longstanding opponent of emigration, rose and described Cain's ideas and the African Civilization Society as "pernicious and devilish." In his judgment, emigration and the pan-African strategy simply confused people and divided their efforts, which should focus on America, the place where they would win their liberation and attain their greatness.[13]

While the African Civilization Society concentrated on promoting emigration in the late 1850s and early 1860s, this program never moved beyond the initial rapprochement with Martin Delany and others to achieve concrete results in Africa. This disharmony resulted because the Civil War presented new opportunities for the organization to fulfill its domestic agenda: to elevate the conditions of African Americans. Martin Delany is the best example of this change in sentiments. By late 1862 he opted to reorient his pursuit of nationalist goals by urging the federal government to enlist separate regiments of black troops, and he eventually became a recruiting officer for the Union army.[14] The regeneration of Africa would have to wait while the African Civilization Society faced the challenge of working directly with the mass of black Americans now poised on the edge of a new and unprecedented birth of freedom.

During the Civil War, African Americans in New York City showed considerable interest in the plight of southern freedmen; the African Civilization Society encouraged and organized emancipation efforts. Reverend Cain worked tirelessly along with Rev. Henry M. Wilson to arrange a series of meetings in churches around the city to publicize the history and mission of the society to provide freedmen's aid. The first such meeting was held in Cain's own Fleet Street church. The practical effect of the organization's efforts were soon felt as people donated clothing, books, and other items for its campaign to provide relief in southern contraband camps. The society also made arrangements to send copies of the *Weekly Anglo African* and the *A.M.E. Christian Recorder* to black soldiers to keep them informed of news from the home front and to promote literacy.[15]

One of the most important southern initiatives taken by the African Civilization Society during the war years was the establishment of freedmen's schools. Washington, D.C., was the location for the first of these schools, and Richard Cain, the society's assistant superintendent of schools, was responsible for establishing them. He traveled there in January 1864 to begin the work, accompanied by Mrs. Caroline W. Groves, an experienced teacher. After a series of meetings at three local AME Churches, Cain witnessed the people's enthusiasm for his plans and proclaimed them "ripe for our work of opening colored schools with colored teachers."[16] On January 25 the first society-sponsored school opened in the district in a hall rented from Union Bethel AME Church. Mrs. Caroline Groves was the principal; within ten days the enrollment grew to eighty students. Two months later three society schools operated with eight teachers, serving almost four hundred students. By the end of the war the society teacher corps grew to twenty-four, and they served in ten day-and-night schools with about one thousand students. The largest of the schools, with over two hundred students, was in Washington, but the society provided additional schools in Alexandria, Georgetown, and Frederick, Maryland. As funds became available the plan was to establish other schools further south. While in the Washington area Reverend Cain started auxiliaries of the African Civilization Society and by April 1864, four existed. They assisted in the educational work by raising money and providing books and other materials; in one case an auxiliary purchased land and constructed a schoolhouse.[17]

The educational efforts of the African Civilization Society were philosophically underpinned by black nationalist ideas. In reviewing the society's work, Rev. Henry Wilson, secretary of the organization, contended, "There is work to be done for the elevation of our people which none but colored men and women can perform." To that end its emphasis was to send black teachers to work among the freedmen. This was not a rejection of white assistance because, as he pointed out, "Our white friends are doing a good work . . . but they cannot do the work which we are called to perform."[18]

The African Civilization Society program of freedmen's education was successful, and Cain's work was generally well received, but there were still detractors. This was especially the case among the more assimilationist black leaders. For instance, well-known black abolitionists George Downing and Charles Lenox Remond declared Cain "the tool of Colonizationists," who had been used "to dupe the colored people of the District [of Columbia]," because he introduced the African Civilization Society there. They also criticized "the propriety of Colored Churches and Colored Schools; intimating that more harm had resulted to the colored people by their separate organization than good." These criticisms of Reverend Cain were moreover an attack on the fundamental assumptions motivating all black nationalists: that African people had a distinct cultural identity and ought to organize among themselves to promote their interests as a people. Responding to his critics, Cain concluded that "the 'common people' are more wise than the would-be leaders. They comprehend the fact that their elevation depends more upon their own efforts than anything else." By contrast, Cain asserted too many leaders "would have them [blacks] stand still and let others think for them, let others direct their destiny." This was most unfortunate because without independent thought and action, African Americans would be deprived of both "honor and nationality."[19]

Another major effort mounted by Cain during the Civil War years to expand the educational infrastructure of the black community occurred in conjunction with Wilberforce University. Wilberforce was created in 1856 by the northern Methodists for the education of African American students. It flourished until mid-1862 when war-related financial problems forced many students to leave the school and the school closed its doors for the next year. Cain was enrolled at the school in 1861 when financial exigencies abruptly ended his education. Wilberforce was in debt for ten thousand dollars, and the Methodists were intent on selling it when Bishop Payne, perhaps African Methodism's most scholarly bishop, agreed to purchase the property located near Xenia, Ohio.[20] Rev. Richard Cain and Rev. Lewis Woodson, both black nationalist activists, formulated fund raising campaigns to secure the necessary monies. Cain's plan was promoted most aggressively through the *A.M.E. Christian Recorder* and won the special favor of Bishop Payne because of its mass orientation. Payne also called for a series of "Grand Festivals" held between December 25, 1863, and January 1, 1864, in cities with substantial black communities as part of the fund raising campaign.

Several of the AME churches, including Cain's own Fleet Street church, collaborated to hold special fund raising programs on January 1, 1864, to link the destiny of Wilberforce with the emancipation of African Americans in the South. These efforts were successful; by the fall of 1863 the school reopened its doors. In recognition of his labors for Wilberforce, Reverend Cain was elected to the school's board of trustees, and by late 1864 the school debt was reduced by one-half. [21]

That Richard Cain devoted so much of his energy to make the Wilberforce acquisition successful is understandable because the school embodied important aspects of his own black nationalist ideology. He believed that "every nationality on this continent have [*sic*] an institution for the instruction of their people, controlled and managed by themselves," except blacks. Cain argued that such a void could exist only because of the African Americans' unfortunate lack of "national pride." Then in words similar to those written by David Walker in his famous 1829 *Appeal,* Reverend Cain postulated the need for "an institution where we can have a *faculty of distinguished colored gentlemen* teaching all the sciences, and elaborating systems, and theories of scientific investigation, producing something new, improving by research on old systems." Wilberforce was necessary because racial prejudice amounting to a pervasive "*Negrophobia*" was found in most white schools, causing Cain to conclude that "it is crucifixion to our children to send them to them." Finally, as the South was being daily transformed by the progress of the war, Cain saw the increasing need for black teachers, missionaries, preachers and businessmen to work among the freedmen. It was equally essential that these needs be fulfilled by an institution such as Wilberforce, which Reverend Cain believed was destined to become "*the colored people's Institution.*"[22]

Richard Cain was captivated by the unfolding drama of civil war and emancipation and urged northern African Americans to go into the South and assist the freedmen with concrete plans to secure and expand their newly won liberty. Although he had spent time in Washington working with the freedmen, as a wartime pastor in Brooklyn who watched men and women venture into the southern field of labor as early as mid-1863, Cain increasingly felt isolated. When in the spring of 1863 he witnessed the departure of Reverends James D. S. Hall and James Lynch from New York as the first two AME missionaries to South Carolina, he had mixed feelings. Reflecting upon that emotional experience, he recalled: "I shall never forget that hour while reason holds her sway, or memory has a place. As I paced the deck of that noble ship, I felt like a 'lion bound.' If it was only my happy lot to be in that noble band, to share their hardships and partake of their joys. Oh! How consoling it would have been to my panting soul."[23]

Cain's pastoral responsibilities kept him in Brooklyn but failed to dampen his enthusiasm for the freedmen's cause. In fact, even as the war continued, he urged other African American leaders to begin making concrete plans for the freedmen's future. Responding to the proposed October 1864 Syracuse National Convention of Colored Men, Cain warned against meetings that simply passed resolutions. "We want more than resolutions in this crisis," he said. There must also be "movements inaugurated immediately to carry them into operation" because only "more practice and less theory will meet our present necessity." Cain wanted the upcoming meeting to consider "the proper training of the youth" and to include classical training and manual skills education, so that they learned "honest *industry* will bring its reward."[24]

Reverend Cain also understood that land ownership was essential to secure the safety and destiny of African Americans. He therefore stressed the formulation of plans whereby African Americans could "possess the *soil,* be the owners of lands, and become independent, or rather self-dependent." To that end, Cain suggested that the convention form a company to purchase land in the South or southwest from the federal government; this land could then be subdivided and resold to poor black families. Reverend Cain attended the Syracuse convention as part of the Brooklyn delegation, but at the close of the three-day meeting he must have departed frustrated with the results. Much of his energy was spent along with Rev. Henry Highland Garnet defending the work of the African Civilization Society from delegates like George Downing who continued to criticize them as the dupes of the colonizationists. The convention resolutions proclaimed sympathy for the freedmen, vowed to work on their behalf, and recommended that African Americans settle on public lands. The National Equal Rights League was formed. Beyond this formation, the specific plans Cain proposed in advance of the meeting failed to materialize. This failure was why during one session he declared, "The interest of the freedmen had not been sufficiently considered by this Convention," a point he juxtaposed with the African Civilization

Society, which in his judgment was doing "a noble part in caring for them and their children."[25]

Not long after the Syracuse convention Reverend Cain's aspirations to travel to the South were fulfilled; in early May 1865 he was transferred from the New York conference to South Carolina. Reaching Charleston by way of Savannah and Hilton Head, Cain arrived in the company of James Lynch, an AME missionary in South Carolina since 1863, and other AME clergymen. Their guiding spirit was Bishop Payne. After being driven from the city in the mid-1830s by the stultifying regulation of free black life, Payne described his return to Charleston after three decades as being "led by the triumphant genius of freedom." On May 15, Bishop Payne officially organized the South Carolina Conference of the AME Church. It was widely known that this step was actually reestablishing African Methodism in a city where the church's connection to the 1822 Denmark Vesey slave conspiracy led to its destruction by the white elite. The seriousness and significance of the hour was not lost on Reverend Cain. With the spirit of slavery so obviously ebbing and the symbolism represented by this first AME conference in the state, Reverend Cain's belief that "revolutions do not go backwards" seemed confirmed and he enthusiastically proclaimed, "The new era has dawned."[26]

In the years immediately following the Civil War, black Carolinians transformed their religious lives, as did their counterparts throughout the South, by abandoning the churches that they attended while they were slaves in favor of new ones under their own control. To coordinate the AME cause, Richard Cain was appointed superintendent of missions for South Carolina. Reverend Cain displayed great enthusiasm in discharging his new responsibilities and took an active part in founding churches in Charleston, Sumter, Columbia, Georgetown, and many of the state's more rural precincts.[27] His monumental achievement was supervising and nurturing the growth of Emanuel AME Church, founded in Charleston in 1865. Organized from the remnant of the original African Methodist congregation of Denmark Vesey's era, this congregation became the flagship of African Methodism in the state and grew rapidly. By 1866 the church had over two thousand members and had nearly completed a large and impressive edifice. His great zeal and success in expanding the church was widely recognized. In an address before the Board of Bishops in 1888, a year after Cain's death, a speaker described Cain as "an untiring worker for his church [and] the chief instrument in building up our work in South Carolina."[28]

Even with Cain's skillful leadership, the success of African Methodism was not a foregone conclusion; there were many physical, psychological, financial, and organizational impediments that church missionaries had to overcome. At first the African Methodists also had to contend with competition from the northern Methodists, and their encounters were sometimes quite contentious. Rev. Theodore W. Lewis, the leading Methodist Episcopal missionary in Charleston, attended the first South Carolina Annual Conference of the AME Church. While there Reverend Cain recalled that the white minister "harangued" the black, former southern Methodists "with a tirade of abuse against the African M.E. church, and besought the people to have nothing to do with it." Cain charged that Lewis maligned the church further by claiming that it excluded whites and mulattoes and attempted to intimidate blacks. He and a colleague also claimed the northern Methodists alternatively attempted to purchase the loyalty of black church leaders with financial inducements or threatened them with the loss of their church property to prevent them from joining the African Methodists.[29]

African Methodist Episcopals categorically denied that their denomination excluded members according to race or complexion, but they nevertheless capitalized on its racial origins and character. The story of how the church was born of Richard Allen's refusal to abide racial discrimination in the Methodist church, the struggle of its fledgling northern congregations for survival, and now their mission to redeem the freedmen gave the African Methodists compelling advantages. As a nationalist leader, Richard Cain encouraged African Americans to take charge of their own religious destiny, and he knew that this could never be done by affiliating with the white Methodists. In his judgment, the rapid advance of African Methodism in South Carolina occurred in part because that denomination embodied "the great central and predominating idea of self-government and religious liberty." Furthermore, he contended that those who rejected the entreaties of both northern and southern Methodists to join with the AME showed "powers of discerning between true manhood and a spirit of cringing servility to the old spirit of caste." Cain and African Methodists generally welcomed the opportunity to fully participate in church affairs, to influence policy at every level, and to select their own leaders. They also saw in this racial enterprise a powerful vehicle, the resources of which could also be used to positively transform their lives and uplift the entire race.[30]

African Methodist missionaries were keenly aware of their responsibility for achieving both spiritual and secular goals in the South. While adding souls to the church, Reverend Cain reminded them that "all the good to the race in the future depends on the proper formation of character." Thus, as missionaries they were the guardians of the "moral purity—the intellectual and social development of the race." Raising the moral standards of black communities, eliminating illiteracy, and inculcating the Protestant ethic were issues Cain and others frequently addressed. Particular emphasis was placed on preparing young men and women for futures brighter than any previously known by African Americans. Reverend Cain also stressed the weighty responsibility shouldered by ministers, missionaries, and teachers. They must "by a thorough education, prepare the colored youth for the high duties of a citizen, a merchant, a lawyer, or millionaire."[31]

Cain used a variety of means to promote the social transformation of the black community. As a nationalist, he always encouraged African Americans to think for themselves, and he early on saw the need for a black press, so in mid-1866 he purchased the *South Carolina Leader* newspaper, renamed the *Missionary Record* in April 1868. Under Cain's editorship, which lasted into the 1870s, the *Missionary Record* was the "organ of the Colored People and exponent of their views and desires." It was also "devoted to Christian Graces, Literature, Arts, Sciences, Politics, And the Progress of Civilization."[32]

The *Missionary Record* was the first successful newspaper published in South Carolina by an African American. In an 1866 meeting with church leaders and Freedmen's Bureau officials, Cain pointed out that the newspaper was produced entirely by blacks, all of whom but himself had been slaves and had virtually no knowledge of business before this venture. He was satisfied, as were many in the audience, that this example powerfully demonstrated the potential African Americans had for achievement, once given an opportunity. The newspaper's editor provided practical information, business advertisements, church news, and serialized literature. Routinely he also used this organ to admonish African Americans, to defend the interests and reputation of the race against its detractors, and to provide the latest political news and opinion. His work as an editor was an important adjunct to his direct involvement in politics.[33]

Shortly after the war ended Pres. Andrew Johnson appointed Benjamin Perry as provisional governor of South Carolina to begin implementing his Reconstruction policies. A constitutional convention was convened in September 1865, which reluctantly acquiesced in the abolition of slavery and authorized the legislature to create a "Black Code" to stringently regulate the lives of black Carolinians. By December the legislature met and amended the criminal code to provide for these strictures. Following Governor Perry's admonition that "this is a white man's government, and intended for white men only," the constitutional convention also excluded blacks from voting and holding office.[34]

These developments propelled Cain into the political fray. Writing to the *Christian Recorder,* he denounced these policies as unjust because they placed Americans and their "posterity at the mercy of designing politicians, and political tricksters." Cain contended that these men had fomented "the mightiest rebellion on which the sun has ever shone" and would spare no effort to maintain Democratic heresies such as the Dred Scott decision and to deny political rights to black Carolinians. Recalling the suffering at Andersonville and "the streams of blood shed at Port Hudson by black men for the nation's life against traitors," Cain lamented that if Governor Perry's policy "is to be our reward, then have we bled in vain." Finally he implored northerners to oppose the spirit of despotism which was yet abroad in the South and to thwart its plan to place "the iron yoke of political disability on our necks and our children for generations to come."[35]

When the South Carolina Republican Party was created in Charleston in March 1867, Cain attended the mass meetings and addressed party supporters. Later that year he took an active official role in South Carolina's first statewide Republican Party convention, which began on May 7, 1867, in Charleston. The purpose of this meeting was to create a working organizational structure and to appoint representatives to write a state party platform. Cain was elected a vice president and served on the Committee on Permanent Organization and on the Resolutions Committee. The latter committee crafted resolutions into a draft party platform, calling for the state to promote land ownership amongst the landless, publicly finance education, and abolish corporal punishment and imprisonment for debt. This draft was amended at the July Republican convention sessions and became the basis of the statewide platform.[36]

The 1867 Reconstruction Acts required the former Confederate states to revise their constitutions before they could be readmitted to the Union. Cain was elected to Charleston's interracial delegation to the state constitutional convention where he joined the ranks of men such as William McKinlay, Robert C. DeLarge, Francis L. Cardozo, and Alonzo J. Ransier. All had been part of Charleston's antebellum free black middle class or elite, and each was destined to play an important role in South Carolina's Reconstruction politics. The convention began on January 14, 1868, and Cain proved a vigorous participant who tirelessly advocated the cause of black Carolinians and working class people generally. Given his longstanding black nationalist philosophy, Cain was deeply troubled over the freedmen's unfulfilled aspirations to acquire land; he quickly became their champion and devoted more attention to this issue than to any other at the constitutional convention. Daily he watched the operation of the emerging sharecropping system enrich the landowners, while further impoverishing farm labor and reducing black Carolinians' chance to direct their economic destiny. This is one reason he resolutely, yet unsuccessfully, opposed a request from the convention for military officials to declare a debt moratorium. Cain believed that contracts legitimately made ought to be fulfilled, but also that in the economically troubled postwar years land-poor planters would be forced to sell some of their properties to the freedmen. Without the proposed debt relief, he stood to lose several thousand dollars in land he was then purchasing.[37]

To stimulate the sale of land, Reverend Cain proposed that the convention petition the federal government for a loan of one million dollars from surplus funds he believed to be available from the Freedmen's Bureau. Under his plan this infusion of cash would be used by the state to purchase the largest plantations, subdivide them, and then resell the property to the landless, regardless of race. This plan would eliminate the need for a Freedmen's Bureau, reduce racial animosity rooted in economic conflict, and also demonstrate the capacity of black Carolinians for self-reliance. This resolution was passed overwhelmingly by the convention. Unfortunately, direct communications with Republican senator Henry Wilson of Massachusetts revealed that Congress was unsympathetic to such a proposal and the delegates finally agreed to take a different approach. As a substitute, the constitutional convention now authorized the legislature to create a land commission to help freedmen obtain and keep a homestead. Once a title to a home had been secured, Richard Cain and other delegates wanted to ensure that it would not be lost due to indebtedness. To this end they inserted a homestead exemption clause in the constitution that prevented the sale of a residence and appurtenances on one hundred acres in the countryside and up to the value of two thousand dollars in the city due to debt or court judgment.[38]

Reverend Cain vigorously promoted the unfettered right to vote to further protect the freedmen's interests, but not all black delegates agreed. Men such as Rev. Benjamin F. Randolph from Orangeburg argued that payment of a poll tax should be a precondition for voting to help defray the cost of public education. William McKinlay from Charleston argued that only literate citizens could understand the importance of the ballot and elect competent officials. He advocated that a literacy requirement be instituted beginning in 1878. Cain was not persuaded by any of these arguments and opposed any limitations on voting rights. A man "may not understand a great deal of the knowledge that is derived from books," Cain admitted. He might "not be generally familiar with the ways of the world," but he could tell right from wrong and was entitled to the God-given right of selecting those who rule over him. Enough of the delegates agreed, and in its final form the section on voting rights provided for universal manhood suffrage.[39]

Elections were held in mid-April 1868 for the legislature and statewide offices. The constitution was ratified, and the Republican slate swept into office under the leadership of the new governor, Robert K. Scott, formerly of the Freedmen's Bureau. Generally, black politicians did not aggressively pursue high-profile offices at this time. Of eight statewide executive offices, only one position, secretary of state, was contested by black candidate Francis Cardozo. By contrast, there were many blacks who ran for legislative seats, and Richard Cain was elected as one of Charleston's two state senators.[40] He quickly developed a reputation for outspoken political independence and severe criticism of Republican ineptitude, corruption, and abuse of power.

One of the best examples of Cain's activism is his reaction to the Charleston election of November 10, 1868, and its aftermath. The Republican mayoral contender, Gilbert Pillsbury from Massachusetts, ran on a ticket with equal numbers of black and white alderman candidates. The Democrats, who now called themselves the Citizen's Party, ran Henry Lesesne, a local political leader and attorney, but they included no blacks on their ticket. The campaign was not issue-oriented, but both parties pledged impartial justice, employment opportunity, and honest administration.[41] On the eve of the election to the surprise and chagrin of many, Reverend Cain actively encouraged the two parties to fuse their alderman candidates into a "Citizens' Union Ticket" to promote a spirit of cooperation for the good of the city. Under the arrangement each party could still field a mayoral candidate if it desired. However, Cain had seriously miscalculated the reaction of black Charlestonians to his attempt at statesmanship. He wrote in the columns of his *Missionary Record* that "within the past week we have been the subject of abuse by our own race more bitterly then we ever could have conceived." He was denounced on the streets as a traitor and a Democrat, and those who most bitterly opposed Cain's attempt at nonpartisanship even threatened to murder him and to burn down his home.[42]

Although Cain initially supported Pillsbury in the election, he was not impressed with many of the men on his ticket and thought they merely saw him as a means to secure offices for their own personal benefit. At the very end of the campaign, Reverend Cain seems to have even switched his allegiance to Henry Lesesne.[43] When the votes were counted Pillsbury had won, but only by twenty-two votes. On election day the balloting was marred by violent outbreaks; enough fraud was committed by Republicans to call the electoral results into question, and in a public meeting, Reverend Cain denounced the perpetrators.[44]

The Pillsbury administration would not assume office for six months because the incumbent city council voided the fraudulent election. When D. T. Corbin, the other senator from Charleston, sponsored a bill to legitimize the election results, Cain opposed this as a partisan ploy that he believed would only heighten political tensions in Charleston and further harm the business atmosphere. He favored a new election or a court-ordered solution. On May 1, 1869, a decision by the Court of Common Pleas validated the election results and ordered the incumbents to turn their offices over to the Pillsbury administration which was inaugurated only days later as Charleston's first Republican government.[45]

By 1869 Reconstruction was well underway in South Carolina, and by this time many of its most intractable problems were also evident. In Charleston Gilbert Pillsbury inherited a sluggish economy, a considerable public debt, and very high unemployment. With the Republican ascendancy, throngs of black workers, sometimes as large as six hundred able-bodied men, gathered daily at the city inspector's office and expected employment. As a witness to these scenes, Richard Cain sarcastically observed that "the promises made before election, are hard to be kept. It would require a mint of money, and more work than two such cities as this will require, to give employment to one tenth of the voters who elected Mr. Pillsbury, and his friends. We suggest, therefore, that laborers do not exact too much from . . . the Mayor." Unemployment was troubling enough, but Cain was deeply disturbed by some black workers' emerging dependency on government employment. In response to this, he used the *Missionary Record* to urge three hundred of those who applied for city work to go into the countryside to seek jobs as phosphate miners and in agriculture "where they would make more money and appear to more advantage in society."[46]

Within two weeks of Gilbert Pillsbury's inauguration, the city council lapsed into petty squabbling as councilmen led by Thomas J. Mackey challenged the mayor's authority to dispense patronage and make appointments. During the entire era of Reconstruction, local Republican politics in Charleston were highly factionalized with politicians fighting one another over patronage positions for themselves, friends, and family members. The infighting, which included the boycott of meetings and physical confrontations, also displayed the grossest forms of incivility and lasted for several council sessions. Cain described the scenes as degrading and humiliating because they were perpetrated "by men professing to be Republicans." He was so frustrated at one point that he advised the council, "You should at once resign, and let the people choose those who will adhere to principles of equal justice."[47]

Cain also found deeply disturbing the tendency of these Republican politicians to bestow multiple patronage positions on themselves and their favorites, while so many on the streets were out of work. The politics of patronage, unabated throughout the period, caused considerable conflict within Republican ranks and contributed to its ultimate demise by internally weakening the party.[48]

Reverend Cain promoted working-class interests through state government. He was elected to the state senate in 1868 and became a proponent for the immediate establishment of the land commission as provided in the 1868 constitution. After some delays, the agency was formally organized in March 1869, but its often controversial operations only achieved minimal success. One of the main problems was that Charles Leslie, the first land commissioner, was corrupt. Cain was one of the most severe critics of Leslie's stewardship. He decried Leslie's lack of accountability and his flagrant disregard of proper accounting records, all of which severely limited the ability of the agency to benefit the landless. Despite its great difficulties, the creation of a land commission distinguished South Carolina as the only southern state to use the power of government to promote land ownership by the former slaves.[49]

By 1869 many of South Carolina's black political leaders found their relationship with white Republicans increasingly tense and sometimes acrimonious. One of their main grievances was that white Republicans did not share political power and patronage equitably. Beginning at this time, black Carolinians abandoned their political reticence and demanded that they be given more offices since they comprised the very heart and soul of the Republican Party. As a nationalist activist, Reverend Cain overwhelmingly supported this position. He was especially suspicious of white northern politicians who were "willing that competent colored men should have a share in government," but only in minor and mostly insignificant jobs.[50] Calling for black Carolinians to be more aggressive in the pursuit of office was but the latest of Cain's efforts to fulfill his black nationalist philosophy. The more aggressive posture he and other black leaders adopted yielded concrete results as African Americans were elected and appointed to high-profile positions. As just two examples, in 1870 Charles Leslie, the embattled white head of the land commission, was replaced by Robert DeLarge and in December, Joseph H. Rainey assumed office as South Carolina's and the nation's first black congressman.[51] A new phase of Reconstruction in South Carolina had begun.

Although the political gains of the era would be temporary, much of the success of the period was the direct result of elite leadership provided by men like Richard H. Cain. South Carolina's cadre of black political leaders was disproportionately composed of men who were free before the Civil War. Most of these black leaders were native southerners, but a small number were northerners who entered the South after emancipation; most important, a free status provided them with formative experiences that served them well during Reconstruction. Certainly Cain's matriculation at Wilberforce University, his training and experience as an AME clergyman, and his involvement in northern activist organizations set him apart from most black Carolinians and prepared him for community and political leadership in his adopted state. The fact that African Americans composed the majority of

South Carolina's population ensured them an important role in statecraft. Their influence was not the product of mere numbers alone and owed much to the aggressive leadership of men like Richard Cain. Black nationalist ideology was the touchstone of his political activism; it was the basis for his critique of white Republicans and of his admonition to black leaders to be more demanding. Fundamentally though, Richard Cain was a churchman, and his effort to build the African Methodist Episcopal Church in South Carolina was one of his greatest legacies. By the late 1870s the AME Church had risen to become the second largest black denomination in the state.[52] It not only flourished during Reconstruction but even survived the political declension that followed to become an incubator for the birth of future black leaders and the continued fulfillment of Cain's nationalist philosophy.

“This Dreadful Whirlpool” of Civil War: Edward W. Gantt and the Quest for Distinction

Randy Finley

On January 26, 1861, Edward W. Gantt warned a Washington, Arkansas, secession caucus that “a rapidly expanding monarchical element” of “Black Republican Despotic Northerners” would ultimately destroy a “fraternal Union.” “I believe this Union ought to be dissolved!” he thundered. Within thirty-three months, after bearing arms for the Confederacy and while many still clung to the cause, Gantt turned tail and joined the Union camp. In an October 1863 address to Arkansans, he urged an end to the war and the abolition of slavery. “We ought to end the struggle and submit. We are fairly beaten and ruin approaches us,” he counseled. “Negro slavery has accomplished its mission here,” he prophesied. “Each day makes new graves, new orphans, and new mourners. Each hour flings into this dreadful whirlpool of wrecked hopes, broken fortunes, and anguished hearts,” he lamented.[1]

Gantt began 1861 as a Lincoln-loathing secessionist, but by 1863 he assured the sixteenth president that “my only object is to induce the withdrawal of my state from its allies in rebellion and its reentry into the Federal Union.” In 1860 he owned eight slaves, but by 1866 he headed a local Freedmen’s Bureau post and upheld blacks’ civil and political rights. In 1862 he led Confederate troops into battle in Missouri, but two years later he campaigned in Pennsylvania and New York for the reelection of Abraham Lincoln. Analysis of Edward W. Gantt reveals the ideological tensions and psychological traumas that political leaders confronted in the tumultuous Civil War era.

Throughout his life, Gantt longed to gain recognition, to become one of the “better” men in his community. As a pretender to the southern white elite, he was devoted to duty, but duty became murkier in this age that witnessed the slaughter of six hundred thousand Americans and the emancipation of four million African American slaves. The world that in 1860 seemed so full of promise, so secure, so orderly to Gantt had by 1863 imploded into a world filled with despair, uncertainty, and anxiety. This is the story of how one southern elite responded to the cataclysm of civil war.[2]

Born in 1829 in Hickman County, Tennessee, to John and Nancy Gantt, Edward learned much from his father, who toiled as a teacher, lawyer, and captain of the local militia. In 1846 the family moved to Maury County, Tennessee, where John opened up a law office and labored until his death the next year. Emulating his father, Edward joined the Tennessee bar and established a law office in Williamsport, Tennessee, at mid-century.[3]

Tennesseans focused on national politics in that year when a civil war could have easily erupted. The carefully crafted Missouri Compromise of 1820, which had preserved the Union for three decades, did not apply to the five hundred thousand square miles gained in the Mexican War of 1846. The discovery of gold in California spawned a population "rip-tide" westward which propelled California to seek admission to the Union in 1849. When many southerners demanded that slavery be extended into the new territory, many northerners balked. Congress debated raucously. Senator William H. Seward of New York demanded that "slavery . . . must be abolished, and you and I can and must do it." Such a prospect prompted Sen. John C. Calhoun of South Carolina to respond that prohibition of slavery would tether the South to "poverty, desolation, and wretchedness" and subject southern whites to "the greatest calamity." Secession was in the air.[4]

To fashion a proper response to the burgeoning crisis, members of the South's elite converged in Nashville, Tennessee, on June 3, 1850, to plot the attack. Representatives from nine states—Virginia, South Carolina, Georgia, Mississippi, Texas, Florida, Alabama, Arkansas, and Tennessee—attended. W. F. Cooper, convention secretary, described the assembly as the "talent of the South," and historian Melvin J. White concurs, noting that "it was not an assemblage of young politicians, but of gray-haired Governors, Judges, ex-members of Congress, jurists, and orators of prominence." But at least one molting politician attended. Honing oratorical gifts so necessary for a successful southern leader, Edward Gantt impressed the voters of Maury County so much that they chose him as one of the youngest delegates to the 1850 assembly.[5]

The convention met for nine days, urged extension of the Missouri

Compromise line, and extolled southern rights. But no groundswell for secession arose, causing historian Michael Holt to label the meeting a dud. The boycott by Delaware, Maryland, Kentucky, Missouri, North Carolina, and Louisiana unraveled portentously southern unity. Even those present contentiously bickered among themselves. John J. McRae of Mississippi urged "preservation of the Union" by the "preservation inviolate of the Constitution," while Robert B. Rhett scandalized moderates with his fire-eating scald. "A slave-holding people," he stormed, "must rule themselves or perish." Rhett prophesied the "beginning of a Revolution" and the "grand Drama of the dissolution of the Union." But passage of the Compromise of 1850 chilled such molten rhetoric. Orchestrated by Sen. Henry Clay of Kentucky and Rep. Stephen A. Douglas of Illinois, the piecemeal measure postponed the Union's death knell for at least ten years.[6]

Gantt, a fledging lawyer, participated minimally. The power and dignity of such men as Maury County scions Gideon J. Pillow and William Polk (brother of Pres. James K. Polk), both wealthy slaveholders and large-landed planters, provided Gantt with models to emulate. Here were southern gentlemen who commanded great power and prestige, precisely the kind of figures Gantt longed to become. If the Nashville convention stoked the ambition of Gantt, Tennessee appeared to provide him with no quick access to political and economic power. He knew and loved the South; but he, too, longed to wear a white-vested suit and gain political prominence. He yearned to be a Polk or a Pillow. So he decided, as did thousands of others in the 1850s, to remain in the South, but to journey southwestward. Arkansas beckoned.[7]

The Cotton Kingdom seeped steadily southwestward throughout the early 1800s, and by 1850 the river bottoms of Arkansas experienced economic flush-times. Arkansas's population soared, expanding by 107.5 percent from 1850 to 1860. Emigrants from Tennessee to Arkansas doubled in that decade, causing historian William Lynch to label Arkansas "the child of Tennessee." But Gantt, unlike most Tennesseans, did not stop in the Delta of eastern Arkansas along the Mississippi River. Driven by fears that he could not penetrate the settled eastern elite, he instead trekked to the southwestern corner of the state and settled in Washington, Arkansas, in 1853. Most other emigrants to southwestern Arkansas in the 1850s came from Alabama, Georgia, and Mississippi and gave the region a lower-South bias.[8]

Washington, Arkansas, county seat of Hempstead County, experienced remarkable growth in the 1850s. The county population almost doubled, increasing from 7,672 in 1850 to 13,989 in 1860. The local newspaper in 1854 described the town's "six stores filled with goods of every description, two drug stores, two groceries where all sorts of qualities of liquor are sold, two silversmith shops, two boot and shoe shops, one tin shop, one tailor shop, one gin shop, two cabinet shops, a printing press, no bars, and good hotels." In the editor's view these establishments, along with three churches and three institutions of higher learning, made Washington an ideal place to live.[9]

Gantt knew that he was still in the South in his new home. The local newspaper constantly advertised slave auctions and "Negroes for sale." No less frequent were notices regarding runaway slaves. For example, F. J. Smith of Fulton, Arkansas, offered a $100 reward for his "negro boy, Bob," who had fled in June, had whip marks on his back, and was "copper color, though not of mixed blood." Mules, so important to local farms and plantations, sold from $150 to $175 per head, and often were driven through the town's streets. The weather, ever so volatile yet critical to southern agriculture, was constantly monitored. In June 1854, for example, the *Washington Telegraph* complained that too much rain had kept the crops in a "deplorable condition," yet two months later in August the same paper decried that "everything is parched up, and the very air, what there is of it, comes to our brow like a hot plaster to a sore skin."[10]

But Gantt also knew he had come West, for the southwestern part of the state was much wilder and undeveloped. Citizens had just begun to push for improvements on the Red and Ouachita Rivers. Leaders clamored for railroads in the region to improve commerce and trade. The absence of railroads, unsure river conditions, and poor roads thwarted mail delivery. Deer, turkey, and bear roamed the thickets and forests on the outskirts of town.[11]

Historian Charles Sellers labels lawyers the "shock troops of capitalism," and Gantt indeed peddled the free-enterprise system as he drafted citizens' wills, sued for breach of contract, and filed liens on debts. Advertising in the *Washington Telegraph* for the first time in April 1853, he and partner, Bernard F. Hempstead, promised to "attend to all business confided to their care in the state of Arkansas." Competition among attorneys was fierce; by 1861 over twenty lawyers vied for area cases.[12]

Discontented merely to practice law, Gantt aspired to both legal and political recognition. In May 1853 he announced that he would run for the unexpired term of prosecuting attorney, held by E. A. Warren of the Sixth Judicial District, which consisted of six counties. When the more seasoned Washington politician Orville Jennings also wanted the position, Gantt withdrew. Later that year, he decided to seek the full term of prosecuting attorney of the Sixth Judicial District and defeated two opponents in August 1854. He won reelection in 1856 and 1858. His eloquence and campaign diligence resulted in his victories. In the grueling July and August heat of 1856, for example, he addressed eleven public rallies.[13]

Gantt impressed the area's elite, just as he had dreamed. The *Camden Herald* in 1854 praised his "fidelity and ability and commendable zeal in enforcing the criminal law." Court records reveal a typical array of prosecutions, such as keeping firearms without a license, selling spirits to slaves, enticing away slaves, failing to keep a road district in repair, and Sabbath breaking by playing cards.[14]

With his career and status rising, Gantt wanted a wife. He courted Margaret Reid, the twenty-year-old daughter of Dallas County planter Thomas J. Reid. Moving from North Carolina to Arkansas in 1853, Reid soon owned over thirty slaves valued at $19,500 and possessed over 2,300 acres of land. Marriage into such a family would strengthen Gantt's standing among the men who mattered, so the betrothed wed on October 31, 1855, in the Methodist Episcopal Church, South. The couple had two sons (Reid and Edward W.) and two daughters (Saulie and Cora).[15]

Gantt relished his new life. He acquired a "voluminous library" and by 1858 owned three carriages that eased his travel along the judicial circuit and also favorably impressed any observer. By 1860, he owned eight slaves valued at $7000 and real estate assessed at $10,000. A law clerk and his wife, R. G. and H. F. Patillo, and a young law student, H. W. Wilson, boarded with the Gantts and augmented the household's coffers. These additions reassured others and himself that he was establishing a favorable reputation in his new home. But the Sixth Judicial Circuit prosecuting attorney was only a stepping stone for Gantt. Just as with Abraham Lincoln, the taste for higher office was "in his mouth." He yearned to go to Washington, D.C., as a congressman from Arkansas.[16]

To enter Arkansas politics on a statewide basis demanded obeisance to or opposition to the "Family" or "Dynasty," a nepotistic oligarchy that had dominated Arkansas since 1833. "Family rule had not benefited the state," notes historian Dewey Stokes who cites "irresponsible if not criminal banking programs" and inattention to the infrastructure and school system as the chief complaints against the regime. By 1860, the Dynasty, led by Robert Ward Johnson, faced its most serious challenge from Thomas Hindman and a cadre of opponents. Gantt joined the insurgents and announced his candidacy for congressman from the Second Congressional District.[17]

Once again, Gantt traversed southern Arkansas to gain the Democratic Party's nomination. At the convention in Arkadelphia in April 1860, Hindman supported Gantt and the Family favored Charles Mitchell. Following a disorderly and rancorous meeting, the convention decided to let the voters choose between Gantt and Mitchell in an August election.[18]

Historian James Woods argues that the contest between the Family and the insurgents was not really an election; rather "it was war." Although Hindman kept his distance, Gantt followed his lead rhetorically and denounced the Family for betraying most Arkansans. He insisted that Congress abide by the Dred Scott decision and protect slavery in the territories. Mitchell, an older and less vigorous campaigner, accused Gantt of "compressing the fewest ideas into the greatest amount of words" and characterized him as a "weak, diluted, imitation" of Hindman. On August 6, 1860, Arkansas voters defeated the Dynasty. Gantt received 54 percent of the vote. The people of the Second Congressional District had decided to move Gantt from Washington, Arkansas, to the halls of the nation's capital in Washington, D. C. The prospects for Edward W. Gantt never looked brighter.[19]

The crucial presidential election of 1860 interrupted Gantt's efforts to gain national recognition in Congress. Both the Johnson and Hindman factions in Arkansas supported John C. Breckenridge, the southern Democratic candidate, so Gantt followed Hindman's lead and canvassed the state in support of Breckenridge. Speaking to numerous Breckenridge clubs, he opposed the election of Lincoln, but assured his listeners that the dissolution of the Union was not imminent, even with a Republican victory. The campaign piqued voters' attention, exemplified by a Washington, Arkansas, rally and barbecue attended by over a thousand. Old Whigs and urban-commercial river town dwellers favored John C. Bell, the Constitutional Union candidate, while career Democrats supported Breckenridge. In the final tally from Arkansas, Breckenridge received 28,783 votes; Bell garnered 20,094; and northern Democrat candidate, Stephen A. Douglas, earned 5,227 from Arkansans. It was a different story nationally, however, as Republican Abraham Lincoln was elected with 39.8 percent of the popular vote.[20]

Despite Lincoln's repeated assurances that his election did not portend any menace to the South's peculiar institution, many in the region had serious doubts. Fire-eaters sensed that now was the moment they had dreamed of for the last ten years. From December 10, 1860, to February 1, 1861, seven lower-South states seceded from the Union. Meeting in Montgomery, Alabama, in February 1861, delegates elected Jefferson Davis as the Confederate president. Hindman and Gantt again stumped the state and openly favored secession. The moderate *Arkansas State Gazette* described their addresses before the state legislature on November 24 and 25, 1860, as "ultra inflammatory, bold, unequivocal, and unmistakable in their meaning." Although many in the south and east agreed with the Arkansas secessionists, large blocs of antisecessionism resided in the western and northern sections of the state.[21]

As Gantt crisscrossed the state, he highlighted the cultural conflicts that rocked North and South. Perceiving Yankee imperialism as monarchical, fanatic, and despotic, he insisted that the republic of 1776 was in jeopardy, that the principles the Founding Fathers had bled for—"equality of white men and their capability of self-government"—were in jeopardy. "I believe the Union ought to be dissolved!" he declared. "If the South resists, and I hope and believe she will, I will bring to her all the best energies of my nature, my present, and future hopes and prospects, my life, my all, and laying them upon her altar, offer them up freely in defense of her insulted honor, wounded pride, and priceless freedom." Honor, pride, and freedom, then, were the ideological touchstones for Gantt.[22]

What is most interesting, and unknowable, is whether Gantt really believed these words. Honor, pride, and freedom dripped easily from the lips of many in the nineteenth century, but did he really fear these ideas were at risk and worth dying for? Or was he, ever the effective demagogue, using them merely to fan secessionist sentiment? Was he a Hindman lackey, following the master's lead? Historian James McPherson insists that both northerners and southerners were deeply devoted and committed to their ideologies. An intensive analysis of southern diaries and letters convinced him that Confederates were devoted to securing liberty, independence and self-government, slavery, and white supremacy; maintaining the ideals of 1776; defending their homes; and deflecting Yankee cultural barbarism. At least publicly, Gantt seems to support McPherson's hypothesis.[23]

Although Gantt's interior motives remained clouded, his actions did not. Throughout the early months of 1861 he roamed the state, concentrating on the mountainous northern and western parts of Arkansas where Unionism thrived. When, after the fall of Fort Sumter in April 1861, it became clear that Lincoln would use force to restore the Union, a second Arkansas convention approved secession by a margin of sixty-five to five on May 6, 1861. When word of secession reached a political rally in Washington, Arkansas, the *Washington Telegraph* observed that "one by one the crowd dispersed and an air of sadness settled over our town as if every one felt conscious of some event from which all levity should be banished." Perhaps they pondered what honor, pride, and freedom would cost.[24]

Gantt immediately resigned his congressional seat. He informed Confederate president Davis that "we are invaded, in immense confusion, and need a hand." As his quest for power, prestige, and status continued, he offered his services to the new president and requested a commission as major general.[25]

Although President Davis ignored Gantt's request, the men of southwestern Arkansas mustered in Arkadelphia, formed the 12th Arkansas Infantry Regiment, and elected Gantt as their colonel. The usual soldierly drilling, complaining, more drilling, and more complaining made up the regiment's daily routine. A nineteen-year-old Lockesburg lad David Burton Coulter feared the war would be over before he could enter the fray. He joined Company G of Gantt's regiment. He enjoyed a barbecue that local citizens gave to honor enlisting soldiers and claimed he fought for the "traditions and hospitality of the southern people." However, disease exacted a huge cost to the regiment from its inception. From eighty to one hundred men per day contracted measles, diarrhea, and chills, and Coulter cursed "the scourge of measles" that plagued his comrades. The regiment's sick soared from four to five hundred during October 1861.[26]

Roscoe G. Jennings, regimental surgeon, praised Gantt for diligently requisitioning medicine for the sick men. He also applauded Gantt for refusing to move the men forward until better guns had been procured and for going to New Orleans in September 1861 to personally inspect the new guns.

"Our regiment is splendidly drilled," Jennings crowed, "and surpasses any other I have ever seen." He genuinely admired Gantt and called him an "excellent officer." Jennings observed, "He is extremely popular with his men. He is a man that will succeed at anything, and he has such indomitable energy." When rumors spread that Gantt was to be promoted to brigadier general, Jennings hoped they were true.[27]

The regiment received orders to head for Union City, Kentucky. It marched from Arkadelphia, to Little Rock, to De Vall's Bluff, where it embarked on steamboats to Memphis, Tennessee. The men drilled in Memphis for a fortnight, took on as many supplies as they could, then headed for Kentucky. Lt. David Burton Coulter was not going to miss his fight.[28]

Gantt, too, rejoiced at the prospect of making a greater name for himself on the field of battle. He had drilled his men into shape and had earned their respect. Rumors of his approaching appointment as a brigadier general pleased him. Only criticism by the *Arkansas State Gazette* that his regiment had misbehaved while in Little Rock concerned him. The newspaper held him responsible and used the incident to declare him "incompetent and unfit for military command." Gantt could rationalize the negativism as merely partisanship and could perhaps convince himself that it was the *Gazette's* attempt to get back at him for goading Arkansans into the war. Ever the wary politician, he trusted the citizens of the state would reject this canard.[29]

Gantt and his men had been sent to Kentucky in order to help maintain control of the Mississippi River between St. Louis and Memphis. This two-hundred-and-fifty-mile stretch of the river included the confluence of the Missouri and Ohio Rivers with the Mississippi. A critical intersection where the North would concentrate men and munitions to fan southward, its defense was crucial for the Confederacy in 1861 and 1862.[30]

The 12th Arkansas Infantry Regiment, led by Gantt, saw their first battle on November 7, 1861, at the Battle of Belmont, a "three shack" Missouri hamlet on the Mississippi River. Union commander, Ulysses Grant, attacked and at first drove the Confederates back; then Confederate Leonidas Polk's men repelled the Yankees and forced them back across the river. Gantt's regimental surgeon described the battle as a series of "repeated charges and an alternation of successes and reverses." Although Gantt's men saw no direct action, a nearby bursting shell nearly killed Gantt.[31]

On December 5, 1861, Gantt gained command of an additional

regiment and moved southward to Fort Thompson, a part of the defense of Island Number 10 in the Mississippi River near New Madrid, Missouri. Even though Gantt's new regiment was "imperfectly armed," he immediately peppered his commander, Gen. Leonidas Polk, with requests for munitions and materiel. David Coulter recalled a winter spent building breastworks and scouting the countryside. The discipline and hard work of his fellow Arkansans pleased Gantt, but he lambasted the Missouri militiamen as "wretched, dispirited, half-armed, undisciplined, careless, and inattentive."[32]

General Polk thought Gantt could handle any challenge. He nominated Gantt for a promotion to brigadier general on December 7, 1861, assuring Secretary of War Judah P. Benjamin that Gantt "has more military capacity than any other of those who are in command of his regiment." But Benjamin had decided that promotion required personal knowledge of the candidate's abilities; hence, he ignored Polk's recommendations and vetoed Gantt's advancement. Although Gantt did not know of his rejection, distinction in a military victory now became a prerequisite for the promotion he needed to continue his quest for power, prestige, and status.[33]

Island Number 10 lay in "a double hairpin turn" in the Mississippi River. James McPherson has noted that "as long as the Confederates held this island, no Yankee boats could go down the river." Gantt trusted that his 1,036 infantrymen, 120 pieces of heavy artillery, and 100 cavalrymen could keep the Yankees at bay. Beginning in March 1862, Union commander John Pope bombarded the island; but the Confederates held. He ordered his engineers to chisel a canal through the Missouri-side swamps to bypass the island, and for three weeks his men slopped and chopped their way through the Missouri muck and mud. In a daring raid during a fierce thunderstorm on April 1, 1862, Col. George Roberts and fifty hand-picked men unexpectedly slipped to the Missouri shore and overran Confederate defenses. They destroyed the guns that had protected Island Number 10 and sent rebels scrambling. David Coulter and countless others fled the island that night as they crossed in boats and rafts and then escaped into the surrounding swamps. But Gantt would not abandon his post without orders. Union soldiers cut through to the Tennessee bank of the Mississippi River and engulfed Island Number 10. In a totally untenable position, the Confederates on the island capitulated on April 7, 1862. Seven thousand Rebel soldiers, including three generals, one hundred heavy guns and twenty-four field pieces, seven rifles, "mountains of food supplies," tents to shelter twelve thousand, and "horses and mules beyond number" were captured. One of the three officers who formally surrendered on April 8 at a ceremony at Tiptonville, Tennessee, was Edward W. Gantt. The unthinkable, for Gantt, had occurred.[34]

Union soldiers escorted Gantt and other captured officers to Fort Warren, Massachusetts, a prison for captured southern officers located on an island just outside of Boston. Although a lack of food and clothing plagued the facility at the beginning of the war, the situation had improved by Gantt's incarceration in the spring of 1862. Adequate food, less-crowded cells, and even alcoholic beverages for inmates became mainstays. Prisoners could stroll the island at will after they promised to forego escape attempts.[35]

Although this was no hellish prisoner-of-war camp such as Andersonville, Georgia, the psychological trauma to Gantt must have been immeasurable. Psychologists of the twentieth century have documented the traumas suffered by prisoners-of-war: a strong sense of unreality, vulnerability, helplessness, and impotence flood the hostage. Self-esteem and self-confidence plummet. As a white male of the southern elite, his manhood and identity would have been shattered. All that he had worked for to this point seemed for naught.[36]

On August 27, 1862, Confederates negotiated Gantt's freedom by exchanging five northern second lieutenants for his release, revealing perhaps his perceived importance. Returning to his family in Washington, Arkansas, both Gantt and local friends remained confident that an appointment as an officer to another regiment was imminent. As early as February 1862 the *Washington Telegraph* refused to condemn Gantt for any military losses. Gantt awaited word from the Confederate capital of his new assignment. Neighbors bolstered his spirits. His hometown newspaper continued to sing his praises as a man of "great energy and character, devoted to his military duties." In a public speech to a local audience on November 26, 1862, Gantt defended his leadership in Missouri. Once again, the local newspaper agreed that Gantt "had behaved with energy and gallantry, and in all respects as become a patriotic soldier." Such praise from the editor and fellow citizens must have boosted his bruised ego. Still he waited for his appointment. It never came.[37]

It is unclear why Confederate leaders refused to reappoint Gantt. He had been accused of flirtations with the wife of a fellow officer, and perhaps some power struggle with his colleague spawned his rejection. Roscoe Jennings,

Gantt's regimental surgeon, wrote in letters to his brother about Gantt's "womanizing" and possibly there were other powerful men offended by his flirtations. Charges of drunkenness also stalked Gantt's efforts at reinstatement. On August 27, 1862, Gantt defended himself against charges of public intoxi cation and dereliction of duty by offering rebuttal witnesses in his defense. "In all my life put together of wine and ardent spirits, I never drank so much as one gallon," he tellingly revealed. "With all the opportunities, I have not tasted even the lightest drink for four months. I could never accustom myself to it. It has only been in extreme cases, since in the service, that I have touched it." This sounds like the "denial" of an alcoholic, but it cannot be proven with certainty why no promotion materialized.[38]

If defeat at Island Number 10 and the subsequent surrender and imprisonment had not been damaging enough to Gantt's psyche, by the spring of 1863 he recognized that he would receive neither a promotion nor reinstatement in the Confederate Army. What to do with the rest of his life? In the early summer of 1863, after days and nights of soul-searching, he fled to Vicksburg, Mississippi, and surrendered to Gen. Ulysses Grant. Although Grant had more pressing matters at hand, he recognized the political usefulness that Gantt's defection could mean for northern morale and for ushering Arkansas back into the Union. As the Union Army extended its control over Arkansas in 1863, Gantt's voice for surrender and restoration to the Union could be crucial. Political rehabilitation began.[39]

For Lincoln and the North, Gantt and other southern prodigals confirmed to war-weary Yankees that the Confederacy was crumbling and the war would soon be over. They also assured southern Unionists that Lincoln required only emancipation of slaves and a cessation of fighting for a return to the Union. For Gantt, support of the northern cause allowed him to provide for his family, to regain political power, and to remold an ideology which would help him rationalize the tragedies and defeats of the Civil War.[40]

Gantt journeyed to Washington, D. C., and conferred with President Lincoln on July 15, 1863. "My only object," Gantt wrote Lincoln after their meeting, "is to induce the withdrawal of my state from its allies in rebellion and its reentry into the Federal Union." Lincoln sent Gantt back to the occupied parts of Arkansas to drum up support for a return to the Union.[41]

Gantt addressed the people of Arkansas through pamphlets and speeches in 1863 and 1864, encouraging them to reenter the Union. In an address in

Little Rock in October 1863, published by the Loyal Publication Society of New York and disseminated throughout Arkansas and the nation, Gantt blamed Hindman, the Johnson Family, and Jefferson Davis for the catastrophe that Arkansas faced. Although he ignored the role he had played in pushing Arkansas into the Confederacy, he now counseled submission. "We are fairly beaten back," he insisted, "and should at once surrender." He demanded that southerners face their calamity squarely. "Our cities are gone to wreck, peopled alone by the aged, the lame, and halt, and women and children, while deserted towns, and smoking ruins, and plantations abandoned and laid waste, meet us on all sides, and anarchy and ruin, disappointment and discontent lower over all the land." He believed, "Wrecked hopes, broken fortunes, and anguished hearts" would only increase if the fighting continued.[42]

Gantt consoled wealthier Arkansans, saying that he, too, would be reduced "from competence to penury" with the emancipation of his slaves. "The inconvenience will be great for a while. The losses heavy," he commiserated. But in a visionary moment, perhaps glimpsed in the prisoner-of-war camp in industrialized Boston, he predicted that new immigrants and factories would transform the Arkansas and southern economies. "Machinery in the hills of Arkansas," he predicted, "will reverberate to the music of machinery in New England, and the whir of Georgia spindles will meet responsive echoes upon the slopes of the far-off Pacific." He pacified his listeners by saying, "Differences of section and sentiment will wear away and be forgotten, and the next generation will be more homogeneous and united than any since the days of the Revolution." Here was a new cause—industrialization—for Gantt to embrace.[43]

By the end of 1863 Gantt swore to any who would listen that many Arkansans had abandoned the Confederacy and reembraced the Union. Confederate flags were "flung to the breeze" and many joined Union clubs and even the Union Army, he insisted. This is what Lincoln wanted to hear. On December 11, 1863, Gantt became the first Confederate officer to be pardoned by President Lincoln. Many northern leaders, especially radicals, cheered Lincoln's pardon and embraced the Arkansan. He corresponded with Secretary of Treasury Salmon P. Chase and Secretary of War Edwin W. Stanton, revealing his importance to northern Republican leaders. Republican strategists in Ohio and Pennsylvania—states crucial for the reelection of Lincoln in 1864—believed that he would reassure war-weary northerners that slavery and secession would soon pass. Northern newspapers such as the *New York Herald* and *New York Times* reported favorably on his trustworthiness. "Gantt stands high with the President," Gen. Frederick Steele informed Rep. S. H. Boyd of Missouri, "for the course he has taken." Lincoln trusted him implicitly and used him to plan with General Steele the return of Arkansas to the Union. He had journeyed far: from the prisoner-of-war camp in Boston to the East Room of the White House. Once again he was desperately scrambling to improve his status and gain political power, even as the bloody Civil War continued.[44]

Many Arkansans and southerners could not fathom how Gantt had changed so drastically. His own family, for a time, mistrusted him, but they eventually accepted, even if they did not understand, what he did. But many of his closest friends throughout the state and the South, particularly his neighbors in southwestern Arkansas, were not so understanding. Gantt's "barefaced perfidy" and "utter abnegation of all principle" saddened John Eakins, former friend and editor of the *Washington Telegraph.* He recalled ironically a speech by Gantt in 1861 at the court house where Gantt harangued "the tories amongst us now." "Most astonishing of all is Gantt on negro slavery. He is done with it. He swings off to the rankest abolitionism." The editor concluded that he is "good to hold up as a terrible warning of the depths to which a human nature can sink, when principle is abandoned. Let the youth of the South contemplate him." The *Little Rock Daily Pantograph* agreed: "It is disgusting to the people to see or hear the name of Gantt." The editor further damned him and called him blatant, foulmouthed, vulgar, intolerant, impudent, insulting, and utterly unprincipled. "Gantt has shown himself up completely," charged Thomas B. Henley, a Confederate congressman from Helena. "He deserves to be drawn and quartered." Contempt for Gantt spread throughout the South, exemplified by the *Savannah (Ga.) Republican*'s denunciation of him as a "traitor, one who deceived his countrymen." Such loathing of the turncoat Gantt hindered the already problematical Reconstruction in Arkansas.[45]

Gantt had prepared for this inevitable abuse. Passions had festered for the last four years and would take years to calm, he assured himself. Military events in 1863 exacerbated tensions as Little Rock and Fort Smith fell to the Yankees in September 1863. Delegates from twenty Unionist counties met at Fort Smith a month later and suggested that a constitutional convention meet on January 4, 1864, at Little Rock. Lincoln addressed the nation regarding southern reconstruction on December 8, 1863, and issued his lenient ten percent plan which allowed a state to return to the Union when ten percent of those who voted in 1860 swore allegiance to the Union and agreed to the emancipation of slaves. Gantt encouraged Sen. William K. Sebastian of Arkansas to return to Washington and resume his Senate seat, which was vacated in 1861. He also recommended to radical Sen. Charles Sumner that Arkansas should be "annexed" and allowed to rejoin the Union.[46]

Meeting in Little Rock in January 1864, Arkansas Unionist delegates unanimously abolished slavery, maintained much of the old state constitution, elected Isaac Murphy as the provisional governor, and called for state elections on March 14, 1864, to ratify the new constitution and elect new state officers. Although Gantt applauded the convention's work, he was then leading an Arkansas delegation to the White House and collaborating on a reconstruction plan with President Lincoln. He continually impressed Lincoln, so that the president ordered Gen. Frederick Steele, Union military commander in Arkansas, to meet immediately with Gantt and finalize the plans for the March 14–16 vote. Although Rebel guerrillas hassled some voters and thousands of others boycotted the election, 12,179 unionists approved the new constitution and elected Isaac Murphy the new governor, while only 220 voters opposed the new regime.[47]

Throughout 1864 Gantt journeyed in and out of Arkansas as he promoted Arkansas's return to the Union and Lincoln's reelection. An address in Cincinnati, Ohio, in January 1864 was typical. He implored northerners not to lose heart, "to speak no word of peace to my southern brethren save that which thunders from the mouth of every cannon, or flashed from the point of every gleaming sword." Such bellicosity reveals that he had clearly divorced himself from the brutality of war. Diligently courting northern leaders, his rhetoric revealed that he had disengaged himself from the carnage of the battlefield. He merely wanted to regain and maintain political power at all costs. Southerners, some perhaps who had fought under Gantt's generalship, would have surely despised his coldhearted abstractions.[48]

Many radical Republicans in Congress were more reluctant than Lincoln for a quick southern return to the Union. In June 1864 a congressional committee refused to seat Arkansas's newly elected congressional delegation. An assassin's bullet in April 1865 changed forever the course of Reconstruction in Arkansas and in the South. Ever the opportunist, Gantt immediately and successfully wooed the new president, fellow Tennessean Andrew Johnson. "In ninety days," he assured the new president in June 1865, "the most radical will not have the nerve to say that Arkansas is not a state." He toured Arkansas and advised the president of the successful restoration of acceptable officials to power. Spurred by his rejection for promotion in the Confederate army he recommended no pardons for Confederate military or government leaders be granted without careful consideration. Fearing that Governor Murphy would propose far too many for amnesty, he hinted to the president that he alone could best counsel him on whom to pardon and whom to reject. He worked feverishly on mining useful contacts in Washington with the Republican radicals, exemplified by his letter to Secretary of State William Seward in which he urged the pardon of Augustus Garland. "Everything prospers well here," he promised the secretary of state. "Our state is nearly organized—only a few more offices to fill."[49]

Gantt also boosted the morale of Unionist Arkansans and ushered Rebels back to the fold. At a Fourth of July address in Little Rock, he extolled the "power and magnificence" of the federal government. Later that year, he insisted that "every act which a state in perfect vigor can do is now being done, and the dawn of returning prosperity breaks upon us." President Johnson agreed and issued an executive order on October 30, 1865, to Governor Murphy. "There will be no interference with your present organization of state government," the president promised.[50]

In March 1865, Congress established a Bureau of Refugees, Freedmen, and Abandoned Lands to facilitate Southern blacks as they moved from slavery to freedom. As Sen. Charles Sumner of Massachusetts demanded, "There must be no slavery under another *alias.* A way from slavery to freedom" must be found. The Freedmen's Bureau, supervised by the War Department, faced daunting challenges as the Civil War ended and Reconstruction began. It sought to help freedpersons find jobs, collect wages, establish schools and churches, reunite families, join in legally sanctioned marriages, obtain civil rights, and participate in politics.[51]

From 1865 until 1869, seventy-nine officials manned the two dozen Arkansas agencies situated in areas of highest black population density. Agents were about equally divided between civilians and former army officers, but their ideologies and attitudes toward Reconstruction and freedpeople varied greatly as evident in their performances. On the one hand, Chicot County agent Thomas Hunicutt extorted payments and sexual favors from the freedpeople before he enforced their contracts with planters. On the other hand, Helena agent Henry Sweeney lobbied for blacks' schools and churches, favored freedmen in contractual disputes with planters, and threatened to call in the army if whites denied blacks' voting rights. Local agents either furthered or restricted blacks' freedom in their earliest moments of emancipation.[52]

Having won the approval of northern Republicans with his volte-face support of the Union in 1863, Gantt was a natural choice for a bureau position. Appointed general superintendent of the Southwest District of Arkansas in September 1865, he assayed the violence-riddled southwestern part of the state until October 1866 and epitomized the challenges that a bureau agent faced in the war-ravaged South. His record as a bureau official at Washington, Arkansas, was, like many other agents, a mixed one. He accomplished much, yet left untouched just as much.[53]

In one of his first addresses to blacks in his jurisdiction, he outlined his understanding of the bureau. "Some of you feel that the Freedmen's Bureau is a change of master for you. That the Superintendents are like so many overseers. This is all wrong. The Bureau wishes to let you alone as much as possible. Its object is simply to protect you until laws and public sentiment gives you all the protection that any other man has." Gantt extolled blacks to embrace the work ethic to reify their freedom. Embracing free labor ideology and the good life promised by northern capitalists, he toiled to transform master's whips and domination into contracts and mutual respect. Enthusiastically he reassured superiors that "men tell me every day that they are astonished at the cheerfulness with which the negroes labor."[54]

Noting that southern whites' "*prejudices give very slowly,*" he spent much time auditing contracts between freedmen and planters. For example, a typical 1866 contract provided that the black laborer receive half of the crop, one hundred pounds of pork and one hundred and fifty bushels of corn in return for a year's labor on the plantation. The employee also swore to "take good care of the stock, poultry, and household and kitchen furniture." Fearing that planters' use of parentless black teenagers as "apprentices" was but a subterfuge for chattel slavery, he vetoed such arrangements. He spent hour after hour at his desk explaining contract provisions to freedmen, and he spent even more time canvassing the countryside on horseback to make sure that planters fulfilled their obligations. As long as he monitored planters' agreements with freedpeople, blacks realized a fair share of their labor.[55]

Realizing that economic independence composed only one component of freedom, Gantt also lobbied for and received funds to build a hospital for freedmen which offset the loss of planters' medical care. He also recognized the freedmen's desire for schools and utilized local churches as classrooms until school buildings could be provided. As early as November 1865, the 283 students enrolled in two schools for blacks in Washington, Arkansas, indicate that he had correctly gauged the intensity of blacks' support for schools.[56]

Gantt also championed the newly protected black family, no longer subjected to the whim of a planter's sale or rape. He encouraged blacks to solemnize their relationships as husbands and wives in church-sanctioned marriage ceremonies. As four white ministers of the Methodist Episcopal Church, South, administered wedding vows, Gantt hoped that such marriages impressed both blacks and whites with the significance of the union.[57]

As a bureau agent, Gantt mediated between planters and freedpeople. He feared that without agents' intervention, former slaves would be "starved, murdered, or forced into a condition more horrible than the worst stage of slavery." He banned the use of corporal punishment by planters, insisted that blacks live where they wished, and urged local white judges to accept blacks for jury duty. In nonjury disputes, he often adjudicated. Although southwestern Arkansas blacks faced innumerable challenges in the aftermath of the Civil War, Bureau Agent Gantt frequently aided them in their movements toward freedom.[58]

Gantt recognized that the Freedmen's Bureau was a political cul-de-sac for his personal career advancement. With every effort to aid blacks in their newly gained freedom, he antagonized many of the white elite who merely waited for the radical regime to exit. Driven to reestablish a statewide base that could lead to higher political office, he moved his family to Little Rock in 1866 and became a prosecuting attorney for the region from 1868 until 1870. If he hoped his new job would be less controversial than his Freedmen's Bureau tenure, he was quickly disillusioned.[59]

As prosecutor, Gantt tried to mold the judiciary to ensure justice for both blacks and whites. Many whites bitterly opposed his efforts to place blacks on juries and to make the judicial system colorblind. He often issued warrants for the arrest of absent jurors, but the white judge dismissed such charges. A statewide newspaper campaign countered and attempted to smear him with accusations of sexual misconduct with a niece in a Baltimore, Maryland, hotel. Other whites demonized him and blamed him for all their woes. "I have been threatened too often with assassination," he confessed, "not to be constantly on the lookout." He revealed to an *Arkansas Gazette* reporter that he often carried as many as seven guns and that he never illuminated his house after dark. "I am going to stay here," he adamantly swore, "till my time comes to die, whether it be from old age or at the hands of some cowardly assassin." His fears were not unfounded. In December 1868, for example, he was severely beaten by two local businessmen who detested his Reconstruction efforts.[60]

Yet Gantt refused to surrender. Ever watchful of the morality of the newly freed blacks, Gantt instigated morality crusades against bawdy houses, adultery, and illegal cohabitation. He canvassed the state in 1867 and recruited members for the Republican Club. At a Grant and Colfax rally in Little Rock in 1868, he exhorted over three thousand blacks to support the Republican ticket and to persevere in their struggles for freedom. Gantt mobilized the judicial branch in an all-out war against the Ku Klux Klan. Violence escalated in Arkansas as the elections of 1868 approached when over two hundred murders occurred. Working with the newly elected governor, Powell Clayton, he supported efforts by informants to infiltrate the Klan. One such spy, Albert Parker, penetrated the White County Klan in 1868 and was murdered. Although Gantt diligently prosecuted the case, local prejudice precluded a guilty verdict.[61]

By the summer of 1870 the physical, mental, and psychological strains of Reconstruction had taken their toll on Gantt. Wishing to remain in politics, he could find no lasting solutions to the problems Arkansas encountered in Reconstruction. He resigned as prosecuting attorney in October 1870, but he prosecuted an occasional case for the state, as in 1872 when he tried to indict Pope County marauders. Once again, however, he failed. "A court surrounded by armed men, who deny its jurisdiction," he lamented, "can hope to do little for the settling of the differences of the people."[62]

Sensing Gantt bordered on nervous collapse, Governor Clayton appointed him in 1873 to compile the laws of Arkansas. Law books and legislative records provided a haven for the exhausted Gantt. The digest included over twelve hundred pages of constitutional and legislative enactments from Arkansas. Gantt and his assistants codified provisions regarding aliens, asylums, bastardy, elections, evidence, juries, liens, and a multitude of other topics. Here Gantt's mind and spirit recuperated. He had tried, and failed, to gain national political prominence. He had tried, and failed, to win glory and fame on the battlefield. He had tried, and failed, to bring justice to former slaves. He had tried, and failed, to reconstruct Arkansas peacefully. He had tried, and failed, to transform Arkansas into Massachusetts by industrialization. He was tired. Research in the law consoled him. He would regroup, as he had done so often before; reconstruct himself yet again; then try once more to gain political power and prominence.[63]

On June 10, 1874, at about 4:00 A.M., Gantt suffered a heart attack and died. The *Arkansas Gazette* eulogized him as "a lawyer of ability, an eloquent, impassioned, and impressive speaker. His loss will be deeply deplored." As a sign of respect, the Little Rock Bar Association accompanied his remains through the streets of the capital city to the local train station. His body was carried to Tulip, Arkansas, in Dallas County and interred.[64]

Gantt, along with other southern scalawags—Joseph Brown of Georgia, William Holden of North Carolina, Albert Brown of Alabama, and James Alcorn of Mississippi—worked with carpetbaggers as conduits between both the defeated Confederacy and the triumphant North and the newly freed blacks and enveloping white racists. Unlike the typical scalawag, Gantt was neither a Whig nor a Unionist in the 1860 to1861 secession crisis. He also did not reside in the mountainous region of Arkansas where few slaves lived; rather he journeyed from a region where thirty percent of the population comprised blacks. His most important contributions were in his attempts to persuade the victorious North that a Carthaginian peace was not needed. He insisted that the South had seen its errors and was ready to embrace smokestacks and railroads. He also helped Arkansas freedpeople begin their arduous trek toward genuine freedom. If leaders like Edward W. Gantt had not existed, it is easy to imagine a much harsher Reconstruction for both white and black Arkansans.[65]

James Carroll Napier (1845–1940): From Plantation to the City

Bobby L. Lovett

After slavery, educated and wealthy black men and women rose to influential leadership positions and soon constituted an elite in their communities. Because of their education, wealth, and influence, these African Americans were expected to lead their fellow freedmen and to develop strategies to pursue equality and justice. W. E. B. Du Bois called them the "Talented Tenth." It was this elite that pushed for educational access for all blacks. Elite African Americans struggled to gain status, class recognition, equal rights, and fair treatment, because they were the ones—particularly mulattos and descendants of mulattos—among the post-Emancipation blacks most likely to face discrimination in transportation, housing, accommodations, and politics. Excluded from upper-class white society because of their race, they fought for their rights and for the rights of all black citizens. James Carroll Napier tellingly demonstrates the trials and successes faced by a member of Nashville's black elite.

James C. Napier (1845–1940) helped shape the African American community in Nashville, Tennessee. This segregated city had a viable and visible black elite, but Napier proved to be the most important and conspicuous member. He and a small group of elite blacks dominated politics, culture, and business for two generations and helped the freedmen make the painful transition from slavery to freedom. Their guidance, achievements, contributions, and activities—even if only performed on one side of the town—helped shape the whole history of Nashville, Tennessee.

Born on an iron plantation as the grandson of a slave master, J. C. Napier was raised in a biracial environment. Yet he spent most of his life in Nashville, a segregated community. He was educated in the city's free black schools and outside Tennessee at liberal institutions such as Wilberforce, Oberlin, and Howard. But as the son of mulattos, Napier learned to hold moderate positions on social and political issues. To some extent, he was an opportunist, a loyal follower of Booker T. Washington, and a believer in the philosophy of racial accommodationism. He, like other black elite, was a social conservative and paradoxically a fighter for the civil rights of African Americans. The interesting life of James Carroll Napier mirrors Afro-Nashville's history through slavery, Civil War, Reconstruction, Jim Crow, and the Great Depression.[1]

J. C. Napier's father, William Carroll Napier (1824–1895), was born a slave on September 24 to Dr. Elias W. Napier and his slave seamstress, Judy (1808–1895?). William Sumner, a free Negro hack man, recalled: "There was a family of colored children living with old man [Elias W.] Napier, and all said to be the children of this white man by a Negro woman." In 1844 William Carroll married Jane Elizabeth Watkins (1825–1909) in a slave ceremony. She was born on April 11 as the daughter of slave Rebecca and master William E. Watkins. The 600-acre Watkins farm was "an elegant place on the Cumberland River" in Davidson County, six miles west of Nashville, along the Charlotte Turnpike. Watkins owned stock in this turnpike, half of the 3,053-acre Piney Furnace in Dickson County, and real estate in Nashville. On June 19, 1845, Jane Watkins and W. C. Napier gave birth to James Carroll.[2] J. C. Napier recalled that he was told that his grandfather was "a man of considerable force of character and influence."[3]

Dr. Elias W. Napier died at age sixty-five on August 7, 1848. The will and inventory provided for the sale of over sixty slaves (ages twelve to sixty-five years). The will freed thirty-one slaves and praised the "yellow [mulatto] female servants for serving me well and taking care of my property in Alabama and Tennessee." The will proscribed freedom for Judy, her five children, and many other "yellow" slaves, and gave them "certain sums of money [that] may be found in their possession at my death." The will provided household and kitchen furniture, corn, bacon, corn meal, sugar, coffee, salt, and other supplies from the smokehouse to Judy and her boys. This mulatto family was to move to the deceased master's small farm and stay there until March 1, 1849.[4] Since the Nat Turner slave rebellion in Virginia in 1831, Tennessee had steadily tightened the restrictions on slaves and free blacks, requiring the latter to leave the state within a year after emancipation.

Judy Napier and her children left Davidson County and moved to Cincinnati in 1849. Ohio had just lifted restrictions against free black migration and offered schools for African Americans. The Napiers had some basic education because they had attended school with the white Napier children, and W. C. Napier had learned to do business by transporting his father's goods to be sold in the Nashville market. The Napier family soon left southern Ohio and sought their fortunes separately. Judy and some of her children moved to Virginia to join the free black community where the boys found work as teachers. One son moved to St. Louis, Missouri, also becoming a teacher. The family returned to Nashville in time for the November 1850 census.[5]

Not unusual phenomena in wealthy middle Tennessee were industrial slavery, hired and quasi-independent slaves, free blacks, miscegenation, mulattos, extended biracial families, and a powerful slavocracy that led private and complex lives without outside interference. Churches were few and far between. For example, in Davidson County's eleventh civil district, home of some of the county's largest slaveholders, no organized churches existed before the Civil War. A quarter of the slaves in Nashville were hired persons or quasi-independent slaves with a limited amount of freedom. J. C. Napier recalled, "Slaves had more money than is generally thought." However, mulattos, perhaps because of their blood connections to elite whites, had better privileges and opportunities to acquire freedom and self-sufficiency. In 1860 mulattos constituted 10 percent of the black population in Tennessee. Overall, blacks constituted 25 percent of the city's population. Nashville had four quasi-independent African American churches and almost as many businesses as in Afro-Cincinnati. William C. Napier soon joined other free black hack (taxi) drivers near the corner of Cedar and North Summer Streets, where they hustled fares. He also rented a part of his father-in-laws's farm and hired slave Alfred Watkins to graze the livestock while he was in town developing his business.[6]

As sectional agitation heightened in the late 1850s, Jane insisted that she and the children return to Ohio. On June 13, 1859, W. C. Napier (with fellow mulatto hack owner Jerry Stothard as cosigner) gained a loan of two hundred dollars from Jane's father. "We boarded the steamboat *Wenoah* near where Fort Nashboro stands," recalled J. C. Napier. Steamers left the foot of Broad Street in Nashville for Cincinnati on Tuesday and Thursday. Jane and the children traveled to Cairo, Illinois, and then to Cincinnati before pushing on to more friendly towns like Oberlin and Wilberforce. Blacks composed much larger percentages of the population at Oberlin, where they could attend public schools, the antislavery First Congregational Church, and Oberlin College, which admitted women in 1833 and African Americans by 1835. The rural Wilberforce community housed a training and finishing school for blacks, Wilberforce University, which was started in 1855 by the Ohio Methodists. The institution had 207 students, including J. C. Napier and mulatto "children of Southern and southwestern planters" by 1859.[7]

With the approach of national elections in 1860, the sectional issues of slavery and freedom became paramount in the national forum, profoundly affecting the future of free blacks such as the Napiers. Men who made their living as "slave stealers and catchers" increased their focus on free blacks when southerners became more paranoid about the potential for slave rebellions. In Nashville a gun was fired to signal the curfew for all blacks and to notify the whites that "all is well." In 1860 Gov. Isham G. Harris failed to force all free Negroes to leave Tennessee—a recent legislative act had been successful in adjacent Arkansas. After Abraham Lincoln won the national elections in 1860, the mortified governor dogmatically pushed Tennessee into the Confederacy. Harris pressured and even jailed loyal Unionists, increased the county slave patrols, and gained a legislative act to draft free black men, ages eighteen to forty-five years, into military labor units. Yet free black men found ways to avoid the draft, and W. C. Napier and other African American entrepreneurs quietly continued their businesses in a town crowded with Confederates. Unfortunately, Jane and the children had to leave Ohio and return to Nashville in 1861 when the financially strapped Wilberforce school was shut down. Meanwhile, "Jane E. Watkins and W. C. Napier" were officially married in Nashville-Davidson County on June 30, 1861.[8]

In February 1862 the Union army under Gen. Ulysses S. Grant moved from Ohio, crossed the Kentucky border, and easily captured Fort Donelson, Tennessee. J. C. Napier recalled: "When the Battle of Fort Donelson was fought, I had just returned from Ohio. I witnessed the entry of the federal troops [into Nashville]." The boastful Confederates were easily defeated and then humiliated as Governor Harris rode through the Nashville streets, shouting the Yankees were coming. John B. Lindsley, head of the medical school at the University of Nashville, wrote in his diary, "The defeated Confederate army passed through the panic stricken city, while the Union men alone seemed to have their wits about them. Large bodies of the retreating army were hastening through" to Murfreesboro—about thirty miles to the east.

Lindsley sent his free black servant, Nelson, to get W. C. Napier to help transport stores and patients. Early in the morning of February 20, Napier came back to beg for help because some retreating Confederate soldiers wanted to confiscate his two carriages. His son, James Carroll, had been cursed and called racial epithets by the Rebel troops. Lindsley hurried over and used his rank as "Post Surgeon" to order the men away. He had "[William] Carroll's carriages brought over to the hospital for the sake of protection." Then the mayor stopped by to get one of the carriages to go to a "conference with the federal authorities." Lindsley "unwillingly obeyed them by letting James Napier (Carroll's son) go." William Carroll came up with the other carriage and continued to transfer the Lindsley goods. On February 23, 1862, the sixteen-year-old J. C. Napier drove the mayor and city dignitaries to the riverfront, so they could row over to Edgefield and surrender Nashville to units of the Union army. The mayor returned and advised: "Now folks, go home. Be quiet and peaceable. Be assured of one thing—the Negroes are safe." But the slaves were not safe. Jane Napier's father reported that some seventeen slaves, including Alfred, left the Watkins farm on November 7, 1862, "for federal service." Next door, the Union cavalry forced Mark Cockrill to give up twenty thousand bushels of corn, two hundred tons of hay, horses, cattle, and two thousand pounds of bacon. Rural slaves deserted their masters in such numbers that the African American population in Nashville increased from about four thousand in 1860 to over twelve thousand by 1865.[9]

The activity of war was so intense that there was hardly any way for free or slave blacks to remain detached. J. C. Napier saw military governor Andrew Johnson take control of the capitol building in March 1862, and he remembered Johnson as a man of "unvarying, simplicity, honest, and courage." In November 1862 the Union post commander twice used William C. Napier as a spy to go to Murfreesboro and reconnoiter the Confederate army. William Carroll also was employed to secretly count the Confederate troops camped along the Harpeth River. There was snow, sleet, hail, and rain by January 8, 1863, and hundreds of blacks streamed into the city after the Confederate defeat at Murfreesboro. Between September 1863 and January 1866, some 20,133 black men, ages eighteen to fifty-five years, were recruited into the Union army in Tennessee as U.S. Colored Troops (USCT). Some local free Negroes would help form the 17th USCT Infantry Regiment in Nashville. Tens of thousands of fugitive slaves and free blacks served voluntarily and involuntarily as Union civilian workers. In a meeting with freedpeople, Governor Johnson threatened impressments if more of them did not volunteer on military labor projects. W. C. Napier "gave a week" of his time and labor among the thousands of African Americans who constructed the Northwestern Military Railroad, designed to transport supplies seventy-five miles from the Tennessee River terminus to Nashville's warehouses. This logistic project was the initial preparation for General William T. Sherman's "March through Georgia." After Sherman took Atlanta in September 1864, the Confederate army of Tennessee decided to attack Nashville, hoping to draw the federals out of Georgia. Sherman shipped part of his army back to Nashville to prepare a defense, but continued with his main army to the Georgia seacoast. When they prepared a defense, the Union soldiers at nearby Fort Gillem (today's site of Fisk University) took some of William Carroll's horses and cows from the Watkins farm and many hogs from his own house in Nashville. The Union army of about forty-two thousand men, including thirteen thousand USCT, won the "decisive Battle of Nashville" on December 19, 1864. This helped bring the end of Civil War closer.[10]

African Americans in Nashville already acted like free men and women by 1864. They were confident enough to organize the "Second Emancipation Day" celebration, with William C. Napier heading the official welcoming party for the speaker, John Mercer Langston. After arriving in town on December 30, 1864, and conferring with Governor Johnson about Reconstruction issues, Langston agreed to Johnson's request to go to the USCT camps and tell the soldiers "for me that they were the bravest men under the sun." He gave an encouraging speech on January 1, urging Tennessee to end slavery. On February 22, 1865, a state referendum abolished slavery. In June W. C. Napier was one of the signers of the call in the *Nashville Colored Tennessean* for county delegates to attend a State Colored Men's Convention scheduled for August 12, 1865. Simultaneously, W. C. and Jane Napier made provisions to send James Carroll back to Ohio, where he enrolled in the Oberlin College preparatory (high school) department (1864–1866) and the collegiate department (1866–1868). The rules included hard studying, plain living, early risings, and no segregating of students by color. Langston likely had helped William Carroll get James Carroll into Oberlin. However, AME bishop Daniel A. Payne had visited Nashville in December 1863 to establish two AME Churches and discuss Reconstruction issues with Johnson, and, during his travels, Payne actively sought Negro students "of hopeful piety and respectable talents" to send to Wilberforce and Oberlin.[11]

After his sophomore year at Oberlin College, J. C. Napier returned to Nashville and inevitably became a Reconstruction leader. In the fall 1868 elections, William C. Napier participated with moderate African American leaders who insisted "native whites" be included in party affairs. This faction of native elite free blacks (including mulattos Nelson Walker and Henry Harding) wanted to continue racial accommodationism with moderate whites, their benefactors of antebellum and Civil War times. But the masses of African American voters had no problem with non-resident Republicans controlling local affairs, and so the Radical Republicans turned to more pliable black leaders (dark skin, former slaves) like Randal Brown and Allen S. McTier. The Radical Republicans organized a torchlight parade and helped Brown and four other blacks win city council and county offices. Soon, the Republican governor selected a three-man committee to hear war claims against the federal government. The Davidson County committee included two African Americans, James C. Napier and James H. Sumner. A year later, however, a group of conservative blacks, led by Elias Polk (former house slave of Pres. James K. Polk) helped the native Conservatives (Democrats) regain control of the government. The Radical Republican blacks scorned the "old house slaves" for supporting the former slave masters in politics.[12]

The black elite, particularly the free mulattos and former house slaves, had held a privileged relationship with elite whites. In the early years of emancipation, elite blacks and mulattos wanted to be treated equally in public and to have access to first-class accommodations. They wanted the right to *not* be segregated by "race" in first-class situations. When the Radical Republicans won the local 1868 elections, elite black Republicans forced them to operate integrated cars to the Fourth of July picnic sponsored by the party. Of course, pro-Confederates and many other southern whites could care less about the Fourth of July celebration. The leftover complexities from a century of widespread miscegenation in slavery would haunt the post–Civil War South, leaving the ruling whites pondering what to do about the large presence of very light-skinned freedmen in their midst.

In 1870 the Democrats, Conservatives, and other Redeemers changed the state constitution, passed new electoral requirements, and spawned anarchy in the countryside. In March 1870, the Tennessee Colored Men's Convention selected J. C. Napier to read a petition before the Reconstruction Committee in Congress. The petition urged: "As a people we have made appeals to the authorities of the State for protection, but they have been . . . fruitless. The legislature has passed many acts which militate directly against the interest and happiness of colored people." We want "the repeal of the common carrier's act, whereby respected [elite] colored ladies and gentlemen, holding first-class tickets, are compelled to ride in the smoking car and submit to the jeers and taunts of those [working-class people] who are not our equals in morals, refinement, or education." They asked that Tennessee be placed under a Reconstruction government. The governor of Tennessee assured the committee that as soon as the franchise was restored to former Confederates the violence would stop. Congress passed the Force Acts to punish terrorists, and the states ratified the Fifteenth Amendment to the Constitution.[13]

The founder of the Howard University Law School, John M. Langston, invited James Carroll to study there. Napier arrived in Washington, D.C. on August 15, 1870, and lived with the Langston family. He and mulatto roommate Josiah T. Settles (1850–1915) of Memphis supported themselves by working as claims' clerks in the Freedmen's Bureau. In 1872 James C. Napier received the LL.D. degree from Howard University and was admitted to the bar in the District of Columbia. He was one of fourteen graduates and a member of Howard's second law class.[14]

J. C. Napier returned to Nashville to pursue better opportunities, although things were tough for the Republicans in Tennessee. Between 1871 and 1881, all three governors were Democrats and former Confederate officers. But the Republicans still controlled the national government. Napier collected letters of reference and lobbied for another federal job. On May 27, 1872, he was appointed a federal revenue assistant for Kentucky, Tennessee, Louisiana, and Alabama. Later he became gauges clerk for the internal revenue district, making daily visits to the local distilleries. Napier gained more visibility in September when Langston returned to Nashville to campaign for the reelection of Pres. U. S. Grant and deliver speeches to the annual Tennessee Colored Agricultural and Mechanical Association Fair. In November local black men turned out in great numbers to help reelect Grant—the first president for whom they had voted since 1868 and, before that, 1832. Also, Sampson W. Keeble (1833–1888) of Nashville won election as the first African American member of the Tennessee General Assembly.[15]

While biding his time until the first generation of local leaders passed from the scene, James C. Napier was admitted to the Tennessee bar by 1875. In 1876 when Napier co-chaired the committee on resolutions for the county Republican convention, the *Nashville Daily American* mockingly pointed out that the gathering was no more than "a little Republican junta of not over forty persons, representing . . . anybody else but themselves." This pro–Democratic Party newspaper recommended that "colored men should [not] speak for any other but themselves." Napier said that "the Democratic Party [is] hostile to the interest of the colored people."[16] Pres. Rutherford B. Hayes visited Nashville in September when he was on a southern tour to sell the "Compromise of 1877." This compromise had allowed Hayes to win the disputed 1876 election. As the local African American spokesman to respond to the president's speech, J. C. Napier insisted, "All that we ask is an equal chance in the start and race of life, an opportunity to work and test our capacities and, when we prove worthy, to have accorded us the recognition and merit due." Hayes responded that "the white people of the South have no desire to invade the rights of the colored people." Even the Yankee soldiers had been awed by the "sea of dark faces that seemed to drown out the white man's very existence" in the South. The president proceeded to withdraw the Federal troops from the turbulent region and institute "southern home-rule."[17]

In effect, the nation turned the "Negro problem" over to the South. The northerners had no real good reason, other than a moral one, to continue to fight the southerners on this question, and the northern missionaries had been sent South to prepare blacks to stay in the South—not to migrate to the North. This change in political fortunes forced African Americans to rely less on the Republican Party at the national level. Thereafter, black leaders increasingly were inclined to work out compromises with local white leaders and accommodate regional white conservative attitudes about race relations. James C. Napier and many local African American elite would become political fusionists and embrace racial accommodationism. In Nashville, this philosophy long preceded Booker T. Washington.

When Reconstruction began to wane, blacks in Nashville searched for alternatives to gain their full freedom, the right to class status, and equal access to America's vast wealth. They even pursued radical solutions to eliminate widespread African American poverty and overcrowding in the urban areas. In 1877 J. C. Napier helped organize the Colored People's Cooperative Emigration Club to resettle surplus urban poor freedmen on western homestead lands.[18] Though they mostly were interested in casting off the poverty-ridden, homeless, loud, and idle freedmen on the street corners of Nashville, the Napier family gained visibility through the Colored People's Cooperative Emigration Club.

In 1878 the thirty-three-year-old J. C. Napier decided to run for office and marry. He smartly chose the Fourth Ward, where working and middle class blacks continued to vote. In the former contraband camp areas of south, east, and west Nashville, multitudes of impoverished freedmen remained, and the number of them registered to vote was too low for a black candidate to win public office. To gain one of the two seats in the Fourth Ward, Napier defeated Charles H. Sanders 246 to 233 votes on September 28, 1878. The *Nashville Daily American* reported that Napier was the only black elected in the thirteen races for the council. Napier immediately left for Washington, D.C., to marry seventeen-year-old Nettie D. Langston, John M. Langston's only daughter and a student of Howard University and the Conservatory of Music at Oberlin College. On October 2, 1878, the ceremony took place in the Congregational Church with an overflowing crowd. A Nashville newspaper mockingly said that no dark-skinned Negroes were invited to the wedding. Later, the U.S. Treasury Department notified Napier that he could not retain the federal job *and* serve in the city council unless approved by the president. Napier gathered enough letters of support to retain his federal job. He quickly learned to respond to the needs of the masses, proven by his 1879 council resolution to study the need for more schools for African Americans.[19]

In the November 1880 presidential elections there was a large black voter turnout in Nashville for the election of Republican James A. Garfield. A local African American, Thomas A. Sykes, won election to the General Assembly, and J. C. Napier and another black won both council seats in the Fourth Ward. On March 27, 1881, black leaders petitioned Garfield, asking for protection from racial violence and a halt to the attempts to disfranchise African American voters. They protested, "Not a single presidential appointment is held by a colored man in . . . Tennessee." They recommended that, "J. C. Napier be appointed as Postmaster at our City of Nashville." Napier began soliciting letters of recommendation, including one from Republican mayor Thomas Kercheval. President Garfield promisingly responded that America had no place for second-class citizenship for any of its people. But an assassin killed Garfield.[20] Through the tenure of Hayes, Garfield, and Arthur, African American citizens found no end to the nadir of Reconstruction.

In the 1880s James Carroll pushed education and civil rights. His protest against the exclusion of black teachers in the Nashville school system caused the superintendent to recommend to the school board that something had to be done about the "agitation by an elite colored man." The board voted to add more colored schools and hire some "competent colored teachers" after expanded white schools accommodated displaced white teachers. Napier became a member of the Republican State Executive Committee in 1882. He and his fellow black councilman, Charles C. Gowdy, influenced the city to create an African American fire company and place gravel on the streets in the black community. Napier became chairman of the council and after Gowdy resigned his seat to become chief of the new African American fire company, Napier was the lone black in the city council. In 1884 J. C. Napier was reelected by engaging in fusion politics with the city's reform coalition, believing this action would "bring together the better [elite] classes of white and colored people." The reform coalition defeated Mayor Kercheval and his political machine. On January 15, 1885, he was among dozens of black leaders, including Frederick Douglass, who met in New Orleans to sign an appeal for federal support of schools for African Americans. Napier lost his federal job after Democrat Grover Cleveland became president in March 1885. The next September, Napier lost his reelection bid, partly because the black vote split after Kercheval persuaded a black preacher to run against Napier, and the newly enlarged council districts and poverty had disfranchised most blacks. When national literary figure Charles Dudley Warner visited the city in the spring of 1886 and met with a group of the black elite, J. C. Napier served as spokesman. "We want to be treated like men, like anybody else, regardless of color. We want the public conveyances open to us according to the [first-class] fare we pay. We want privileges to go to hotels and the theaters, operas and places of amusement," said Napier. When President Cleveland visited Nashville in 1887, James Carroll and brother Elias W. were part of the African American honor guard that marched in the parade, but this display of loyalty did nothing to advance Napier's desire for a federal job.

Also, J. C. Napier was almost on the wrong side again when local blacks pushed for a public high school. In September 1887 a black mother and her son were turned away from the city's only high school, but African Americans held mass protests at St. John AME Church until the city capitulated and added a high school curriculum at Meigs Colored School. Napier supported this initiative, even though he had originally supported a proposal for a publicly supported high school at elitist Fisk University.[21]

James C. Napier continued to be a moderate politician and racial accommodationist like most of Nashville's black elite. Even when lynching became a common white response to the civil rights push by the second generation of post-Emancipation blacks, J. C. Napier chose his words carefully. He willingly worked with moderate and liberal men "from the better class of whites," just as his father had done. Napier became involved with the Open Letter Club, formed in the late 1880s by the noted writer George Washington Cable. The Open Letter Club, headquartered in Nashville with a Vanderbilt University English professor as coordinator, included members such as Frederick Douglass, John R. Lynch, and other white and black elite. Cable wanted "to bring the discussion of Southern racial injustice into the open forum." On a visit to Nashville in December 1889, Cable dined with elite blacks at James Carroll and Nettie Napier's. The local newspapers found out about it and branded Cable "a renegade to the South, a traitor, a defamer of the South" and "the stench of the gutter for socializing with our colored elite." Cable said he merely meant to break bread with the brethren, many of who were "as white as any white man." After the Vanderbilt professor denounced racial mingling, Cable disbanded the Open Letter Club in 1890. Neither Warner, Cable, nor any liberal white wanted to risk status on behalf of African American rights. Although disappointed, J. C. Napier still believed in political change and assured white Republican candidates that they "had the unanimous support of the Colored voters." By this time, most black men had been disenfranchised. Napier continued as a delegate to the Tennessee Republican League Convention, chaired the Davidson County Republican Convention, and ran as the Republican nominee for the circuit court clerk position. On January 2, 1891, the Emancipation Day speaker, J. Mercer Langston, Napier's father-in-law, told the Nashville audience to rebuke the Democrats, stay with the Republican Party, and have faith until the "President sends troops into the South."[22] No troops came.

Matters deteriorated for blacks and for the Napier family in the 1890s. The recently amended Morrill Land Grant Act (1890) appeased white southerners by sanctioning separate colleges for blacks. The patriarch of the family, William C. Napier, died on December 20, 1895. Frederick Douglass and J. M. Langston died the following year, and the U.S. Supreme Court declared in *Plessy v. Ferguson* that separate but equal public facilities were not unconstitutional. Thereafter, the passage of Jim Crow laws reached a crescendo in the South. The southernization of the American nation in race relations further crystallized after the Spanish-American War (1898–1899). Tennessee refused to arm blacks or allow them to participate in its regiments. Race relations continued to free fall.

With Jim Crow decisively in place and the southernization of America sweeping forward, the Republicans again attempted to remove J. C. Napier from the state executive committee. But Napier enlisted the help of Richard Henry Boyd, head of the National Baptist Publishing Board, who appealed to African American churches. Boyd and the Rev. Luke Mason helped take charge of the Sixth Congressional Republican Convention, which selected black nominees and insisted that Napier be a delegate to the National Republican Convention. In 1900 some 112,236 of Tennessee's 480,243 blacks could still vote, but most of them were too intimidated by bullies, too poor to pay the poll tax, and too uninterested in a corrupt electoral process, which seemed to leave their plight unchanged. Local blacks' flirtation with the Greenback Party, the Populist Party, and other third-party movements in the 1880s and 1890s had come to naught.[23]

By this time James C. Napier had built a secure alliance with Booker T. Washington. Washington's third wife was Margaret Murray, an 1889 Fisk University graduate and a friend to Nettie Napier. After marrying Washington, Margaret frequently spent several weeks with James Carroll and Nettie at their summer home outside Nashville and spoke to local women's groups. Soon after Frederick Douglass's death, Washington was propelled into the national African American leadership position after his Atlanta Cotton Exposition speech of September 1896 when he advocated acceptance of the elite white man's racism in return for his support of education, jobs, and other concessions for blacks. To emulate the Atlanta Exposition, in 1896 the officers of the Tennessee Centennial Exposition included a "Negro Department," which Napier chaired. In August Napier resigned "for health and business reasons." He wanted the white directors of the exposition to finance an exhibit (similar to the one in the Atlanta Exposition) where blacks could "correctly" demonstrate their progress since slavery. Napier believed that what elite blacks "had done and were doing" best demonstrated progress since slavery. But the directors turned to a more pliable African American, Richard Hill, a schoolteacher and son of a former slave fiddler. A "Negro Building" was constructed and included a real cotton field with former slaves picking the crop. Hill proclaimed, "Jim Crow is for our protection" from mob violence. For "Negro Day" in September 1897, he hired Booker T. Washington to repeat his Atlanta Cotton Exposition speech. Napier concurred with Washington by saying that "your idea of the relations of the races in this country seems to be the popular one, and takes well whenever it is expressed whether before a black, white, or mixed audience."[24] His affiliation with Washington would prove beneficial. By 1898, Napier sought greater national exposure in an unsuccessful race for Congress.

J. C. Napier became one of Booker T. Washington's most loyal associates. After Washington and others formed the National Negro Business League at the Atlanta conference in 1900, Napier became a member of the executive committee and in 1902 helped start a Nashville chapter to arouse "business interests among [Nashville's] Negroes." On November 5, 1903, the members met in Napier's downtown offices and organized the One Cent Savings and Trust Company Bank, which opened on January 16, 1904, in the Napier Court building. He was a board member and the cashier of One Cent Bank until he died. The National Bankers Association would be formed and affiliated with Washington's Negro Business League. When critics of Washington such as W. E. B. Du Bois verbally attacked Washington at a convention in 1903, Napier refuted their "bloodthirsty speeches," even though Napier had supported Du Bois's Niagara Movement as "the birth of a new spirit of united purpose and effort." But he said nothing in March 1907 when Washington appeased a conservative Vanderbilt University audience by promising that "the elite colored man will never intrude himself into your social circles where he is not asked or where he is not wanted."[25]

Despite his close ties to Booker T. Washington, James Napier and his local associates believed that "separate but unequal" discriminated against all classes. Even Washington secretly worked against the Jim Crow system. In late 1903 he urged Napier to help persuade the president of the Pullman Car

Company, Robert Todd Lincoln, to hold a conference about segregated trains. Napier and others wrote letters, but Lincoln refused to meet. In December 1903 Napier wrote to Washington, "I think that the time has come when we should take a bold stand in favor of law and order and insist on their rigid execution as applied to the Negro whether in his favor or against him." Napier, R. H. Boyd, and thirteen other black leaders organized a streetcar boycott in Nashville on July 5, 1905, formed the Union Transportation Company, and operated several eighteen-passenger electric cars. In July 1906 the boycott leaders endorsed the Afro-American Council (a chapter had been formed by Nashville Negroes in 1891), and made the One Cent Bank, which J. C. Napier headed, a depository for the "Council's Defense Fund." In 1907 the streetcar boycott came to an end, partly because working-class blacks could hardly afford to support it.[26]

Washington and his followers continued their political emphasis and focused on election of Republican William H. Taft to the presidency. African Americans had lost much faith in Pres. Theodore Roosevelt after he had dismissed the Twenty-fifth Regiment of black troops in November 1906. The soldiers were accused of shooting some whites during an August 1906 riot in Brownsville, Texas, although they took up arms in self-defense against the town's taunting racists. Local black leaders still somewhat admired Roosevelt, perhaps because he allegedly offered J. C. Napier the position of consul-general to Bahia, Brazil, in 1908. But northerners were agonizing over the way the southern demagogues had handled the race problem since the Compromise of 1877. Lawlessness, lynching, riots, and political corruption in the South embarrassed the nation. As Roosevelt's handpicked successor, Taft told *Alexander's Magazine* in May 1906, "I cannot put myself among those pessimists who regard the settlement of the political [Negro] question in the South as beyond hope." Wealthy northern philanthropists began pouring money into the South to improve life for southern whites and blacks. In 1907 when Anna T. Jeanes, the daughter of a wealthy Philadelphia merchant, gave a million dollars to support education in the rural South, Taft and Napier became members of the racially integrated board of trustees.

Napier continued to be dedicated to his family and business while maintaining political activism. In May 1908 Taft dedicated Fisk University's Carnegie Library and revealed, "I am deeply interested in the success of the Booker T. Washington doctrine, which is for the colored race to cut a path to success by making others see how essential and indispensable he is and how useful to the community which they are a part." He insisted that a section of the downtown Ryman Auditorium be reserved so that black leaders could hear the speech but announced his intent not to push black federal appointments when opposed by whites. Napier predicted that "if made president, it is my firm belief that he [Taft] will use the whole power of his position to influence sentiment in the South to acceptance in good faith of the Fifteenth Amendment." Napier argued that African Americans had nowhere to go and nothing to gain by deserting the Republican Party.[27] On October 30, 1908, the *Globe* urged the "Colored Brethren" to "stick to the Republicans because the Democrats are dominated by our ancient enemy [neo-Confederates]." On March 4, 1909, newly inaugurated President Taft asserted that "the colored men must base their hope on the results of their own industry, self-restraint, thrift, and business success, as well as upon the aid and comfort and sympathy, which they may receive from white neighbors of the South."[28]

In late 1909 when racial accommodationism had won out in the White House and in Afro-Nashville, Napier and other black leaders met a train in east Tennessee that carried Booker T. Washington on a triumphant statewide tour. The *Globe* called Washington "the Champion of the [Colored] People's Cause."[29] Black leaders clung to the Republican Party, their fragile alliance with northerners, and racial accommodationism. Napier remained the foremost leader in Afro-Nashville. He had been selected four times as a delegate to the Republican National Convention, including three times from the state-at-large.

African American leaders in Nashville admired Napier, approved his determination to achieve national office, and regarded him as their best hope for national recognition. Napier lobbied for a federal job in the Taft administration in 1909. The *Globe* insisted that "the Negroes of the entire state are asking recognition of their political leader [J. C. Napier], the one man who has without fear or favor, stood up boldly . . . for the success of the grand old [Republican] party." In 1910 President Taft offered him an administrative post in Liberia, but Washington secretly advised him to decline because of the "fevers there." Washington perceived some of the current black federal office holders as his enemies, and he particularly wanted to place an ally in the Treasury Department.

Taft nominated Napier for a U.S. Treasury position in early 1910. Through 1911 a total of twenty-four letters were exchanged between the anxious Napier and the president's office, with Taft personally responding to two of the letters. On March 15 the president's secretary told Napier not to worry—the appointment would be approved soon. Napier shared the letter with Washington, who returned it with a note of support on March 23. Napier already had sent a check for $100.02 to Tuskegee, which led Washington to respond that "I am greatly tempted to frame it as a souvenir," because "the brethren [Negroes]" hardly donate anything to Tuskegee. Napier invited Washington to come to the house for dinner, but the Fisk trustee conveniently responded that he would be too busy "studying the Fisk situation." Napier then turned to pester the Democrats of the Tennessee congressional delegation for their support, and he even solicited letters from his local white Napier relatives. His man in Washington, D.C., Robert W. Thompson, used his "National News Bureau" to assure all concerned persons that Mr. Napier was "not a candidate for any job now held by a colored man; of course, if there is to be a change, [he] would like to be considered." But on April 17, 1910, Thompson assured James Carroll and Nettie that "we shall all rejoice to see you both as members of the social and official circle of the nation's capital." Although some senators cynically questioned whether the light-skinned Napier was "really a Negro," the Senate approved his nomination as register of the Treasury. This brought before Napier the old wounds of the post-Emancipation problems of miscegenation, race, and class. But he said nothing to the racist senators—at least publicly; besides, by then elite mulattos had resigned themselves to assimilate into the categories of "Negro Race" and "Colored Race." The whites, too, had rejected the open miscegenation of the Old South and publicly proclaimed the idea of "racial purity" in the Age of European Imperialism and Social Darwinism. But black elites were busy building a life of wealth, influence, class, and privilege of their own within the proscriptions of Jim Crow America. When elite blacks attended parties and receptions in Nashville for U.S. Register-designate J. C. Napier and Nettie, fine carriages and rare automobiles picked these guests up at the railroad stations. At a Nashville reception for Nettie and James Napier, Richard H. Boyd testified that "Mr. Napier . . . is a Negro of whom the whole race is proud."[30]

On May 1, 1911, the African American elite in Washington, D.C., held a banquet in the Odd Fellows Hall to honor James C. and Nettie D. Napier. The exultant Napier testified that "the colored people of this country never had a firmer friend" than W. H. Taft. To appease opponents of Booker T. Washington, Napier noted that Douglass, Langston, and Blanche K. Bruce would "turn over in their graves to see the 'Jim Crow' car roll into the District of Columbia, the very Capitol, with impunity." In September 1911 Napier learned that Solomon P. Harris was elected to the Nashville city council—the first black councilman since 1885. In November Napier visited the Georgia Colored State Fair. He joined other African American leaders to question the less-than-equitable distribution of federal funds to support black farmers and agricultural programs at black colleges. He sent Taft a report entitled "The Industrial Advancement of the Colored People of the United States," and on March 12, 1912, appeared before the House Committee on Agriculture. Napier often had lunch and discussion at Gray's Restaurant with fellow members of the "Negro Cabinet" including Judge Robert H. Terrell, James A. Cullo, Ralph Tyler, Kelly Miller, Calvin Chase, R. W. Thompson, and others. In early 1912 Napier and the "Negro Cabinet" approached Taft about precluding any "public misunderstanding" about the president's race policy. Taft responded cautiously but did block the appointment of an ex-Confederate to the Supreme Court. In April 1912 Napier joined New York's Equality Congress to petition the president and the secretary of war to form an African American National Guard unit. At the meeting, he proudly exchanged old currency for new bills with his signature as register of the treasury on them. He spoke at Howard University, the Colored Young Women's Association, Wilberforce University, and toured Florida with Booker T. Washington on an "educational pilgrimage." He helped to gain approval for the Tennessee Agricultural and Industrial State Normal School for Negroes and was involved in promoting Walden University, a black institution in Nashville.[31]

The campaign of 1912, which pitted former president Theodore Roosevelt against incumbent president Taft for the Republican nomination, placed Washington in a dilemma. Washington had served as a black adviser to Taft and to President Roosevelt. Some African Americans in Nashville formed a Colored Progressive Club to support Roosevelt, while others supported Wilson. Napier stuck by Taft. After Woodrow Wilson won the presidency, Washington wrote to Napier, "I am sincerely sorry for Mr. Taft." On

January 14, 1913, Nettie and James Carroll attended their last presidential reception at the Taft White House. During Wilson's administration, federal offices became segregated. Napier resigned, and all the members of the "Negro Cabinet" (except Judge Terrell) lost their federal jobs. Not until 1953 did another black (a Republican) serve in the treasury position.[32]

Back home in Nashville, J. C. Napier immersed himself in local civic, business, and civil rights affairs. He resumed the job as cashier of the One Cent Bank without a salary and practiced law. In 1913, Republican governor Ben Hooper appointed him to represent Tennessee at the Emancipation Celebration of Ex-Slaves in Philadelphia. In his effort to block a pro–Du Bois candidate from joining the Howard University Board of Trustees, Booker T. Washington successfully nominated Napier for the seat. Napier succeeded Washington as president of the National Negro Business League in 1915, and at the organization's convention on August 15, 1917, he insisted that blacks migrated north because of "mob-law, the 'Jim Crow' system, poor housing, poor schools, inadequate education, disfranchisement, and general abbreviation of citizenship, with which none of us are satisfied in this Southland."

Speaking at an African American rally in Hadley Park on April 15, 1917, Napier conceded that support should be given to President Wilson during World War I. Nettie helped to form an African American women's unit of the National Council of Defense, with which her husband and R. H. Boyd helped. Yet Wilson wanted to censor the African American newspapers for justifiably accusing America of racial oppression. In 1918 when a black was lynched in a town near Nashville, Napier led over two thousand African Americans to present a petition to the governor. He and others participated in the Tennessee Law and Order League to stop lynching. Nettie led a women's protest that forced the officials to allow some African American exhibits in the Women's Building of the State Fairgrounds, involved herself in the women's suffrage movement in 1919 and 1920, and soon became president of the Frederick Douglass Memorial and Historical Association to restore and maintain "The Old Warrior's" home. On January 18, 1919, Napier and ninety-two others established the Nashville branch of the National Association for the Advancement of Colored People. The next year he helped charter a chapter of the Commission of Interracial Cooperation (CIC). He influenced the CIC to support a $160,000 campaign for new buildings and a streetcar line to Tennessee A & I State Normal College. In 1920 the National Convention of the Lincoln Voters League honored J. C. Napier and John R. Lynch (1847–1939) "for their national leadership."[33] Still, Napier would not become *the* national leader he so desired.

Napier faithfully supported the efforts of black educational leaders at Fisk, Meharry, and Howard. When the students went on strike against the racially conservative president of Fisk University in 1924, he fully supported the president. W. E. B. Du Bois, whose daughter was in attendance at Fisk, led a rebellion to fire the president. Napier persuaded John Hope (then president of a college in Atlanta) to try and calm his friend Du Bois down, but Du Bois continued the attack. After being pressured by public rallies in the black community, on April 16, 1925, the president resigned. Despite this disappointment, the eighty-year-old Napier forged ahead as chairman of a drive to raise twenty-five thousand dollars for Fisk University in order "to prevent the lowering of standards at the school and to guarantee the continuance of the institution in Nashville." James Weldon Johnson, sometimes called the "father of the Harlem Renaissance" and then a professor at Fisk University in 1931, recognized Napier as one of "Fisk's greatest supporters" by granting him the honorary doctor of laws degree. He supported Howard University's president against a faculty rebellion, which he considered to be "unholy and hostile effusions against the Administration of the school." By 1931 the aged Napier attended few board meetings at Howard, and the president had to mail copies of the June 1932 commencement address by Pres. Herbert Hoover. Napier had served as chairman of the Hubbard Hospital Association to raise money to build the first teaching hospital at Meharry Medical College in 1912. When the faculty threatened to quit in 1933 after their pay was decreased during financial difficulties, the eighty-eight-year-old Napier quieted the discord. The Meharry president said, "I appreciate it all the more because of your age and because it is not as easy for you to get around as it is for some people."[34]

Napier had little or no influence left in the Republican Party of Tennessee, which continued the "lily-white" strategy to push blacks out of the party in an effort to attract more southern whites. This especially was the tactic used during Herbert Hoover's administration. Although Napier remained loyal to the Republican Party, the party had no use for him. By the 1930s the rising stars in black Republican clubs in Tennessee were eclipsing Napier.

When Pres. Franklin D. Roosevelt visited Nashville in 1934, J. C. Napier was selected as the African American respondent. Nashville blacks reacted favorably to Roosevelt and the New Dealers—the New Deal programs awarded many projects for Afro-Nashville, including a new high school building, improvements at Tennessee A & I State College, restoration of Union army Fort Negley, and construction of the Andrew Jackson Housing Project, managed by an African American. Another local federal housing project on Lafayette Street was later named for him. In 1938 the Democratic mayor tried to honor J. C. Napier by nominating him for a city commission on federal housing; however, a loyal black Democrat, Coyness L. Ennix, was more acceptable to Tennessee's senator K. D. McKellar. Napier graciously sent his letter of resignation.[35]

After three months of illness, James C. Napier died on Sunday, April 21, 1940. Funeral services were held in Fisk University's chapel on Wednesday, April 24. The president of Tennessee A & I State College cancelled classes for the day because J. C. Napier was listed as one of the founders of the institution. Frankie Pierce and her City Federation of Colored Women's Clubs insisted that the city public schools be closed; the mayor agreed, and sent a police escort for the funeral processional.[36] Some forty-five thousand former American slaves still lived in 1940, but for the Napier family, "the long journey from iron plantation to city," from slavery to freedom, had ended.

James Carroll Napier had the influence, wealth, and education required to become a member of the black elite. He was one of the "aristocrats of color" who influenced the history of Nashville in many important ways. Although born a slave to mulatto parents on a middle-Tennessee iron plantation, he grew up as a free black. Life was far milder for him than for most blacks. Napier had seen the Civil War years close-up until his family had sent him behind the lines to Ohio to attend college. He returned to the city just as Reconstruction began, and then quickly rose in the political ranks of the Tennessee Republican Party, heading the black-dominated Davidson County Republican club, attending national Republican conventions, and serving on the executive board of the Tennessee Republican Party until 1908. When local blacks began their civil rights protests with vigor, Napier was chosen regularly as their spokesman from 1874 to 1920. When they pushed for more educational opportunities in the 1880s, he assumed a leadership role. As one of only two African Americans in Tennessee with a formal law degree, Napier soon gained national recognition and even became register of the U.S. Treasury in 1911. He was also an opportunist, aligning himself with Booker T. Washington, promoting his own image through incessant letter-writing campaigns, and trying constantly to stay employed in the federal service. Yet he was too old and too little recognized to become the successor to Booker T. Washington in 1915. Still, Napier's life of ninety-five years highlighted and accompanied the many phases and stages of African American history in Nashville-Davidson County, from slavery to freedom. The journey of his mulatto family from the iron plantations of Dickson County to Nashville exemplified how many antebellum blacks made the difficult transition from the rural to the urban environment. J. C. Napier and other black elite were not the sole history makers in the African American community, but he and they were the symbols and the shining stars in the unfolding of that history of tragedy and triumph.

Although the Napier family members represented the elite among people of color, nevertheless, they too suffered the racism, discrimination, and rejection practiced by whites. In this precarious environment, the black elite, including J. C. Napier, bore the heavy burden of providing the leadership in culture, business, and politics for African Americans. Despite personal self-interest and egotism, members of the black elite tried to maintain the graces of a ruling class while facing awful political and social dilemmas. Their lives reveal the complexities in a place and at a time so tragically fixated on the color of a person's skin.

Robert E. Lee Wilson and the Making of a Post–Civil War Plantation

Jeannie M. Whayne

By the time he died in 1933, Robert E. Lee Wilson of Mississippi County, Arkansas, had amassed a vast plantation and mercantile enterprise that rivaled any in the South. He had risen from obscurity as the orphan son of a Civil War veteran, beginning with a 160-acre homestead as his patrimony. He eventually amassed 65,000 acres of land and was worth millions of dollars. Oral tradition has it that young Wilson crossed over the Mississippi River sometime in the early 1880s to find his homestead shrouded in deep forests, surrounded by swamps, and periodically threatened by flood water from the Mississippi River. A veritable treasure of wild game and water fowl inhabited the area, including a dangerous assortment of predators such as wild cats, savage razorback hogs, and poisonous water moccasins. Malaria and typhoid fever were common ailments plaguing almost every resident. The coming of the railroad and the growth of the lumber industry opened up new possibilities, particularly for those with some capital, plenty of energy, and unusual vision.

Although he was of relatively modest means and from a family of few pretensions—his father having owned only one slave, a small homestead, and some 2,700 acres of swamplands—Wilson fashioned a plantation system that incorporated a peculiar paternalistic ethic of his own creation, a paternalism that resembled that of corporate firms like the Pullman Company or Mississippi's Delta and Pine Land Company as much as that of the planters of the antebellum era. By the 1920s his plantation and business enterprises were carefully organized and systematically managed with a comprehensive network of farm overseers and office supervisors. He subdivided the 28,054 acres he owned in south Mississippi County alone into fifteen different farms, each having its own overseer who reported to a single general overseer who reported to the farm manager in the office at the Lee Wilson & Company headquarters in Wilson, Arkansas. He operated businesses in five other towns in south Mississippi County, including two towns named for his daughters, Marie and Victoria. He owned and operated a short-line railroad and various business enterprises, which included a drug store, a dry cleaner, an automobile dealership, a lumber company, a planing mill, a cotton compress, a power and light company, and several general stores and gins; all of the enterprises reported to the Lee Wilson & Company general office in Wilson. He also acquired a controlling interest in several banks in the county.

For his farm laborers and other employees, he provided adequate housing, health care, excellent educational facilities, and places of entertainment. His farm hands lived in housing complexes organized around one of the fifteen plantations and drew their mules and implements from central barns located on the respective plantation. His white-collar and mill workers also lived in housing owned by Wilson, who became known simply as "Boss Lee." He developed a reputation as a benevolent despot who could be harsh, unyielding, and prone to strong language, but he was also capable of great generosity. He expected hard work and loyalty from all those under him, whether white or black, farmer or laborer, white-collar or servile worker. While he constructed a complex and orderly system of management, he paid close attention to every detail himself and frequently intervened in decisions made on the various farms, in the office, or at the banks. He was, simply put, omnipresent.

Wilson was born near present-day Wilson, Arkansas, on his father's 160-acre homestead. Josiah Wilson "entered" the homestead in 1846 and had his title certified in 1848. Josiah also accumulated approximately 2,700 acres of swampland in Arkansas and owned land near Randolph, just across the Mississippi River in Tennessee.[1] He suffered losses prior to his death in 1872 and had little to leave his children, William Henry, Robert E. Lee, and Victoria. Josiah's widow, Martha Parson Wilson, moved her family to Randolph, just north of Memphis, where both she and Josiah had family. The children were left orphans a few years later when she died in 1878 during one of the periodic yellow-fever epidemics that struck the Memphis area.[2] Wilson, only thirteen at the time of his mother's death, was raised by an uncle and attended schools in Tennessee, receiving only the rudiments of an education.[3] Some time in the early 1880s, young Wilson left Tennessee and started working his Arkansas homestead, apparently cutting timber and farming—both on his own land and as a field hand on nearby farms.

In the mid-1880s Wilson opened a honky-tonk that proved to be anything but profitable, discovering after a year or so that "the employees stole all the receipts and he had only $150.00 he could get his hands on." With what cash he had remaining, he "bought a groundhog sawmill and set it up at Golden Lake," and with no money left "he made arrangements with a store owner to feed the laborers, and charged it against their payroll. He got out two barge loads of lumber on the river . . . This enabled him to pay the indebtedness and some left over, which he invested in timberland at $1.25 per acre."[4] By this time he had married Elizabeth "Lizzy" Beall, the daughter of a prosperous farmer and lumberman, and went into the lumber business with his father-in-law, Socrates.[5] In 1888 he was managing Socrates Beall's sawmill interests, and by 1898 he was in full partnership with him. Together they owned forty million feet of standing timber in the Golden Lake area and another seventy-five million feet of standing timber around Barfield, all located in south Mississippi County. In May 1899 Wilson helped organize the Osceola Land & Lumber Company in partnership with two men from Osceola and two men from Cairo, Illinois. James L. Hale of Cairo became president, with Wilson as vice president.[6] Meanwhile, he began to the lay the foundation for his plantation empire. As he brought his cutover land into production, he incorporated as Lee Wilson & Company, constructed cotton gins, opened commissaries, and put to work some white tenants but mostly black sharecroppers in his cotton fields.

Wilson's rise to a dominant position as planter and employer was largely owed to his acquisition and subsequent transformation of cheap, marginal land. His real property holdings in south Mississippi County increased from the 160-acre homestead he inherited from his father in 1872 to 28,054 acres by 1922.[7] In addition, he owned thousands of acres in north Mississippi County, including his very profitable plantation at Armorel and a few thousand acres in surrounding counties. Wilson acquired most of his land while it was still forested or as cutover land, much of it for fifty cents an acre. As one of the main proponents of the creation of drainage enterprises in the St. Francis River basin, he was able to turn his swamplands into valuable agricultural acreage.[8]

The efforts to drain the swamps of eastern Arkansas began in the antebellum era and were orchestrated by landowners with little aid from the state or federal governments. In 1850, however, the United States Congress passed an act calling for the donation of unsold swamplands to the states with the understanding that the states would sell the lands and use the proceeds to construct levees. Under the act Arkansas received 8.6 million acres, but many of the levees constructed in the 1850s deteriorated during the Civil War. County levee districts, dominated by large landowners, attempted to repair the levees after the war, but a series of significant floods in the 1880s (1882, 1883, 1884, and 1886) demonstrated the deficiencies of the uncoordinated efforts of individual counties. The state responded to pressure from landowners in 1891, passing legislation making it possible for counties to form consolidated levee districts. The idea was that more comprehensive and coordinated projects that crossed county lines would allow for better drainage. In 1892 representatives from the levee districts of eight northeastern Arkansas counties—Mississippi, Craighead, Crittenden, Cross, Lee, Poinsett, St. Francis, and Phillips—formed the St. Francis River Levee District, and in 1893 the state passed an act incorporating the district. The 1893 act also donated two hundred thousand acres of unsold swamplands within the eight-county area, swamp lands remaining from the 1850 act of Congress, to the levee district, anticipating that the district would sell the land to fund its initial operations.[9]

Lee Wilson, still a young man in the 1890s, did not become a member of the district's board of directors until 1929, but he was closely allied with John B. Driver, an organizer of the consolidated district in 1892 and president of the St. Francis Levee District board from 1897 to 1901.[10] Wilson began to purchase swamplands from the district in the 1890s and was a strong advocate of drainage. Like other land owners in Mississippi County, however, he became impatient with the slow progress being made by the St. Francis Levee District and became involved in a controversial effort to create a new intracounty drainage district in 1901. Realizing certain inadequacies in the state's drainage laws, Wilson corresponded with officials in Illinois and secured copies of that state's drainage laws.[11] Arkansas did not allow counties to sell bonds to fund levee building, and lacking any other means of funding initial construction, most county drainage enterprises were small affairs. Given the existence of thousands of acres of swamplands in Mississippi County, more ambitious and costly projects were necessary if these lands were to be reclaimed.

Wilson was not alone in his desire for reform of the state's drainage laws.

In early 1902 Mississippi County judge Logan D. Rozelle appointed a three-man committee—S. E. Simonson, W. B. Calhoun, and Wilson Burchfield—to pursue reform of the state's drainage laws. Working in concert with the committee, Wilson and four other prominent men, including J. T. Coston, filed a petition to reform those laws. Simonson and Lee Wilson were close friends, and Coston was Lee Wilson's attorney. One of the other petitioners was John Driver, whose presidency of the St. Francis River Levee District board ended the year before. Together they lobbied for state legislation permitting the creation of county drainage districts with the power to sell bonds and levy taxes. In 1902 the state responded by passing legislation modeled on those laws in force in Missouri.[12]

Wilson and his compatriots discovered that not only did they have to contend with the opposition of some timber companies and land speculators who did not want to pay higher taxes on lands they did not intend to develop, but they also had to deal with land owners situated on higher ground who resented the prospect of paying taxes for drainage that they believed would help them only nominally. Feelings ran so high in Mississippi County that despite the passage of enabling legislation in 1902, Wilson and his cohorts were unable to secure enough local support to organize a large area in south Mississippi County. The law required that land owners within the proposed district must agree to the formation of the district. A few smaller areas in the county formed districts between 1902 and 1908, but strident opposition emerged when two major drainage districts were proposed.[13]

As late as 1908 the opposition seemed relentless. One opponent wrote a letter to the editor of the *Osceola Times* declaring that the taxes would be confiscatory. The opponent challenged the editor to rethink her alliance with the "vampires who have been sucking the blood of the people for several years, and now have formed a syndicate to rob them" and promised that those who opposed drainage would "resort to their guns in defense of themselves and those who depend on them." He further declared, "I am only one of hundreds who will resort to blood shed before starvation."[14]

Indeed, violence threatened to erupt at a picnic that Lee Wilson sponsored on his property, a picnic designed to promote the districts. One of the petitioners for Drainage District 8, W. B. Calhoun, was threatened by a knife-wielding assailant at the picnic, and Wilson himself had to intervene when yet another opponent of the district threatened S. E. Simonson. Perhaps the most infamous episode transpired when Judge Rozelle called a meeting of the county court on July 6, 1908, for a hearing on the issue of forming Drainage District 8. The meeting occurred during a hotly contested political race with one candidate for sheriff adamantly opposed to the formation of the district.[15] Lee Wilson, anticipating the appearance of armed opposition, stationed his own well-armed men in strategic locations around the courthouse. A crowd of opponents brandishing guns and knives arrived at the courthouse, and in this tense and dangerous situation, the proponents and opponents of the district testified. The crowd grew more restive and the situation even more ominous, so Judge Rozelle wisely stayed the proceedings for ninety days and adjourned court. A crowd flourishing a rope followed his carriage down the road as he departed from the courthouse. He was later visited by a committee of men who threatened his life if he granted the petition to create the district.[16]

Rozelle died of natural causes before ruling on the issue, and J.T. Coston and other prodrainage men convinced newly elected governor George Donaghey to appoint prominent young attorney S. L. Gladish to fill his position. Donaghey had spoken in favor of drainage at a gathering in Mississippi County during his campaign for the governor's office earlier that year, and Coston, one of the original prodrainage petitioners, had stumped the state for Donaghey, helping him to secure election. Gladish ruled in favor of establishing the district, and, as a result, he faced stiff competition in the special election held to confirm his appointment in July 1909. For the first time in the history of the unincorporated town of Wilson, the entire population, including convicts leased by Wilson to work his plantation, voted in the election. The result was that Gladish was narrowly elected.[17] Gladish authorized the selling of bonds to fund construction of District No. 8 to a firm in Springfield, Illinois, and other bonds to fund construction of the even larger Drainage District No. 9 to a St. Louis financier. Opponents of the two large districts filed numerous injunctions that Gladish heard in his courtroom over the next six months. Finally, in December 1909, the last of the injunctions against the two districts was lifted and construction began in earnest.[18]

The controversy over drainage did not end there, however. Wilson's relationship with the St. Francis Levee District Board was complicated by a struggle for control between the "upper" and "lower" counties. His friend, John Driver, president of the board from 1897 to 1901, was replaced by

O. N. Killough of Cross County in 1902. Killough represented the "lower" counties—Cross, Lee, Phillips, Crittenden, and St. Francis—within the district in the struggle with the "upper" counties—Mississippi, Poinsett, and Craighead. The issue, of course, was where to position the levees and how to apportion the taxes. In 1909 W. B. Miller of Poinsett County became president of the board, and Lee Wilson served as chairman of the Mississippi County branch of an association composed of the three upper counties known as the St. Francis Valley Drainage Investigation Association.[19]

During much of this period of struggle for control over the levee board, Wilson was engaged in lawsuits against the federal government—litigation that involved the St. Francis Levee Board's right to sell him acreage within what was known as the sunk lands. The land in question had been "sunk" by the New Madrid earthquakes of 1811 and 1812 and lay principally within Mississippi and Poinsett Counties. In 1908 the Interior Department announced its ownership of approximately 120,000 acres of that land and declared its intention to open the area for homesteading. Hundreds of landless men and their families descended upon northeastern Arkansas and literally squatted on lands that they believed would be open for homesteading, despite warnings from the Interior Department that the land was in dispute and that final certification of their homesteads would be delayed.[20]

In 1914 the federal government brought suit against Wilson and four others to "quiet title" to the land in order to establish once and for all the government's ownership of it.[21] While various others claimed approximately 80,000 acres in the disputed area, the Wilson case involved his alleged ownership of only 853 acres in the Moon Lake area of Mississippi County, which he had acquired from the St. Francis Levee District.[22] The federal government claimed that the land had never belonged to the St. Francis Levee District nor to the state of Arkansas, which had donated the land to the district in 1894, and thus the conveyances were null and void.[23]

The state believed it had the authority to donate the land to the St. Francis Levee District because the land in question had been conveyed to the state by the 1850 Swamp Land Act. The federal government declared that only surveyed lands had been transferred by that act and pointed out that the land involved in the dispute had never been surveyed. Indeed, they had been recorded by surveyors in 1841 as lakes, and since surveyors are not required to run a survey of bodies of water identified as lakes, they did not do so in this case. When these lands were later determined to be swamps, however, the failure to survey them became crucial. Wilson claimed that the bodies of water were lakes and not swamps and that the St. Francis Levee District Board could claim ownership by riparian right, a long established principle in legal history. Riparian rights applied to owners of land contiguous to a lake who then drained the lake. Such owners could claim ownership of the drained land.[24]

When the federal court ruled in 1914 in the government's favor, Wilson appealed.[25] In 1917 the United States Supreme Court confirmed the lower court's ruling that the land belonged to the federal government (because they were unsurveyed swamplands never conveyed from the federal to the state government as part of the 1850 Swamp Land Act) and that the principle of riparian rights did not apply to the sunk lands of northeastern Arkansas (because they were swamps, not lakes).[26] However, the court implied in its written decision that a remedy for Wilson might exist through congressional legislation.[27] Through his relationship with Arkansas Senator Joseph T. Robinson and Rep. William J. Driver, son of Wilson's old friend, John B. Driver, Wilson was able to influence the passage of legislation that gave "preferential rights" to men like himself who had paid the real property taxes and had made improvements upon lands that they believed they owned during the period that the land was in dispute. Those successfully claiming preferential rights were allowed to purchase the land that they claimed for an appraised value, which included any timber that might have been removed but excluded any improvements made on the land.[28] Although it appears that Wilson was never able to secure the land specifically identified in the case that he lost in Supreme Court in 1917, he surfaced as a "riparian claimant" in congressional legislation and was able to purchase at least 1,160 acres.[29]

The 1920s was a decade of challenge and consolidation for Wilson. While his real property holdings did not increase within south Mississippi County, the value of those holdings more than doubled, largely as a result of the drainage ditches constructed in the 1910s by the various drainage enterprises, particularly Drainage Districts 8 and 9, which allowed Wilson to expand his plantation enterprise. Similarly, his personal property increased in value from $85,515 in 1922 to $232,205 in 1931.[30] However, Wilson did not escape the economic problems confronting other planters in the agricultural sector in the 1920s—the decline in cotton prices, the flood of 1927, and the drought of 1931.[31]

Wilson was no stranger to economic catastrophe. In 1911, even as he battled the federal government for ownership of the swamplands and expanded his farming enterprises, he was still very much dependent upon his lumbering business, and a downturn in that marketplace caused him to have to borrow $300,000 from financiers in Springfield, Illinois. No sooner was that accomplished than the 1912 flood broke the levee near Wilson, submerging his lumberyards and bringing him to the brink of economic disaster. According to one Wilson employee, Robert Robinson, who wrote in April 1912: "Our company has received as severe losses as anyone I suppose, the town of Wilson being three to six feet in water; all of the lumber flooded and covered with sand, making it hard to sell. Of course it is not worth nearly so much. . . . Our Mississippi [River] Mill is ten feet in water at the present time and our damage there is going to be quite heavy as we had about twenty five thousand dollars worth of lumber there. The high waters, of course, have put a quietus on shipping, and business is going to be very light for the next few months."[32] Not only was Wilson's lumber business damaged by the flood, but his farming operation came to a stop. Wilson survived by putting his tenants and sharecroppers to work on two thousand acres of high ground he owned near Armorel in north Mississippi County.[33] The next year the levee broke again. This time he turned to a St. Louis businessman for a $100,000 loan.[34]

The upturn in the market for agricultural products during World War I made it possible for Wilson to recover. He paid off his debts and plowed much of his profit into the further reclamation of his land and the expansion of his plantation enterprise. Farmers elsewhere behaved in a similar fashion during the prosperous war years. Many of them bought more land, purchased additional equipment, and built new barns and other farm structures. Wilson's real-property holdings did not increase in south Mississippi County between 1911 and 1920, but his personal property wealth there increased from $35,167 to $147,000. Rather than purchasing more land in south Mississippi County, Wilson expanded his business and farming enterprises there. In 1911 he listed only three businesses on the personal property books for south Mississippi County: the Wilson Bank, the Wilson Drug Store, and Lee Wilson & Company. In 1920 he listed seven enterprises, including stores in the towns of Wilson, Marie, Bassett, Keiser, and Evadale.[35] By this time he not only had controlling interest in the Bank of Wilson but also helped launch a bank in Keiser. In 1922 he gained controlling interest in Farmers Bank and Trust in Blytheville.[36]

Because of the precipitous drop in prices paid for agricultural products which accompanied the recession following World War I, farmers and merchants who serviced the farm economy suffered severe losses. The Bank of Wilson received numerous requests for extensions on loans to various parties, including two letters from farmers in February 1919. John Joiner wrote that "cotton is gone for nothing," and Johnson Mitchell stated, "I have fell down in my cotton and I can't pay."[37] No record of the bank's reply to their requests for extensions survives in the records, but its response to another creditor suggests it was unlikely to have replied in a manner pleasing to either Joiner or Mitchell. Hollipeter, Shonyo & Company of Blytheville, which was in the real estate, automobile, and mule business, had a five thousand dollar loan through the Bank of Wilson and asked for an extension in December 1919; the company wrote the bank that, "you know how the conditions have been this fall for the collections and we are not right now in shape to take it up."[38] The bank responded immediately that "it is not at all satisfactory to carry past due paper" and demanded payment.[39]

One of Wilson's own entities, the Keiser Supply Company, faced difficulties, and on March 12, 1919, manager L. L. Harwell wrote to Wilson that "we have quite a few accounts that are due and the jobbers are beginning to DUN us pretty lively." Harwell suggested that they draw on one of their cotton factors, Wilson-Ward Company of Memphis, but Wilson instructed him to apply to the Bank of Wilson for a three thousand dollar loan instead.[40] Later that year Wilson helped organize the Bank of Keiser with Harwell as president, perhaps as a hedge against future cash flow problems for his enterprises in Keiser.[41]

The recession turned more serious in the next year, and the situation became so drastic in the fall of 1920 that some farmers posted signs on cotton gins demanding that the ginners close until prices went up.[42] Indeed, for many farmers and merchants, the 1920s were a continual nightmare of bankruptcies and foreclosures. In 1921, one of the most prosperous planters in south Mississippi County, Walter Driver (no relation to John B. Driver or his son, Cong. William D. Driver), found it "impossible to sell even a part of his cotton at anywhere near the actual cost of production." Ironically, Driver had passed up the opportunity to sell his harvest for ninety-five cents a bale, deciding to wait until the price rose to one dollar. Instead of rising, the price sank to a nickel a bale, and Driver found himself facing bankruptcy. Driver was able to reach agreement with his creditors and avert total disaster, but he never fully recovered.[43]

Lee Wilson, on the contrary, expanded operations in the 1920s. Referred to by one essayist writing in 1923 as "a feudal baron of old," Boss Lee held sway over a town that "had no mayor and no court . . . no municipal laws." Everyone in the town was "his employee and his tenant," for he owned every building and home in Wilson. All the homes, whether three-room cottages or more commodious residences, had running water and electric lights supplied from his power and light plant. Even the tenant homes in the outlying plantation area had "electric lights, tub and shower baths, hot and cold water, telephone, hedge, flower garden, truck patch, and chicken yard." His land stretched "eight miles wide and twenty-seven miles long."[44]

His substantial landholdings provided him with ample collateral that he was able to leverage in creative ways. For example, in 1919 a bank representing one potential creditor asked one Wilson enterprise, the Bank of Wilson, for a reference regarding another Wilson enterprise, a mercantile establishment doing business under the name of Hill & Wilson. The First National Bank of St. Louis wrote, "In behalf of one of our valued customers we will appreciate an expression from you as to the general standing of Hill & Wilson, Marie, Ark., which town we believe is adjacent to your city, and particularly regarding Mr. Lee Wilson personally. Do you consider these parties responsible for a merchandise account of around $2,000?" Without revealing the connection between the two entities or its own relationship to Lee Wilson, the Bank of Wilson responded that "the firm is composed of R. E. Lee Wilson and O. M. Hill, each have invested in the business $37,500.00. Neither of them have made us a statement as to their individual worth, but we feel that $75,000.00 would be a conservative estimate of O. M. Hill's worth and Mr. Wilson will run over a million. We would consider these people good for the $2,000.00 order your customer has."[45] Similarly, when the Hanover National Bank of New York wrote the Bank of Wilson in late 1919 asking for information about the new bank being organized in Keiser, the response failed to reveal Wilson's connection to either bank. Clearly, Wilson was able to take advantage of the leverage he had at his disposal.

One asset that Wilson was willing to mortgage held special significance for him, and the creditor who advanced him $500,000 must have understood that fact all too well. In May 1922 the American Trust Company advanced the loan at 7 percent interest, and in return Wilson pledged the land where the town of Wilson was situated. The land involved amounted to only 428.35 acres, and the loan was far in excess of what the land and buildings were worth. Thomas Dysart, the trustee who oversaw the loan for American Trust Company, clearly understood that the town of Wilson represented the soul of the Wilson estate. The $500,000 loan almost certainly accounted for Wilson's ability to weather the difficult 1920s.[46]

Next to his ability to acquire and develop land and his facility at establishing businesses and banks, it was Wilson's extraordinary control of labor that most accounted for his rise to wealth and power. Census records confirm that the vast majority of Wilson's plantation labor force was African American. By 1920, 516 (66.4 percent) black and 260 (33.5 percent) white men of sixteen years or older resided in Golden Lake Township, an area that includes the town of Wilson and the main body of the Wilson plantation. Of the 470 black men listing occupations on the census, 277 (58.9 percent) were farming, and only 2 of those farmers claimed to be farm owners. The rest almost certainly worked on plantations and given their location, most would have worked for Lee Wilson. Another 136 (28.9 percent) black men worked in the lumber industry, likely for one of the Wilson enterprises. Thirteen black men worked in some servile capacity, as cooks, house boys, yardmen, and porters. On the other hand, only 62 (29.1 percent) of the 213 white men listing occupations were employed in some kind of farming enterprise, including 5 farm managers and 6 men who operated horse/mule farms. Of these white men, only 19 (33.3 percent) claimed to own their farms and 2 claimed to be homesteaders, leaving only 29 (13.6 percent) who might have worked as tenants for Wilson. A far greater percentage of white men were employed in the sawmills and planing mills (30.5 percent) or in white-collar jobs (16.9 percent). To be sure, they were very likely employed by Wilson in the lumber business or as clerks in one of his mercantile establishments.[47]

Most of those who labored on the Wilson plantation were new to the area. Just as Wilson had arrived at a time when the railroad and lumber industries were emerging in the 1880s, white and black landless men and their families began to surge into the northeastern Arkansas Delta looking for opportunity. Only 17.3 percent of the white and black men in Golden Lake

Township had been born in Arkansas. Most of the rest came from Tennessee (27.8 percent) and Mississippi (30.9 percent). The only meaningful difference between the black and white men in this regard was that the African Americans were more likely than whites to have been born in Mississippi.[48] But black newcomers to Mississippi County would eventually find that they had relatively few opportunities to do anything but work for Lee Wilson and his ilk. African Americans faced intense competition from whites for jobs in the lumber industry and for places on the growing number of plantations, competition that often erupted in violence. Whitecapping activities in Mississippi County resulted in no high-profile arrests or convictions, but references to violence against blacks and a "white-only" mentality surfaced in south Mississippi County's major newspaper, the *Osceola Times*.[49]

One opportunity rarely open to African Americans in Wilson country in the early twentieth century was homesteading. A violent and lethal campaign to keep what few homesteading opportunities that existed available only to whites prevailed in northeastern Arkansas. While newspaper articles referred to the desire of African Americans to homestead, they also recounted the "white only" mentality in the area. A letter from a homesteader wife referred to the burning out of a black homesteader, and although the white homesteaders were fighting a sometimes violent battle with planters, including Lee Wilson, the homesteader union that they created in 1914 included no black members.[50]

A look at personal property tax records provides the best evidence that this opportunity was not open to African Americans. Few African Americans resided in the school district most dominated by homesteaders in south Mississippi County. Only eight African Americans resided in that area in 1920 and only one remained in 1931. None of these few owned real or claimed personal property in either year. To be sure, their inability to secure a homestead cannot be attributed entirely to racism. Maintaining and developing a homestead required capital, and few African Americans had accumulated the requisite capital necessary to secure title.[51] Lee Wilson, of course, had plenty of room for African American sharecroppers, and to be fair to him, he provided an attractive alternative to the uncertainty prevailing elsewhere in the violence-ridden Arkansas Delta. The housing for his tenants and sharecroppers was far superior to that occupied by those on other plantations and many homesteaders.[52] He had a black doctor and clinic available for his

African American sharecroppers,[53] and the schooling provided for black children, while not equal to that provided for whites, was much better than that available elsewhere.[54] He also operated a black dance hall and sponsored picnics and barbecues. Unlike many planters who insisted that their sharecroppers grow cotton and corn only, leaving no acreage allotted for gardens which might help feed the family and prevent pellagra, Wilson insisted that his croppers keep "kitchen" gardens. One of his farm managers would routinely inspect their gardens to make certain that the right vegetables were being raised and that they were properly tended.[55]

A sense of paternalism and shrewd self-interest on his part was responsible for the better circumstances on the Wilson plantation. He considered them "his" people, and thus he provided for them. By furnishing them with medical facilities, for which a small "insurance" fee was charged to their account on a monthly basis, and a venue for entertainment, he kept what money there was at home. He paid in doodlum—his own paper money—which could only be redeemed at one of his stores.

In return for the privilege of better housing and schools, adequate medical facilities, and safety in the violence-prone Delta, African Americans and whites alike working for Wilson traded independence for dependence. Both renters and sharecroppers were closely supervised. Wilson employee D. N. Morris kept a written daily report for the summer of 1933, and it provides a revealing glimpse into the manner in which the Wilson plantation was operated. Morris was the man in charge of the day-to-day activities of the farming operation. Writing in abbreviated language, he reported on July 10, 1933: "Took load choppers to Clarence Henry. Loaded up with seed corn and went to Matt Ingram, Jeff Granville, Sol Jude, Andrew Malone, Gus Malone, Keiser Plantation, Herman Green, W. R. Rutherford, A. L. McBee, Mitchell Jaxon, Priestly Jones, Zeal Hamilton, Will Autman and W. R. Rutherford . . . got them all started planting corn . . . Went back to negroes planting corn, got pair mules for Mitchell Jaxon. Brought hands from Grove Farm to work on Water Tower at Wilson, took home in afternoon and brought choppers back to Wilson."[56] This entry in Morris's notebook also reveals the interplay between the town and the farm operation, but the men mentioned by name in this segment of Morris's notebook were either renters or sharecroppers for Wilson; their names appeared on a list of forty-eight sharecroppers and renters who had accounts in the Wilson store. That list indicated the amount that they owed on their accounts and the number of acres that they worked.[57] Morris scrutinized the activities of the renters as closely as he did the sharecroppers. For example, on July 3, 1933, concerning the four hundred acres rented by W. W. Anderson, Morris reported that hands were "plowing and chopping, most of this is in sharecrops [meaning that Anderson put sharecroppers on the acres he rented from Wilson], and payroll running light. Corn good shape and looking good except about 10 acres belonging to sharecropper which have notified to clean out right away." If Morris was dissatisfied with the performance of a renter or sharecropper, he sometimes took drastic steps to remedy the situation. For example, on July 31, he reported that he had decided to make D. K. Morgan, who sharecropped seventy acres for Lee Wilson, "move and come to Wilson." Morris took Jesse Greer, another Wilson employee and former deputy sheriff, with him "and served notice on him [Morgan] to move which he did the next day. We are going to plow up all of his cotton. . . we took all his tools and mules, in other words, every thing he had and moved them to Ridgeland Farm."[58] Morgan owed Wilson $342.44, and it is likely that he was expected to work off the debt in some other way.[59] Those who worked for Wilson accepted the interference of the overseers and farm managers, for there was little other recourse. Oral tradition has it that if you wanted to leave Wilson's employ, you did so in the dead of night and took nothing with you. George Stith, a black union organizer for the Southern Tenant Farmers' Union, reported that his sister and family worked on the Wilson plantation in the 1920s, and when they decided to depart, they left all their possessions and slipped away late one evening. He reported another incident involving a black farmer who worked for Wilson for nearly twenty years; he gained enough income to purchase land in Missouri and left all his possessions behind when he departed. He prudently opened the gate so his stock could graze, fearing that if they suffered, he could be pursued and prosecuted for that offense.[60]

The point is that you could leave, but if you dared to take along whatever you had acquired during your tenure under Wilson, he would come after you. He did not have to resort to illegal means to detain black sharecroppers; planters and local law enforcement officials had interpreted laws dating back to Reconstruction as giving them the authority to prohibit a sharecropper or tenant to leave the employment of a planter when they owed a debt.[61] Planters typically "furnished" their sharecroppers with money or supplies until the end of the crop year when "settlement" was made, and planters sought the passage of the lien laws as much to limit mobility as to collect a debt.[62] Wilson kept attorneys on retainer, and one of their responsibilities was to prosecute those who owed Wilson money, either because they had borrowed money and defaulted on the loan or because they had absconded with property that Wilson considered his own.[63] But the issue involved more than property. In providing better housing, health care, and recreation for "his people," Wilson demonstrated a high degree of paternalistic concern, and he believed that he was owed something in return. Loyalty, perhaps. Or perhaps he believed that the property acquired by his tenants and sharecroppers was not truly theirs, that they had earned the right to possess the property while under his protection, but to leave the plantation with it was out of the question.

Wilson's reputation for holding labor in place notwithstanding, he would not tolerate abuse of African Americans in his territory, particularly if another white man called his attention to it. In November 1932, Thomas Dysart wrote to Wilson to complain about the treatment that his "negro man" received when driving through Wilson. Dysart was the man who had served as trustee for the $500,000 loan from American Trust Company which Wilson secured in 1922. Wilson investigated the incident and reported to Sheriff W. W. Shaver that two of his unpaid deputy sheriffs, H. B. Carpenter and Jake Thrailkill, were "hijacking every foreign car that comes through Wilson that they think they can get a dollar out of." They had apparently arrested the black man, Virgil Branch, for speeding and for being drunk; took all his money, the horn off his car, a pistol, a Remington double-barreled shotgun, which actually belonged to Dysart; and demanded a seventy-five dollar fine. After questioning several people, Wilson believed that Branch had neither been drunk nor speeding and notified the deputies "to get out of Wilson and stay out," and appealed to Sheriff Shaver "as a friend and a citizen of Mississippi County, to revoke their sheriff deputyship at once."[64] To Dysart, Wilson wrote, "I had Carpenter in my office this morning and I told him to get off the premises and stay off . . . I am positive that no sons-of-bitches like this can stay on any of my property."[65]

Wilson's relationship with Dysart certainly influenced him to take the complaint more seriously than he might have if Dysart had been unknown to him. Whether Wilson believed it or not, evidence suggests that some of his employees treated African American labor too roughly. Earlier that year, Wilson had been notified by Scipio A. Jones, a prominent African American attorney in Little Rock. Jones wrote that he was representing "two colored men and the estate of a third to prosecute a suit against you in the federal court for damages based upon alleged acts of peonage." Jones professed to have "always heard of your eminent fairness to my people," and implied that his letter was meant to give Wilson an opportunity to make restitution for wrongs committed against his clients. The three black men in question had apparently been hired by Wilson's labor agents in Little Rock and transported to Wilson in mid-November of 1931 to help harvest the cotton crop. The text of his letter explains the claim:

> These men allege that the acts of peonage occurred between November 15, 1931 and November 26, 1931, in that they were employed by your agents in Little Rock and their transportation was furnished to your farms at Wilson; that their employment began on November 15, but they were interrupted in their picking of cotton by excessive rainfall and being unable to work they were charged for their room and board and began getting deeper into your debt, and when they sought to leave, they were seized by your agents and employees, brutally beaten and restrained of their liberty until they finally effected their escape. From the beatings administered one of the men died.[66]

Wilson's response to Jones was short and direct: "Replying to your letter of May 25th and note contents relative to my men, farm managers or anybody in my employ mistreating any one. This is not true. You can take any steps that you see fit." No record of the suit can be located, and no further correspondence exists in the Wilson files.

The control that Wilson exercised over his black laborers—whether by physical coercion, by law, or by paternalism—was such that African Americans remained with him when greater opportunity existed for them elsewhere in northeastern Arkansas (thus defying the expectations of neoclassical economists).[67] African Americans in Tyronza Township in neighboring Poinsett County who listed under $500 in property had an average value of $113.00, exceeding their counterparts in Wilson country, who were claiming $98.38 in personal property. The percentage of African Americans in the two populations is worth examining, as well. In Mississippi County there were 863 blacks as opposed to 265 whites, so the black population constituted 76.5 percent of the total population of taxpayers. In Poinsett County there were 290 blacks as opposed to 363 whites. That means that blacks made up only 44.4 percent of the population. And this despite the fact that African American farmers had a much greater chance of owning the farm that they operated in Poinsett County. Furthermore, in the Mississippi County township only 4.4 percent (160 out of 3,581) of black farmers owned their farms, while in the Poinsett County township, only 6.6 percent (42 out of 594) owned their own farms. Despite arguably better economic opportunities for blacks in the latter, they chose the relative security and better conditions in Wilson country—either that or they did not enjoy sufficient mobility to take advantage of what prospects Poinsett County offered. It may be that Wilson was more successful in keeping them indebted and using the law to his advantage, by keeping them in peonage. Neither scenario bears out the neoclassical expectation that blacks invariably took advantage of a free market to improve their material circumstances. The evidence suggests two possibilities: First, Wilson could maintain a black work force on his plantation because he used coercion, in which case the assumption of neoclassical economists' belief that southern labor was sufficiently mobile to pursue opportunity is challenged; or second, blacks could move if they chose, but they chose instead to stay in a paternalistic and controlled environment. They were not gravitating automatically to economic opportunity. Wilson's ability to continue to command a more than sufficient labor force in spite of the at least theoretical evidence of better opportunities for black workers elsewhere must be counted as a key factor in his success and his central role in the building of a new plantation system in northeast Arkansas.

Despite his ability to control labor and land, Wilson faced economic ruin on the eve of Franklin Roosevelt's election to the presidency. An examination of the personal property tax records for south Mississippi County for the period between 1920 and 1933 reveal that Wilson's fortunes declined between 1920 and 1922, rose between 1922 and 1931, and declined again between 1931 and 1933. Those records are not available for north Mississippi County. Because Wilson owned property there, including his prosperous plantation at Armorel, these figures should not be taken to represent his total personal property wealth. In south Mississippi County alone, Wilson's personal property wealth declined from $147,000 in 1920 to $95,245 in 1922, the year after Walter Driver faced bankruptcy. Through whatever means he used to survive the first few years of the 1920s, between 1922 and 1931 Wilson's total personal property wealth rose sharply to $232,205.

Even the flood of 1927, which began in late March and eventually extended nearly a thousand miles from Cairo, Illinois, to the Gulf of Mexico, caused him little grief. It brought devastation to portions of eight states, particularly Arkansas, Mississippi, and Louisiana.[68] In Mississippi County the flood inundated 94,600 acres: it destroyed 46,000 acres of cotton, 36,600 acres of corn, 5,100 acres of hay, and 6,900 acres of other crops.[69] Most of the devastation and flooding occurred in north Mississippi County, where a total of 26,968 people received Red Cross emergency aid, with 11,396 actually residing in Red Cross camps. Curiously, no blacks in Mississippi County were placed in Red Cross camps, and only 935 blacks received Red Cross aid outside the camps.[70]

Because of the extensive reclamation efforts made possible by the creation of Drainage Districts 8 and 9, which were principally located in south Mississippi County, little serious flooding occurred there.[71] According to one news report, "No one living near Wilson was driven from home by the high waters," nor were farmlands in the Wilson area ever under water.[72] Wilson and other prominent planters had men patrolling the levees and drainage ditches because of attempts, some of them successful, to dynamite them and thus relieve the flooding elsewhere.[73] A refugee camp was established in Osceola, but many of the refugees were from outside the county, some of them from as far away as Little Rock.[74] The Wilson Milling Company "donated a truck load of flour and meal," to help feed the refugees and thus "made many new friends for this big hearted Mississippi county institution."[75]

Aside from helping to feed refugees, Wilson also became involved in the creation of an organization designed to extend credit for agricultural purposes for those in the flooded areas of Arkansas, particularly in the hardest hit counties, Poinsett, Phillips, Desha, Chicot, and Lee. Because the flood caused so much devastation in an area that was already crippled by a continuing decline in cotton prices, Herbert Hoover, in charge of disaster relief during the flood, urged the creation of "an organization of some character . . . for the purpose of extending credit to the farmers."[76] The result was the creation of the Arkansas Farm Credit Company, of which Wilson was one of the original stockholders. Because of its insistence on adequate collateral, something that the banker in Wilson would have appreciated, few landless farmers secured loans. Even larger land owners, many of whom had already pledged their land as security for outstanding loans, found it difficult to secure credit through the new organization.[77]

Despite the flood of 1927, Wilson continued to thrive and to exert his influence. A look at a list of Wilson properties demonstrates that he was bringing more of his land into cultivation and expanding his plantation operations. In 1922 Wilson listed two farms: the Marie Farm and the Evadale Farm. In 1931 he listed eight other "farms": Eureka, Fair View, Hickory Lake, Grove, Highland, Mary V., Ridgeland, and the Joe Ab Lake farm. He ran at least two cotton gins, and his mercantile and manufacturing enterprises had expanded as well. In 1922 he had seven such business establishments. In 1931 he operated fifteen such enterprises, including the Wilson Power & Light Company.[78] As banks in the county began to fail in the late 1920s and early 1930s, Wilson stepped forward to help organize two new ones, one in Luxora in 1928 and one in Osceola in 1932.[79] This brought the number of banks in which he had an interest to five. It was also during the 1920s that his son came of age, married, traveled to Europe, and built a Tudor-style mansion in Wilson. His son hired architect George Mann to build the two-story red brick house, which had casement windows, high gables, and a terrace, at a cost of $25,000.[80] Lee Wilson Sr. continued to occupy a nice but relatively modest home. He was able to increase his net worth in the 1920s while many of his neighbors, both large and small, faced bankruptcy.

Wilson was not immune to the problems confronting other planters, however. His success was largely based on his ability to diversify his plantation and business interests. The deepening depression challenged both, as neither farming nor industry escaped unscathed. Meanwhile, the drought of 1930 threatened his plantation enterprise, and the further collapse of farm prices nearly ruined him. In an August 24, 1932, letter to Junius M. Futrell, the Democratic candidate for governor who would defeat the Republican candidate in the fall election, Wilson wrote, "You know the condition of the farmers in this section of the state, for the last two years. In 1930 we made no cotton on account of the drought. In 1931 we made a bumper crop, but did not get the cost of production for it."[81] In a separate letter to his son a week earlier, Wilson had complained about the expense associated with the erection of a new gin, reported that their box factory had lost fifteen thousand dollars and that the lumber business was in trouble. He concluded that the "crops on our property will be about 50% of last year," and that, generally, "things are slower than hell."[82] As a cost saving measure, Wilson reduced the salaries of many of his employees, including his veterinarian, Dr. J. N. Jerome, to whom he wrote on April 26, 1932, "I guess that you realize the conditions that we are laboring under and I hope that you appreciate same. There is nothing we have that we can turn into money at a profit and we don't see any future. Under these circumstances, I am forced to reduce your salary from $180.00 to $150.00."[83]

Indeed, Wilson's economic situation deteriorated sharply in the two years between 1931 and 1933. His personal-property wealth dropped from $232,205 in 1931 to $104,685 in 1933, the next year for which records are available.[84] He had survived the desperate 1920s, the flood of 1927, the stock market crash of 1929, and the drought of 1930, which destroyed his crops and reduced his livestock, only to face the virtual collapse of cotton prices. Wilson's need to negotiate two Reconstruction Finance Corporation (RFC) loans in 1932 totaling nearly two million dollars suggests that much of his prosperity was based on his tendency to operate on the margins—to borrow, in other words. He seized the opportunity to buyout those of his neighbors who did not have his assets, and, luckily for him, when the economy completely collapsed and the bottom truly fell out of the cotton market in the early 1930s, the federal government stepped forward with a generous loan program.[85]

Small wonder then that Wilson would write in a letter to his daughter on November 9, 1932, "HURRAH FOR ROOSEVELT! THE COUNTRY IS SAVED." Wilson understood that the RFC loans were not alone enough to save his enterprise. Cotton prices had to be stabilized, and he had faith that Franklin Roosevelt's administration would address that serious problem. Roosevelt's presidency ushered in a new era of government activism, which would include RFC grants rather than simply loans which had to be paid back. Wilson missed that opportunity, having negotiated his RFC loan prior to Roosevelt's election, but he stood to gain significantly from Roosevelt's Agricultural Adjustment Administration (AAA).[86]

Lee Wilson supported the AAA and told the *Osceola Times* in July 1933 that "the failure to accept the governments proposed cotton acreage reduction" would "result in cotton selling at 5 or 6 cents a pound . . . and absolute ruin for the South." Identifying Wilson as "the largest individual cotton grower in the world," the *Times* suggested that he had "achieved this distinction because of what he knows about raising cotton" and that Wilson intended "to reduce his cotton crop by seven thousand acres."[87]

While Wilson spoke out in favor of implementing the program, other Mississippi County planters had actually helped to shape Roosevelt's response to the agriculture crisis. Cong. William Driver of Osceola played a direct role in shaping the development of the AAA. C. G. Smith of Blytheville in north Mississippi County was appointed one of five regional advisors to aid Agriculture Secretary Henry A. Wallace in implementing the cotton reduction program.[88] But not all farmers in Mississippi County were enthusiastic about it. Since farmers had already planted their crops by the time Congress acted in the first year of Roosevelt's term, the AAA ordered them to plow up crops that had already been planted to limit production and thus raise prices. The county extension agent who represented north Mississippi County found some farmers there initially unwilling to participate in 1933's "plow-up" campaign.[89] S. D. Carpenter, the extension agent in south Mississippi County, reported on the other hand that farmers there in the heart of Wilson country were so enthusiastic that they had oversubscribed, pledging to destroy more acres than they were entitled to under the program.[90]

In 1934, the first year of the crop reduction program, opposition to the program evaporated and farmers throughout Mississippi County became enthusiastic about it. According to north Mississippi County's extension agent, J. E. Critz, farmers there were entitled to receive $380,246 for participating in the plow-up campaign in 1933.[91] Farmers in south Mississippi County, meanwhile, were due benefits amounting to $479,487.[92] Lee Wilson & Company received $75,048.64 in plow-up payments on thirteen of its sixteen farms.[93] The total amounted to 15.6 percent of the payments made to farmers in south Mississippi County for that program.

Largely as a result of the plow-up campaign, the condition of Lee Wilson & Company at the end of 1933 was much improved from the previous year. The Wilson farm ledgers for 1932 and 1933 reveal the difference that the AAA program's cash contribution made. In 1932 the now fourteen Wilson farms generated $180,348.90 in revenues, but all lost money. In 1933 they produced $246,418.70 in revenues and showed a modest profit. That represents a difference of $66,069.80 in general revenues. According to those same ledgers, the company received $75,048.64 from the cotton plow-up program in 1933, accounting for the difference between loss in one year and profit in the next. By 1937 when the next farm ledger was available, the Wilson revenues rose to $351,773.60 and the profits were considerably larger. No sums were identified in those ledgers as crop reduction payments, so it is likely that his revenues ran even higher. Clearly, the AAA helped salvage the Wilson's plantation empire.[94]

Just as Wilson's company was winning its struggle to survive, he contracted a severe strain of amoebic dysentery at a hotel in Chicago and died on September 27, 1933, at a hospital in Memphis, Tennessee. Although Boss Lee would not live to see it, over the next few decades his plantation would be transformed from a labor intensive to a capital-intensive enterprise that relied on heavy investments in machinery and chemicals. A massive exodus of both black and white labor accompanied this transformation, and the face of Mississippi County and, indeed, of southern agriculture, changed dramatically. With the disappearance of workers, the opportunities for the sort of paternalism Boss Lee had embodied all but vanished. Only its shadow remains. In the early 1950s, Lee Wilson & Company began selling off the homes in town, many to former renters and employees. The place no longer resembles a feudal barony. Much of the plantation land is rented to larger concerns, and while the Wilson family continues to wield considerable influence, no single Wilson holds sway in the manner of Boss Lee.

When young Lee Wilson arrived in the county in the early 1880s, it was a wilderness of swamps, thick forests, and wild game. In part through his efforts, the swamps were drained, the forests cleared, and the wild game obliterated. While tens of thousands of immigrants participated in this drama, few of them remained to enjoy its legacy. Yet the transformation they contributed to is a lasting testament to their presence.

Reward for Party Service: Emily Newell Blair and Political Patronage in the New Deal

Virginia Laas

In 1932 former Democratic National Committee vice chairperson Emily Newell Blair was happy to be back in the political fray. Having been out of politics for several years, she was delighted that those in charge of the Democratic presidential campaign sought her participation and included her in their inner circle. Eleanor Roosevelt had invited her to come to Democratic headquarters, and Blair felt that she was once again a significant factor in the party organization. With obvious pleasure, she wrote to her husband, Harry, about Molly Dewson, head of the Women's Division of the Democratic National Campaign Committee: "I must say she treats me as if I was her chief stay. She says she needed me & I've been a great help."[1] Her return to a position among the political elite was a satisfying moment for Blair. She had always been ambitious and had worked throughout her career to find a place for herself and to advance the cause of women. The 1932 election brought her back to the center of power, and she relished the opportunity to be influential once again.

Beyond her personal ambition, Blair was eager to help the Democratic Party. Believing that another four years of Herbert Hoover would be "a national disaster," she was dedicated to the progressive principles espoused by Franklin Roosevelt. In addition to her political ideals was hard reality: her family needed an income. The economic depression had not bypassed southwest Missouri, and her husband's law practice had suffered. A Democratic victory meant reward for party workers, and Blair admitted to Harry that a political appointment could "provide bread & meat for us for 4 years anyway."[2] During the campaign, she worked hard for Roosevelt's election and placed herself in a position to be rewarded for her efforts.

After the Roosevelt landslide, Blair looked forward to settling down with her husband in Washington to enjoy a degree of financial security. The

Democratic Party victory was, for her, the culmination of her years of devotion to politics, and she could justly expect suitable compensation for her contributions to its success. A nationally known writer and outspoken feminist, Blair had been a Democratic Party leader since 1922. Although she had never used her political position for personal gain, the effects of the depression forced her to look to the party for a job. Roosevelt's New Deal offered unprecedented opportunities for women. Blair, however, did not want a reward for herself; she wanted a position for her husband. Rather than move forward with the women in the New Deal, Blair stepped back, wanting her husband to reap her reward.

While Blair's decision to advance her husband at the expense of her own career brought stability to her personal life, it cost her the influence and power she had sought for so long. Hers was not an unusual choice. In the early decades of the twentieth century, as women fought to secure their place in public life, many struggled to find a balance between professional advancement and private happiness. The choices that Blair, like many women, had to make were not easy ones, nor were the results entirely satisfactory. Blair's attempts to earn a reward for her work and to position her husband to reap that reward—actions which resulted in intricate political infighting—demonstrate the added obstacles that women faced when they sought equality with men. Blair's desire to balance personal ambition with marital harmony is also an apt illustration of her contention that women of her generation bridged two eras, from Victorian to modern times. Women like Blair envisioned the twentieth century as a time when they could share power with men and move easily among elite political leaders; they were, however, constrained by the continuing pull of nineteenth-century demands of patriarchy.

Born in the booming mining town of Joplin, Missouri, in 1877, Emily Newell grew up in the nearby but older and more sedate town of Carthage. In 1900 she married her high school classmate, Harry Blair. After his graduation from Columbian Law School (now George Washington University), the couple settled into a conventional, small-town, midwestern life: Harry practiced law and Emily focused her attention on rearing their two children, Harriet born in 1903 and Newell in 1907.[3] Her first venture into the larger world came in 1910 when her article, "Letters of a Contented Wife," was published in *Cosmopolitan.*[4] That piece was quickly followed by others that appeared in magazines such as *Lippincott, Outlook, Woman's Home Companion,* and *Harper's Bazaar.* Within two years, she published at least ten times in magazines and was becoming a nationally known author.[5]

When the suffrage cause in Missouri rejuvenated in 1913, Blair was chosen to be the first editor of their journal, *The Missouri Woman.*[6] After suffrage was gained, Blair moved into party politics and won election as Missouri's national committeewoman in 1921. Democratic National Committee (DNC) chairman Cordell Hull asked her to come to Washington to organize women voters in February 1922; August saw her election as a vice chairperson of the committee.[7]

Remaining vice chairwoman of the DNC until after the 1928 convention, Blair worked hard to integrate women into partisan politics and to win equality within the party hierarchy. During her tenure on the committee, she organized thousands of Democratic women's clubs across the country. Her office initiated a Democratic newsletter and produced innumerable educational pamphlets explaining the major political issues of the day. Blair pushed for political education for women through the party organization and was responsible for seeing that Schools of Democracy, to teach women about the political system, were held in seventeen states. Perhaps her most enduring legacy was the founding of the Woman's National Democratic Club and its clubhouse in Washington, D.C.[8]

During those years, she also continued to write, contributing short stories and features to a wide variety of magazines. More importantly, she published numerous articles on women, politics, and public life.[9] She also wrote a monthly book column for *Good Housekeeping* from 1926 to 1933. Feature stories about her attest to her national prominence, naming her one of "the outstanding women leaders of America" and including her in a survey of "Women in the Washington Scene."[10]

After retiring from the DNC, Blair continued to follow politics closely but concentrated her efforts on writing projects, publishing two books and numerous articles.[11] She also maintained her position as associate editor of *Good Housekeeping,* churning out her book column every month. As the Depression deepened and Harry's legal business dwindled, Emily searched for additional sources of income. She had always thought that her writing career would prosper if they lived in New York or Washington. She had never, however, been able to convince Harry to move.

Pursuing additional income on an extended trip to New York in 1930, she frenetically arranged a lecture series and sought commitments from publishers for future books and articles. She wrote Harry that she had become convinced "once and for all that it is essential to move East or give up all this writing biz. Cant market without these contacts with N.Y. Cant make any profit by taking trips from Joplin to get the contracts."[12] To that end, in early 1931, Emily encouraged Harry to apply for a position as a senior attorney with the Interstate Commerce Commission. Although Emily utilized her political influence, budget cuts had precluded increasing the size of the agency.[13] She refused to be discouraged, urging continued efforts in Washington. A return to Joplin, she thought, would be "suicidal" and would only be "closing the door" to opportunity.[14] Meanwhile, she scrambled to increase her earning power, taking on a lecture series and radio talks. She even considered writing screenplays.[15]

In early 1932 Emily again sought a position for Harry. Pres. Herbert Hoover had appointed Texas Democrat Jesse Jones as director of the newly created Reconstruction Finance Corporation. Having served with Jones on the DNC, Emily could easily push for her husband's appointment. Jones spoke encouragingly to Emily, but once again, no job resulted.[16] At the same time, Sen. Carter Glass, another political friend, assured Emily that "it was his pleasure to do *any thing* in the world . . . to make it possible for us to come to Wash."[17]

Politics opened another avenue for the Blairs. As early as November 1930, Blair recognized that Franklin Roosevelt was the most likely Democratic candidate for the presidency.[18] By early 1932 President Hoover's inability to end economic hard times gave hope to a party long out of office; the Democrats had a chance to wrest control of the government from the Republicans. Not since Woodrow Wilson's reelection in 1916 had the Democrats held the presidency. Winning office meant jobs for the party faithful, and Emily quickly gauged the possibilities.

In March 1932 Blair received an invitation from Eleanor Roosevelt to come to Albany and meet her husband.[19] Although in several campaigns she worked closely with Eleanor, Emily had no personal contact with Franklin. It was a pleasant and memorable experience for Blair. She likened the Roosevelt milieu to what she imagined "English country people" were like: "all very casual, rather full of themselves & very natural & easy. More to the manor born than most people in public life." While impressed, Blair was not ready to give her total endorsement: "He is the center. They treat him rather as a big boy, who must be humored—everyone ready to make his affliction as little noticeable & difficulties as little as possible, a really lovely family atmosphere. As to him I don't know. He is confident that he has the nomination & talks very well & impressively about his program which he outlined to me . . . which sounds very good. And he seems impressive. . . . But I cant get away from fact that he *is* playing politics too much."[20]

Despite any initial misgivings, she became a staunch advocate, starting in her own state to rally support for Roosevelt. Active at the Missouri Democratic convention, she was not reluctant to let the leadership of the Roosevelt campaign know of her work on behalf of their candidate.[21] She redoubled her efforts during the national convention, and Roosevelt noticed. After the convention, in reply to Blair's offer to assist in the general campaign, Eleanor told her,"You did grand work with your delegation at the Convention. My husband is very grateful."[22]

Molly Dewson, the Roosevelt's stalwart organizer of women, discussed with Blair the feasibility of organizing Democratic women and asked for advice, knowing that Blair had successfully organized thousands of clubs during the 1920s. Blair seconded Dewson's idea and gave her detailed advice drawn from her earlier experience. She was also quick to inform Eleanor Roosevelt of the advantages of organizing Roosevelt Women's Clubs in those areas where Democratic women were not organized or where the regular affiliation emphasized local elections over the national ticket. Dewson conferred with Roosevelt and commented that Blair's organizational plan was "very sane." Eleanor, eager to have Blair's help, arranged for the campaign to pay Blair's expenses to come confer in New York.[23]

The Women's Division of the Democratic National Campaign Committee named Blair director of the Bureau of Women's Clubs. Traveling to Washington in September, she helped with the initial organization of that local bureau and worked with Molly Dewson in formulating general campaign strategy. She was particularly gratified, for she felt that Dewson appreciated her work. She told Harry that Dewson "consults me about everything & makes me feel she really wants my advice." At the end of September, she confided to Harry that "Miss Dewson feels that I have been of the greatest help and I think I have, myself."[24] Blair was most impressed with Dewson and the national organization; she told her husband that Dewson had "an immense capacity for detail & is more intelligent than most women in this work." Comparing the current organization to her earlier efforts, she wrote, "They are much more workmanlike in lots of things than we were in 24. . . Careful analysis of all polls—especially Hearst's. More thought in what they are doing. Better planned publicity."[25]

After the initial organization of the club plan, Blair's major contribution to the organization of women was simply the use of her name in generating enthusiasm for the clubs. Others implemented the plan. Later Blair's most important work in the campaign turned out to be with the Speakers' Bureau, headed by Lavinia Engle. She was one of four women speakers sent out on a grueling national tour.[26] Beginning in New York, Blair traveled through Ohio, Indiana, Illinois, Iowa, Kansas, Colorado, Oregon, Washington, and California, speaking daily. She was very effective. One Ohio woman expressed to the Speakers' Bureau her enthusiasm for Blair's appearance: "I have never heard a clearer or more concise statement of the vital issues in the campaign. She made an address which pleased and charmed the women and interested and informed the men as well. . . she has a very pleasing platform presence and inspires her hearers with confidence in her knowledge of what she is telling them. It was really a most successful occasion."[27] For Blair, the exhausting effort was worthwhile. She loved being back in the center of political action, and she was devoted to the Roosevelt cause. Beyond her ideals and ambition, however, lay her family's future. As she told Harry as she prepared to leave on the speaking tour: "the only thing to do was to get into this campaign in a vigorous enough way to be able to get something after election."[28]

Immediately after Roosevelt's election, Blair became actively involved in questions of patronage. In her correspondence with Lavinia Engle, Molly Dewson, Eleanor Roosevelt, and a host of male politicians, she made astute suggestions on appropriate jobs for particular people. Of special interest to her was the push to make Frances Perkins the first woman cabinet member. Promising to do all she could to further the nomination, Blair wrote Dewson, "I will go the limit."[29] Within weeks of the general election, Blair dispatched a flurry of letters to men and women, urging them to support the appointment of Perkins as secretary of labor.[30] By mid-January she reported to Dewson that she had written more than seventy-five letters, and most had responded favorably.[31] Another appointment of special interest to Blair was that of attorney general. She promoted the candidacy of Homer Cummings.[32] Having served with him on the DNC in the early 1920s, Blair applauded his liberalism. As important to Blair personally was the hope that her friendship with Cummings might lead to an appointment within the Justice Department for her husband.

Since late summer 1932, Blair had made it clear to many of her colleagues that she hoped her reward for a successful campaign would be a job for Harry. While she remained dedicated to that cause, there are gentle hints that her own ambition surfaced ever so slightly in the months after the election. Her ambivalence is apparent at the end of a lengthy letter to Lavinia Engle discussing political tactics. Blair wistfully concluded, "I wish I could be in Washington—not for my sake for I desire above all things to stay here, but I know I could do the whole administration a great deal of good if I were there with all my contacts and influence, saying the right thing at the right time. But it isn't the thing one could suggest oneself, is it?"[33]

When Cordell Hull's name was touted for appointment as secretary of state, she teasingly wrote to Harry, "I think I'll go in for being an asst. Secy of State! How's that?"[34] Harry's reply that he had seen her name mentioned in newspaper reports brought an immediate denial of any desire for office. Blair told her husband, "I don't want anything for many reasons. Nor would I ever fall for your suggestion that you'd get into a law office here because you probably would never do it. There'd never be a convenient season & I'm not going to live apart from you."[35] When her friends suggested that Hull might be willing to have Blair as an assistant secretary of state because he had previously worked with her, she demurred, stating that it was a job that "you could not go after—it would have to come to you." Once again, the temptation to seek her own place was apparent in her letter to Harry: "The work would interest me. It would furnish me with an entirely new field to conquer. It would be an important place. And it would pay, I understand $10,000. Perhaps if such a thing came I would feel that I could not turn it down if only for financial reasons." In the next sentence, however, she backed away from her ambition: "I could not and would not take it (and I think the possibility of it offering very slight) unless I were assured that you could and would live in Washington. . . I much prefer that you have the appointment and that I do the freelancing."[36]

Despite these twinges of ambition, she primarily desired a position for

Harry. Chairman of the DNC and close Roosevelt advisor James Farley promised her a position for her husband "entirely satisfactory to me."[37] She effectively used her political connections, either seeing in person or writing letters to influential friends.[38] Meanwhile, drawing on her abundant political skills, she offered Harry very specific advice in gathering letters of support. She told him that when he requested letters to be sent to Roosevelt, he should "ask (adroitly, of course), that they stress your abilities—the point is that the powers that be want to appoint you & the letters must fortify them. Have them say—the writer understands you deserve a legal position with a department or commission, solicitor or counsel. (This leaves it open but defines the kind of work)—& they wish to testify as to your fitness. Also mention it would be pleasing to Democrats of your section."[39]

The Blairs' hopes for a suitable position rose when Roosevelt's initial appointment to attorney general, Sen. Thomas J. Walsh of Montana, died on March 2, 1933, en route to Washington. Roosevelt then named the other major contender for the post, Homer Cummings, to lead the Justice Department. It seemed a particularly favorable choice for the Blairs. With their expectations high, it was a particularly hard blow when Cummings appointed Harry Blair, not to head the Lands Division, but only as one of several lawyers within that division.

Emily immediately called upon the Democratic Party's network of women, including Dewson and Eleanor Roosevelt. In addition to urging the former to write to the President about Harry's appointment, she also sent a long letter to the latter.[40] In the letter to Eleanor, she explained that Cummings would not guarantee that Harry would eventually lead the division and the economic and political ramifications that made his proposal unsatisfactory. First, the lower salary made it impossible for the Blairs to move to Washington. *Good Housekeeping* had dropped Emily's book column, and any position that Harry took must make up for that loss. More important reasons, however, were political. She confided to Eleanor, "It would be rather ignominious for me in view of my past political activities, to have my husband accept a position so much less than one I might myself aspire to, besides being a reflection on his importance in state politics and his standing as a lawyer in Missouri. The people at home simply would never understand it."[41]

Part of the political problem was Emily Newell Blair's relationship to

Democrats in Missouri. Even though she had served as national committeewoman for seven years, she was never a part of the inner power circles in the state. From the beginning of her political career, she had been an opponent of Missouri's senior senator, James A. Reed. Indeed, his opposition to Blair had brought her to national attention. Suffrage, the League of Nations, progressivism, and antibossism were the issues on which Blair built her power base. Reed challenged her on each count. Moreover, by 1933, Kansas City boss Thomas Pendergast (with whom Reed was closely allied) extended his influence beyond the confines of his city and was a major factor in statewide politics. Further, he played a crucial role in delivering Missouri to the Roosevelt cause at the nominating convention. The new administration could hardly afford to offend the controlling powers in Missouri.[42]

Confiding to Louis Howe that "the situation [was] rather delicate," Eleanor Roosevelt contended nevertheless that Blair should be rewarded.[43] She felt so strongly about Blair that she intervened directly with Homer Cummings. Despite recognizing that Blair was "not over-popular with the present organization people in Missouri" and admitting that the two women had not always agreed, Eleanor labeled her "one of the outstanding women of the party." She argued, "I think she is one of the women who deserve recognition and if she desires it for her husband and not for herself, I am backing her." Roosevelt understood that Blair's influence went beyond partisan politicians: "It may not help us in Missouri, but it will help us in other places greatly particularly with independent women who are feeling that the party is giving recognition for good work."[44]

Despite his disappointment at the low level of his position, Harry accepted the job and began work. Pressure to improve his position, however, did not abate. Cummings responded to Eleanor's letter by expressing his sympathy with the Blairs and claiming that it was the only opening he had to offer. He suggested, "Perhaps, when opportunity offers, Mrs. Blair will call at the office. I shall be glad to go over the situation very frankly with her."[45] Blair did see Cummings, and he was frank. She reported their talk to Dewson: "He loves Harry like a brother but he thinks he is a scholar and a lawyer and he wants an executive and an administrator." While she tried to convince the attorney general of Harry's abilities, she concluded, "It's a little hard to 'sell' your husband." Emily took comfort in knowing that Harry could prove himself capable of managing a division within the department, and she seemed reconciled to the inevitable: "Lots of love and heaps of gratitude for all you did. I'm satisfied that all of you have gone the limit."[46]

Cummings had reason to question Harry's ability to run a large division. In personality and demeanor, Harry did not strike Cummings as a forceful leader. Recovering from a bad case of the flu, he had not impressed the attorney general during his interview.[47] Neither did his past experience seem particularly remarkable: Beginning as a court stenographer, he had read law in Carthage before earning his LL.B. degree. He then engaged in a general practice with an emphasis in mining transactions. Living in the heart of a large lead and zinc mining belt that extended into Indian Territory, Blair had gained expertise in corporate and land law. He had not, however, held public office, and his résumé showed little administrative experience.[48] Others who did gain appointment as assistant attorneys general had more impressive records. Harold Stephens, for instance, held a J.D. degree from Harvard, had served as an assistant prosecuting attorney and a district judge, and had written a significant text used in Harvard's administrative law course. John Dickinson's academic credentials were equally impressive: B.A., Johns Hopkins; M.A. and Ph.D., Princeton; and LL.B., Harvard.[49]

Although not completely content with his position, Harry worked in the Lands Division and anticipated future advancement. Emily's acceptance of the situation, however, changed dramatically in early June with the announcement of Jewell Swofford's appointment as commissioner of the U.S. Employees' Compensation Commission. Blair immediately expressed her dismay to both Eleanor Roosevelt and Molly Dewson. To the president's wife, she asserted that the appointment was "the worst blow that could have befallen women in Missouri and will be considered in Missouri, as indeed it is, as a repudiation of me by the Administration." While she acknowledged Swofford's abilities, Blair was "heartsick" that the "only Presidential appointment given to Missouri—either to man or woman—" had gone to a member of the Reed-Pendergast faction.[50] That she was devastated by this unhappy turn of events was evident in her comments to Dewson: "It is my death-knell in politics. That's all." Deciding that it was "undignified and foolish" to continue to press for Harry's advancement through politics, she told her friend that they would remain in Washington until the end of the year, then return to Missouri, "wiser but a little sadder." Her defeat seemed complete: "As for politics—I'm done, state or national."[51]

Ewing Mitchell, who had been Emily's ally in Missouri to rally Democratic support for the Roosevelt candidacy, took up the cudgel for his friend. Mitchell extolled Harry's virtues as a lawyer, emphasizing his administrative abilities. He linked Blair's appointment to Swofford's and the larger issue of the political divisions in Missouri. The Swofford appointment, he maintained, had created "great resentment" among Democratic women in Missouri. The appointment of a staunch Reed-Pendergast ally while pro–Roosevelt supporters had been thus far ignored was seen as a "slap in the face," and their leader, Emily Newell Blair, had been "absolutely crushed" by these unhappy developments.[52] Heartened by Mitchell's support, Emily did not give up the fight; she wrote that she tried to rehabilitate herself politically and "get Harry out of the humiliating position" she had put him in."[53]

Molly Dewson had also been at work for the Blairs. Although she did not have an official title until after the election in October 1933 when she became chairwoman of the Women's Division of the DNC, Dewson was the acknowledged authority in rewarding women for party work.[54] One long month after Emily had expressed her displeasure at Harry's appointment, Dewson could report progress. On July 25, she wrote Emily that she had talked with Cummings who had agreed to raise Harry's salary to seventy-five hundred dollars and name him special assistant to the attorney general—if those terms "would truly satisfy you." The implication that these changes were made simply to placate her bothered Emily. Two other comments in the letter only exacerbated her distress. Although Molly claimed that Harry's new salary would put him "in the top rank," she also stated that Nellie Ross as director of the Mint received eight thousand dollars, while Lucille McMillan on the Civil Service commission got eighty-five hundred dollars, as did Swofford for her position on the Employees' Compensation Commission. It was hard enough for Emily to know that those women were paid more than Harry; Dewson compounded the wound by telling her friend, "Any of these jobs I believe could have been had for you." A still heavier blow came when Mary described her conversation with Cummings, who admired Harry as a lawyer but did not think he was "a leader of men." In trying to comfort her friend, Dewson only deepened the wound, saying that Cummings "spoke of his regard for you and he also said if you were the lawyer you would [have] the qualifications to take charge of a department."[55]

With that letter, Emily reached her limit. Her typed reply amounted to an over four-page, single-spaced wail. Claiming, "I have been though hell this past three months," she described her situation to Dewson. She wrote that she felt as though she had "put Harry in an untenable position for a man with any self-respect" and explained that her husband had plenty of experience in overseeing other lawyers and earned the respect of legal and political colleagues. "For a man like Harry," she explained, "to be relegated to the work of a super-clerkship is gall and wormwood." Missouri Democrats believed that his modest appointment meant that "the Blairs have absolutely no political standing with the administration." With hurt feelings and wounded pride, she felt enormous guilt that she had placed Harry in such an untenable position.[56]

In a pair of letters Lavinia Engle tried to explain Emily's outburst to Dewson, commenting that Cummings had "made Mr. Blair feel that he was put over on them because of his wife and the situation has enough truth in it to make things bad for her." While admitting that Emily "built up some ideas in her own mind that will have to come down," Engle reassured Dewson, "She will come out of it." Loyal to her friend, Engle told Dewson, "Emily is one of the real women in the Democratic party." While she acknowledged that Blair had been "unwise to ask for an appointment for Mr. Blair and not for herself as she was nationally known and he was not," she concluded on a positive note, "She is too true a democrat and too strong a feminist not to see it though."[57]

In trying to assuage her friend's personal and political hurt, Dewson asked if Emily would accept a position for herself, and Blair replied, "It would not solve my personal problems." It would, however, improve her public standing, and she told Dewson that she would accept an unpaid presidential appointment to a post "that I could fill or get which another woman could not." That sort of job could restore her reputation in Missouri and allow her to pursue her "life-long job of promoting feminism."[58] Dewson made it happen: in the first week of August, Blair was appointed to National Recovery Administration's (NRA) Consumers' Advisory Board (CAB), which had been created in June 1933.[59]

With an Industrial Advisory Board and a Labor Advisory Board already established, the NRA decided to create an entity to represent consumer interests in the development of code provisions. The board consisted of twenty members, plus nine consultants and a staff of approximately eighty.[60] Blair's first assignment on the newly created board was handling price complaints.[61] She plunged into the work, reporting at the November meeting of the board that she had responded directly to two thousand letters. She had broken down the complaints by industry and compiled charts and abstracts to assist in code establishment. The minutes of the meeting recorded that her work gave "valuable indication of current consumer complaints," and provided an "immediate and effective channel of consumer education."[62] Blair herself remembered: "I threw myself into the protection of the consumer . . . with as much enthusiasm as I had once had for the inclusion of women in politics. I committed myself to a new purpose."[63]

Her busy involvement with the CAB, coupled with Harry's increasing success at the Justice Department, brought an end to Emily's emotional turmoil. She apologized to Dewson for her unseemly outbursts, confessing that she was "ashamed" to have added to her friend's burdens. Realizing that she had "mixed the personal and the business," Blair understood that Dewson had "gone the limit" to help her.[64] By the end of the year, Harry proved himself to Attorney General Cummings and was rewarded by appointment to the position that he and Emily had thought him originally entitled, assistant attorney general.[65]

Despite Emily's desire that Harry take the lead in their family, events conspired against her. On December 18, 1934, the chairperson of the CAB, Mary Harriman Rumsey, died. Emily's bid to replace her was backed by the most powerful women in the administration: Eleanor Roosevelt, Frances Perkins, and Molly Dewson.[66] Not everyone, however, was happy with the choice. An editorial in the *Consumers' Research Bulletin* ignored her political career altogether, asserting that Blair's "chief claim to fame" had been her connection to *Good Housekeeping* and the Hearst publishing empire. Worse, with heavy sarcasm, the editorial ridiculed her as a lightweight, a society matron.[67]

Despite that criticism, Blair went to work with a will, vowing to Dewson "to make the work as successful as I can." Since the death of the former chairperson, the board had drifted, as Blair described, "No morale, no direction and all that Mary Rumsey started going to pieces." She was determined to improve its operation, assuring Dewson, "I think I can pull it all together and make it effective again."[68] She proved herself an able administrator, winning the praise of board member Frank P. Graham, president of the University of North Carolina, who commented after five months of Blair's leadership: "Mrs. Blair has taken charge in a very fine and workmanlike way."[69] The program, however, was short-lived. In May 1935 the Supreme Court declared the NRA unconstitutional.[70] The president then appointed Blair to a committee of six to oversee its dismantling. Emily Newell Blair's active participation in the New Deal came to an end with the completion of that duty. On March 6, 1936, Roosevelt accepted her resignation.[71]

Harry's promotion to assistant attorney general placed him in charge of the Justice Department's Lands Division. He, too, proved himself to all doubters. When he assumed the post, his staff totaled 59; in three years it grew to 759. A complex division, it handled litigation embracing many agencies, commissions, and bureaus. Legal matters related to Indian affairs were especially significant, involving very large sums of money.[72] Three years of such service were enough for Harry. In January 1937, he resigned from the Justice Department and began a private practice in partnership with his son Newell.[73]

In her autobiography Blair remembered that when her responsibilities concluded, she felt "adrift again." Having "been in the center of events," she had difficulty adjusting to watching others continue to direct public affairs. She was, she felt, "a spectator on the back row of the peanut gallery!"[74] She did not find it particularly comfortable to watch from the sidelines as other women found important places in the Roosevelt administration. Part of her problem was self-inflicted. If she had sought a job for herself rather than Harry, she could have been one of the leading women in the New Deal. At age fifty-nine, she thought her public career was over, and she turned her attention to rewriting her autobiography and contributing a few articles to popular magazines.

Throughout her public career, Emily Newell Blair had worked to place herself and other women at "the center of events." Yet when her turn came and important jobs could have been hers, she drew back. It was time, she thought, "for Harry to take the public front."[75] That decision turned out to be not a completely satisfactory answer in her personal or public life. She had always overshadowed Harry, but he had not been able to replace her as the most important public figure of the family. As she looked back on her career, she observed that her life spanned two eras, from Victorian to modern times. Hers was the generation that won suffrage; another generation replaced them in public life. Caught between nineteenth-century cultural standards of the proper relationship between husband and wife and twentieth-century advances for women, Blair felt "marooned."[76]

Despite her unsettled feelings about her public life, she had been, in many respects, quite successful. She reached the highest level within the party machinery of any woman as vice chairman of the Democratic National Committee in the 1920s; she was responsible for increasing women's participation in politics; she was part of the women's network that played an important role in obtaining jobs for other women in the New Deal; and she wrote about women's issues sensitively and perceptively in national publications. Emily Newell Blair and others of her generation prepared the way for younger women to participate more fully in public life, follow their ambitions, and consider the possibilities of careers beyond the home. When she completed her autobiography in 1937, Blair found satisfaction in her contributions to advancing women; she wrote that "the young woman of today starts free to be and do what she wishes. She does not have the same concessions to make to respectability, the same compromises between domesticity and marriage."[77] While she was overly optimistic in foreseeing the future for women, she was, nevertheless, justified in finding value in her contributions to the advancement of women in public life.

"A Generous and Exemplary Womanhood": Hattie Rutherford Watson and NYA Camp Bethune in Pine Bluff, Arkansas, 1937

Fon Gordon

Black women's history examines the complexity of the intersection of race and gender and has expanded the interpretive frameworks of American history and experience.[1] Recent studies of constructions of gender and class among black women suggest that middle-class and working-class black women shared the need to theorize or "make sense" of their individual and collective drives to resist racial and gender subordination.[2] Examination of Hattie Rutherford Watson's life and philosophy reveals a subtle negotiation of citizenship and civility that one black female elite created.

Hattie (Harriet Louise Gertrude) Rutherford Watson (1885–1974) was born in Rome, Georgia, the elder of two children of Samuel Wilson and Mary Anne Lemon Rutherford, both former slaves. Although the family did not possess an antebellum tradition of freedom, they were, nevertheless, representative of the expanding post-bellum black bourgoisie. Her father, born in Clayton County, Georgia, remade himself variously as a grocer, editor of a weekly newspaper, financial agent for the North Georgia Baptist High School, and financial agent for the True Reformers. Mary Anne, the elder Rutherford, founded the National Benefit Life Insurance Company in 1898 and served as secretary general until his retirement in 1931. Her brother, Robert Herbert, was president-treasurer of the company. Her maternal aunt, Laura Pearl Lemon, was the fourth wife and widow of AME bishop Henry M. Turner.[3] After attending public elementary school in Atlanta, she completed her high school diploma at Spelman Seminary and matriculated as the only graduate of the college course in the spring of 1907.[4] In September of that same year, she married J. B. Watson, seventeen years her senior.

Hattie Rutherford Watson was a member of a network of southern race women who organized to improve conditions for the race and for black womanhood in both secular and religious institutions. Watson was also member of an elite group of wives of college presidents that included Lugenia Burns Hope of Morehouse College, Jennie B. Moton of Tuskegee Institute, and Mabel Campbell Atwood of Kentucky State College. Yet within the culture of segregation their status as married, formally educated, and professional did not protect them nor enable them to shield working-class black women from the incivility and terror of Jim Crow. Stephanie J. Shaw suggests that the black community not only encouraged their educational achievement and class privileges but also imbued them with an ethic of socially responsible individualism in response to racial domination.[5] Consequently, Watson assumed her responsibility as a member of the southern black elite and devised a political and social strategy in her leadership of NYA Camp Bethune, which represented the culmination of thirty years of race work.

John Brown and Hattie Rutherford Watson remained in Atlanta during the first sixteen years of their marriage. Within the first year, Watson served as the first secretary and a charter member of the Neighborhood Union; she remained "actively engaged" for fourteen years.[6] Both Watsons taught at Morehouse College for several years: he taught mathematics and science, and she taught Bible classes. From 1908 to 1923 Watson interrupted his academic career and served as secretary of the Colored Men's Department of the International Committee of the YMCA; liquidating agent for the Atlanta Savings Bank (Hattie Rutherford Watson was his paid assistant); and state agent for the Southern Fire Insurance Company. In 1923 Watson resumed his academic career and presided over Leland College, supported by the American Baptist Home Mission Society, at Baker, Louisiana, for five years.[7]

Leland College, originally a single-building school located in New Orleans, was destroyed by a storm in the spring of 1915. The trustees reorganized the school as a boarding institution, purchased a new site, and erected three new buildings in 1923. The Watsons furnished the enlarged physical plant, secured livestock for the farm and dairy, and expanded the student body. The first session in the fall of 1923 enrolled 68 students, and by the third year enrollment had risen to 219 students. Besides her official function as first lady, Watson taught music and German; acted as college pianist; served as college bookkeeper, purchaser, and registrar; co-edited the school newspaper, the *Leland Bulletin;* served as faculty advisor for the campus YMCA; and raised three varieties of poultry, chickens, turkeys, and geese.[8]

In addition to their duties at Leland, the Watsons were also involved in the larger rural community. Hattie recalled, "Besides the general work with the students, one of the most important labors here has been the cultivation of the people in the immediate community, [who] we found raw and undeveloped. Hardly a young person, [or] adult could read or write. We visited them in their homes and churches and have sought to interest them in the education of their children."[9] Watson's memoir reveals an economically stable marriage characterized by mutual respect, affection, race leadership, and efficient management of resources. Her married and privileged status provided protection[10] and facilitated community activities. The Watson's activities in Louisiana reified their joint educational purpose. Together, they labored for racial justice for thirty-five years; alone, her community career spanned fifty-five years.

In her capacity as NYA director of the Division of Negro Affairs, Mary McLeod Bethune used the federal largesse of the New Deal to initiate "five special camps for Negro girls" located in Florida, North and South Carolina, New Jersey, and Arkansas.[11] To facilitate her feminist agenda and commitment to black education, Bethune secured the cooperation of the "Black Cabinet," the National Council of Negro Women, and the NYA to sponsor the first National Conference on Problems of the Negro and Negro Youth, convened at the Labor Department in January 1937. The conference recommended that "more work and recreational camps be provided for the youth of the nation and for the under-privileged Negro women."[12] The resulting program at the Division of Negro Affairs included educational camps for young black women and federal appropriations extended to black students at all levels, including elementary, secondary, college, and graduate education.

In the aftermath of the Elaine riot in 1919 following World War I, William Pickens described the black experience in Arkansas. As customary in the region, he characterized the state's agriculture as the product of "semi-slave labor" and suggested that black attempts at rail travel on a "slow train thru Arkansas" was "one of the horrors of life."[13] In the decade of the Great Depression, exacerbated by agricultural decline, black Arkansans faced continued rural poverty, crushing debt, sharecropping evictions, relegation to domestic service, and lack of access to adequate education and health care.

NYA Camp Bethune, located at AM&N College, offered academic classes, vocational training, and health care for mostly rural, unemployed, unmarried, young black women, ages eighteen to twenty-five inclusive.[14] NYA Camp Bethune and the other sites represented positive federal intervention in the economics and geography of Jim Crow. Eligibility requirements, in addition to age and marital status, stipulated that the girls or a family member be the recipient of federal relief as well.[15] Informally, the camp promoted race consciousness and emotional nourishment.

There were two sessions of NYA Camp Bethune in 1937. The first session convened from February 1 through June 30 with sixty-two girls enrolled; and the second session met from July 1 through September 30 with fifty-eight girls registered. Mary McLeod Bethune selected the site and appointed Hattie Rutherford Watson as camp director. The Watsons knew Bethune through women's club work and through their positions as administrators of black institutions.[16] Watson supervised a staff of eight during the first session and a staff of seven during the second term.

To simulate a rustic experience, camp lodging consisted of tents with wooden floors and sides, and the tents were equipped with gas heat and electricity. The college dining hall served the young women three meals a day.[17] Although the college and the camp represented stigmatized space within the culture and geography of white supremacy, the school enjoyed prominent status within the state's black population, and the campus grounds were impressively maintained.[18] The reputation of the college as an academic institution and its physical plant were a source of pride for both black Arkansans and black visitors.[19]

During the second session the camp staff included five women and two men. NYA Camp Bethune offered the opportunity for a small cadre of black professionals to broaden their experience and continue their roles as socially responsible adults. The four women who taught physical education, home economics, English, and social science each earned $90 per month. The camp furnished salaried health professionals as part of the NYA provision of medical care.[20] Margie Morgan, the camp nurse, earned $10 more per month. She had three years nurse's training at the Royal Circle Hospital in Little Rock, and the Arkansas State Board of Examiners licensed her as a registered nurse in 1931. Before affiliation with the camp, Morgan worked as a private-duty nurse and earned $145 per month. Her apparent decision to resign a better-salaried position reveals the significance of the camp to the staff. As camp nurse and teacher of health education, Morgan provided daily health exams and lessons in nutrition. Dr. Clyde A. Lawiah, Morehouse College and Meharry Medical College alumnus and a practitioner in Pine Bluff, was camp physician; he provided physical exams and medical care for the campers during both sessions.[21] The only other teacher whose salary equaled Morgan's was Elisha Earl Wheeler, supervisor and teacher of the plant nursery project. Watson earned $135 per month. In correspondence with Florence M. Read, president of Spelman, Watson commended the staff for "working hard and faithfully to make every day count so that girls may be benefited from their stay in camp these few months."[22]

The NYA stipulated the formal structure of the camp. Academic classes met five days each week for three hours. The curriculum consisted of classes in English, social science, physical education, health education, and home economics. The English course consisted of recitation, grammar and spelling, writing assignments, discussion of current events, extemporaneous speaking, and conducting daily plenary sessions. In the social science course, the campers studied and charted "the high cost of low wages." The students practiced the fundamentals of softball, baseball, croquet, and tennis in physical education. Home economics provided instruction in sewing and meal-planning. The vocational training classes met six days, including Saturday, for three hours, and students engaged in needlecraft or handicraft arts and horticulture. The young women worked sixty hours per month, for which they earned five dollars.[23]

Watson augmented the camp program that drew from her personal and professional experience. The young women published a newspaper, the *Bethune Spotlight;* organized themselves into a student government association; created a gallery of accomplished black American women; hosted open houses for the public; and attended the Monday night lecture series. They also led the weekday plenary sessions. The camp assemblies opened and closed with prayer, and both camp songs and religious hymns were sung. One student-led program during the first session featured camper Lee Ivory Caudle who read a paper entitled "Manners on the Street and in Public Places," on definitions of middle-class respectability and femininity.[24] The Monday night lecture series brought in local and out-of-town speakers. Anna M. P. Strong, assistant supervisor of Negro schools for the state, discussed

"The Three Keys to Success: Friendliness, Work, and Hope." She provided "beautiful illustrations . . . to show each key." S. A. Pruitt, a local, self-employed beautician, delivered a "much prized" presentation. She advised the young women on good health habits, which were the "first beauty aid," along with hair care, the proper use of cosmetics, and the selection of sensible clothes and shoes.[25] The Monday night lecture series was described as "one of the high spots in our camp program."

During the first session Watson used assemblies to introduce a personal development series called "Talks on Personality." An editorial review of one of Watson's presentations deemed "talks on this subject coming from Mrs. Watson are meaningful" and exemplify the "most desirable personality traits in her everyday dealings with her camp children."[26] The editorial affirmed Watson's nurturing relationship to the young women. The extent that she was successful in creating a "beloved community" or "camp family" can be measured in the students' references to her as our "camp mother" and themselves as "camp children."[27] Although Watson and her husband had no children in 1937, and, perhaps, because of it, her mentoring included motherwork.

The assemblies frequently hosted guest lectures delivered by members of the AM&N College faculty and administration and state and national figures. Dean of the college, John W. Parker, took as his theme, apparently unaware of the irony, "If I Were A Camp Girl." He advised the young women to follow the instructions of their teachers and to do "more than that which is required of you."[28] Hilda Smith, member of the National Advisory Committee of the NYA, visited during the spring session. Her presentation focused on the history of the NYA camps for women.[29] Mary McLeod Bethune, on a spring tour of resident training centers, addressed a camp assembly at her namesake facility. The young women described themselves as gratified "to hear her speak to [us] from the fullness of her heart and experiences." The account of her visit concluded by restating her philosophy of race uplift— "to be of service to others."[30]

As a group effort, the women constructed a display entitled "Our Picture Gallery." They collected and mounted news items and photographs to "study the lives of famous Negro men and women of today." During the first session the biographies included Mary McLeod Bethune, Marion Anderson, Salaria Kee (the first black nurse in the Spanish Civil War), Gertrude Ayer

(Harlem school principal), Jane M. Bolin (corporate counsel for New York City), and George Washington Carver.[31] Watson reinforced the biographies with assembly presentations about each hero.[32]

Emilie B. Parker taught English and served as faculty adviser for the camp newspaper and its staff of four. The social science teacher, Ruth Ward, sponsored the student government association designated as the city council. The council devised a code of legislation and demerits for the camp community. The literary editor of the *Bethune Spotlight* reported, "The training we receive in participating in the activities of the camp broadens our viewpoint of life. We make our own rules and regulations . . . And [we] become disciplined . . . and more self-reliant [and] useful."[33] The extracurricular activities shared by the campers included bus trips to sites of interest in Pine Bluff, college athletic games, an Easter egg hunt, hikes and wiener roasts, and an occasional faculty-chaperoned Saturday night dance.[34]

NYA Camp Bethune was a significant experiment in federal responsibility for black women that provided a venue to "promote interracial understanding and serve as an ambassador of good-will between the races."[35] Segregated black and white visitors to the camp included the Colored State Teachers' Association, Gov. Carl E. Bailey and other members of the honorary board of trustees of AM&N College, officials of the State Department of Education, and the state WPA. To accommodate officials and parents, the campers hosted a Sunday afternoon "Open House" during both sessions.[36]

Parents of the young women represented a less visible but important constituency to be accommodated. Watson corresponded with worried parents who wanted to know about the camp routine and their daughters' participation, and she reassured parents that their children were safe. Several of her letters reaffirmed the respectability of the facility. In a letter to her daughter Margaret, Ceola Hannah scolded her for going to frequent parties. The younger Hannah, perhaps afraid that her mother would demand that she come home, asked Watson to intercede. Watson wrote, "Your daughter feels that you have the wrong impression in reference to the camp from a statement you made to her in a letter recently. She said you thought she was attending dances too much. Margaret has not been to a dance since being here . . . You need have no fears that your daughter will do anything which will reflect [badly] on you or her. She is very ladylike and I believe she is going to make a good record in camp."[37] In a letter to parent Sam Moore, Watson asserted the efficacy of the camp by insisting, "We feel that the girls are forming good work habits." She continued, "The girls have made much improvement in their personal appearance and health habits since coming to camp through regular and wholesome meals and regular rest and sleep."[38]

Among Watson's gifts was her ability to mentor young women. She maintained correspondence with NYA Camp Bethune, Spelman, and AM&N College alumnae. Former camp alumna Louise Mayo wrote, "I guess you've been looking to hear from us since we left but daddy has been ill ever since I've been home but he is better now. I am still anxious to come back to go to school."[39] Watson responded, "My dear Louise: I was so happy to receive your letter. I have heard from so many of the girls since they left the camp. They all feel near to Camp Bethune and they are all very near and dear to me."[40] In a letter to another former camper, Watson wrote: "I was very happy to receive your card sometime ago and I wish you to know that I am always delighted to hear from my girls. I am still interested in them even though they are not in camp."[41]

The correspondence between Watson and the young women reveals their mutual respect. The campers' veneration for Watson was based on her elder status, authority as camp director, and respectability as wife and first lady. Watson based her regard for the campers on her generational, gender, and racial obligations to them. Watson's motherwork paradigm replicated the mother-daughter relationship. As camp director she fulfilled the role of surrogate mother—the mother every girl wished she had, the parent every girl hoped to be. As the prototypical mother, Watson's maternalism encouraged opposition to racial and masculine subordination. NYA Camp Bethune was an integral part of Watson's professional activities and symbolized her commitment to the education of black youth. The camp experience helped rural, young black women in Arkansas mediate their displacement during the 1930s. Her implementation of the camp was a paradox of gentility within the hardships of Jim Crow.

Watson's administration of NYA Camp Bethune nurtured civility and citizenship. She inculcated the formal course work, vocational training, and extracurricular activities with generational responsibility, gender consciousness, shared historical and racial experience, religious faith, and gentility.[42] Post-bellum women activists valued education, and the generation born in that era made and helped preserve educational venues as important sites of engagement. NYA Camp Bethune provided civil space in response to segregation and exclusion. But despite its evident success, NYA Camp Bethune was not renewed after its two sessions in 1937. The NYA terminated all educational camps for black and white women after two years. AM&N College, however, served as the site for an NYA resident training center for unemployed young black men in 1940.[43]

NYA Camp Bethune briefly secured federal funding specifically for black women, but their official endorsement did not result in further experiments in providing opportunities for black women. At the end of the first fiscal year, Mary McLeod Bethune observed of the camps: "The cultural guidance and recreational benefits of the camp program to a selected group of girls has been of inestimable value." Her report further recommended that the special camps "be maintained and that care be taken to insure the participation of Negro girls."[44] Bethune expanded the educational camps for young women to include camps for black women, just as she expanded college and graduate school aid to black scholars. She fostered a regional and national network among black women that implemented federally mandated inclusion and made possible funding for black women as clients and as professionals.[45]

The brief tenure of the NYA educational camps for black women corroborated the historical nature of black legal standing in American society.[46] American law has historically degraded African American citizenship, and the failure to maintain the camps for black women reified black women's sociopolitical status in American public life. The NYA camps for black women existed simultaneously with the exclusion of domestic service and agricultural labor, the two most important occupational categories for black women, among the recipients of Social Security from 1935. The dissolution of the educational camps also confirms the historiographical consensus among racial and regional studies of the New Deal that recognize the liberal intent and sometime implementation of New Deal planning for blacks, while concluding the substance was largely symbolic.[47]

In addition to her public role as first lady of AM&N College, Hattie Rutherford Watson co-founded and co-edited, with her husband, *The Arkansawyer*, the official student newspaper, and held the position of acting or assistant librarian from 1929 until her retirement in 1962.[48] Her commitment to black higher education was not restricted by her affiliation with AM&N College. In 1929 the board of trustees of Atlanta University elected her as a member. She was also elected alumna member of the Spelman College board in 1931, and she served on the Morehouse board from 1933.[49] Her club work in Pine Bluff included membership in the Social and Art Club of NACW; Delta Omega Omega chapter of Alpha Kappa Alpha Sorority; Jack and Jill of America, Inc.; Pine Hill Community Club; PTA; Association for the Study of Negro Life and History; and the National Association for the Advancement of Colored People. Her professional memberships included the National Education Association, American Library Association, and the Arkansas State Library Association. She was a member of St. Paul Baptist Church for over forty years, and she established the John Brown Watson Sunday school at AM&N College.[50]

After her husband's death in December 1942, Watson continued as assistant librarian, and in the fall of 1952 enrolled in Atlanta University to complete a M.S. degree in library science. She received her degree in 1956 and resumed her position as assistant librarian.[51] In 1962 she retired from the AM&N College library (dedicated to her husband in 1958) and resigned from the board of trustees of her alma mater after thirty-two years of service in1963. The Spelman College board passed a resolution of appreciation, which read in part, "Her generous and exemplary life has represented at its best the womanhood which she so beautifully espoused."[52] The board's resolution acknowledged Hattie Watson's importance as a female elite committed to new understandings of race and gender in the South of Jim Crow.

Tufted Titans: Dalton, Georgia's Carpet Elite

Thomas Deaton

America has long been regarded as the land of opportunity, where the reward for hard work, diligence, and persistence is often prosperity. Unfortunately, for many it is a jaded dream or a lie. The people of northwest Georgia, however, have recently seen the American dream come true for many and draw it within the reach of others because of the development of the tufted-carpet industry in the area. Beginning as a cottage industry, it bloomed after World War II into a billion-dollar bonanza with the aid of technological breakthroughs, cheap skilled labor, and creative entrepreneurs. The work of housewives, mechanics, and small businessmen in homes, storefronts, and converted gas stations laid the foundation out of which innovation, persistence, and product demand would usher in the Age of the Tufted Titans. In the 1980s, Dalton, Georgia, claimed more millionaires per capita than anywhere else in the United States. The tufting industry literally transformed both the region and its people.[1]

In 1895 Dalton was a sleepy little town with fewer than forty-five hundred inhabitants in its one-mile radial city limits. Other than two small thread mills and scattered farming, it attracted sparse attention from potential industrialists. A few miles to the west, fifteen-year-old Catherine Evans hand-tufted a bedspread in a pattern that she had seen on a pre–Civil War bedcover at a cousin's house. The chenille design looked like a row of caterpillars in which a simple design made of eight strands of cotton yarn, when clipped between the stitches, fluffed up. When friends saw it, they wanted one. Soon, others marketed it to general stores and regional department stores. Creative homespun marketing stimulated a surge of orders. A handicraft industry began. Throughout the 1920s and 1930s haulers were loading their Model Ts with stamped sheeting and the yarn to tuft the variety of designs and then spreading the handwork through the hills of northern Georgia and east Tennessee. Days later the haulers would return to pick up the finished work and pay the housewives in either credit to country stores or five to twenty-five cents per spread. Their work was collected at spread houses, where it was washed in large iron kettles, dried and fluffed on clothes lines, folded, and shipped to the expanding customer base.[2] During the Great Depression, while the nation was experiencing bread lines and strife, as many as ten thousand home tufters in the region were supplementing their small farms by earning a few cents on each spread. Already, tufting was making a difference in the area.

In the early 1930s inventive mechanics adapted sewing machines to create the looping and cutting of the tufting enterprise. Most started with the old gooseneck 3115 Singer head, which was used for sewing heavy textiles such as overalls and tents. Using a hacksaw, they would cut off the raceway, bobbin, and hook and replace them with a series of makeshift attachments, "where the needle would come down, a hook would take that thread off the needle after it went through the sheeting, hold the thread and the needle would then go back up and pull more thread in." Then the process would be repeated. The hook or "looper" would be holding four or five loops at a time. A cutter blade with a scissors action came along severing four or five loops behind the tufting needle. The cutter blade could not cut yarn off simultaneously or the thread would jerk out, causing the machine to quit sewing.[3]

As a result of these creative innovations, mechanization of the industry had begun. Although scores claimed the original invention, by 1940 Cobble Brothers had quietly created the first yardage machine. It could tuft bedspreads 108 inches wide with ninety-nine needles on a one- and one-eighth-inch gauge. Also the product mix expanded. To the line of bedspreads they added robes, scuffies, toilet seat and tank covers, and throw rugs. It was a simple transition to larger rugs and tufted carpet. Cotton yarn gave way to synthetics, and when Dupont 501 fiber burst upon the industry, along with developments in dyeing and finishing, the broadloom tufted carpet production stormed passed the older woven carpet industry to become the item of choice in the home of the 1960s. By 2000 tufted-carpet companies were producing 1.833 billion square yards of tufted carpet a year, netting $10.8 billion. Yet with all this growth, what had begun in northern Georgia, only a few miles south of Chattanooga, remained centered in that region. More than 90 percent of tufted carpet made in the United States is produced in Georgia, and North America produces 55 percent of world production.[4]

No other American industry has developed in one geographic location and persisted in that area like the tufted-carpet industry has. Economic geographers Billie Walters and James Wheeler credit agglomeration economics with this persistence in one location and, to a certain degree, for the success of the industry. They cite the drawing forces of a skilled-labor pool, access to suppliers of raw materials, good service from those suppliers, and access to producers of machinery. And it is true that the proximity of the yarn suppliers in the Carolinas, the heavy machine manufacturers of Chattanooga, and the continuing base of those skilled in carpet production aided this growth.[5] Historian Randy Patton recently postulated that the industry rose on the economic base of the nineteenth–century New South commitment to a marketing society as expressed in the old cotton mills of Dalton. Historian Robert McMath focused on the role of Dalton Light, Water & Sinking Fund (now Dalton Utilities) after 1945 under the leadership of V. D. Parrott for bringing the needed water for dyeing and electricity and gas for power. Ordinary cities use 80 percent of its water for residences and 20 percent for industries, but Dalton reverses that.[6]

Other regions in America have water, access to raw materials, and proximity to heavy equipment production as well as better distribution locations. Reg Burnett of RBI Associates, the guru of the industry, loves to point to the strong work ethic of the people of north Georgia, and his senior associate, Amy Cruse, speaks of the "Magic of the Moment." All the necessary conditions collided with men having the right attitude and the capacity to grow. Most of all, the entrepreneurial leaders did not come out of the New South cotton mill background but simply emerged in Dalton. They were not the local economic leaders but working people who seized the moment. They were mechanics, store owners, tinkerers, teachers, and salesmen. When national consultants to Bob Shaw told him that his corporation must move its international headquarters to Atlanta to provide better financial, educational, and marketing conditions, he chose to stay in Dalton to build his "world-class," industry-leading carpet company. It is this synergy of northwest Georgia that holds the broadloom-carpet industry. The true success story of the tufted-carpet industry cannot be told without major attention to the entrepreneurs who crafted and developed it in their own image.[7]

It is impossible to tell the stories of all of these individuals, but a cross section of these leaders provides a view of this unique American industry.

B. J. Bandy, one of the pre–World War II leaders and the first millionaire in the tufting industry, made his fortune in bedspreads. Growing up as a farm boy, he quickly decided that plowing was too hard, so he "learned to telegraph." Bandy married a schoolteacher and taught her to telegraph for the railroad. B. J. and Dicksie saved their money and started several small dry goods stores in Sugar Valley, Calhoun and Hill City, about twenty miles south of Dalton. He also traded and loaned every penny that he could. The post–World War I recession of 1919 hit the community hard and many declared personal bankruptcy. Since no one was paying him, B. J. had a hard time meeting his bills; at one point he owed his suppliers twenty thousand dollars. Yet he was too stubborn or too proud to go into legal bankruptcy. He had heard about Catherine Evans Whitener and the money she was making with spreads. If Mrs. Whitener could go out and sell them, then he was sure that his wife could too. Mrs. Whitener not only agreed to help them, but also gave them three or four spread patterns with which to start.[8]

In late 1920, armed with one bedspread and a railway pass, Dicksie traveled northward. She remembered sitting up all night on the day coach. She disembarked in Washington, D.C., and walked with her suitcase to the first department store she could find, Woodward & Lothrop. To the buyer she announced, "I'm Mrs. Bandy from Dalton, Georgia, and this is my spread. Would you like to buy any?" Even though this was all new to her, they ordered four hundred spreads at four dollars each, which meant she would double her money. She immediately left for Baltimore before the buyer could change his mind. There she sold two hundred more to Hothscheld & Kohn. She was so excited, but rather than go on to New York, she decided to "come back home and hire the people to tuft those 600 bedspreads." They set up shop in a tin building in downtown Dalton and began to learn how to stamp the spreads and get them tufted. They were only one of the many hand tufters and spread houses in Dalton.[9]

By 1932 simple tufting machines with single and multiple needles were being developed, and Bandy quickly moved to the next level. Erskine Boycell of Gastonia, North Carolina, had developed a machine that produced a product similar to the hand-tufted ones. B. J. bought his company and patents and by 1940 he had plants in Cartersville and Rome, Georgia, using two different types of machines. One was a skip stitch type which nearly duplicated the hand-tufted design. The other was a scissors type machine since tufted bedspreads were cut pile. With these two he could create either a loop tuft or the flowering look of the clipped stitch. As other machines were created, B. J. felt that many of the developments in the Dalton area were infringing on his patent rights. Most of the demand was for cut-pile tufting on bedspreads because there was little interest in rugs. The scissors-type machine created cut pile tufting easily and most of the competing machines seemed to be an adaptation of his patent. His attorneys successfully won litigations to protect his patents.[10]

B. J. heard that Polly Prentiss Company in South Carolina might be infringing on his patent. However, his lawyers were certain that the hacksaw invention of O. C. Moore was not covered. They suggested that B. J. and Polly Prentiss join forces to cover the field. Litigation solidified a strong legal position but created a great deal of ill will. The other companies then sued, claiming monopolization. B. J.'s son, Jack Bandy, remembered his father and O. C. Moore talking one day while playing golf: O. C. said, "You know, B. J., if we died tomorrow, no one would come to our funeral." They therefore decided not to enforce the patents, giving the industry "a free tufting ride," except for the patterning and combination devices.[11]

B. J.'s son-in-law, Joe McCutchen, completed their variety of tufting machines by adding an adaptation to the needle-punch machine, which had been developed by Cabin Craft. In this style the sheeting was clamped on an oversized embroidery hoop or wagon wheel which was on an axis so that the operator could move the four-foot hoop around to craft the design with a needle. It used a hypodermic needle through which the yarn came from a bin overhead and was held in the material by the tension of the fabric. Bob McCamy and Fred and Lamar Westcott, guiding lights of Cabin Craft, had started in the textile business with a hosiery mill in Dalton in 1917. When Real Silk of Philadelphia bought them out in 1928, Fred took the lead in making the transition to the emerging tufting industry. For many years Cabin Craft also was a major leader in the industry, using the needle-punch-tufting style, until it sold out to West Point Pepperell.[12]

World War II and its attendant allocations of materials forced Dalton's textile shops to produce olive-drab washcloths, towels, bomb covers, and parachutes. When the war ended, some decided to explore other business options because there seemed to be too many spread houses. However, the postwar period was the time of transition from a small, but successful, craft industry to the wealth-producing tufted carpet explosion. Dalton began to bloom into an industrial textile town.[13]

The news of the end of World War II came to Dalton over the radio waves of its small local station, WBOJ, which beamed its broadcasts just beyond the one-mile radius of the city limits. That night its more than ten thousand inhabitants could have gone to one of Dalton's three movie theaters to watch Roy Rogers in *Don't Fence Me In* or *Her Highness and the Bell Boy* with Hedy Lamar. After that, they might walk home through the gas-lit streets with a feeling of safety, since the two night policemen took care of the only major problem, rowdy drunks. The small African American population (just over one thousand) did not venture out at night. A Klan lynching of an accused black in the late 1930s had produced lasting fear. The median family income for Dalton in 1940 was $2,482. The town was divided by the Western & Atlantic Railroad tracks. The small black community lived on the eastern side along with most of the low income whites. The more affluent families lived in homes facing Thornton Avenue, located at the western edge of the business district. Crown Cotton Mill was adjacent to the railroad and the Chattanooga highway at the northern end of town, surrounded by its mill village. At the southern edge of Dalton, the American Thread Mill offered employment to those residing in Thread Mill Village. It was a small town of mill workers; it seemed an unlikely site for the development of a unique American success story. The positive work ethic of sturdy north Georgia farmers and workers, the developing skills of tinkerers and machine makers, and the right environmental conditions awaited the emergence of innovative leaders.[14]

One of the greatest contributors to the tufted-carpet industry was Eugene T. Barwick. "Innovator," "leader," "visionary," "pioneer," "demon," "crook"—all terms which have been used to describe Gene. Tom Neal of Lawtex believed, "Members of the industry ought to get down on their knees and thank him. He and the industry remind me of the relationship between a shark and the pilot fish. The pilot fish sticks to the underside of a shark, and then, after the kill, they race out to eat all the bits and pieces left. Gene was the shark that blazed the trail and the industry has benefitted from his courage."[15]

Coming from a modest family background, Gene went to the University of North Carolina on an athletic scholarship. He played end on the football team and made the *Sports Illustrated* All-American team. After graduation, he went to work for Sears & Roebuck in Jacksonville, Florida, and "by happenstance" ended up in the floor covering buying department. He advanced then to mail order sales manager in Chicago and then carpet buyer for the central office before being drawn into World War II. At the end of the war, he returned to Sears and became the regional merchandise manager for floor coverings in Atlanta. Because most wool was allocated to the Northern states, he usually bought cotton rugs from the northern Georgia mills. During this time, one of his sources, C. M. Jones, began to have delivery problems. Although Jones made one of the best throw rugs in the business, Gene discovered Jones's business operations were in disarray. A single trip to the mill to implement deliveries brought a broader vision for Gene of what could be done with this infant industry. As he later said, "If they can do that with one needle, why not 1500 needles."[16]

In 1948 Gene left Sears and became the sales manager for Ben Kahn, owner of a small rug tufting operation called Lawrence Products, Inc. in northern Alabama. He received a salary plus bonus and did an outstanding job, but friction developed over marketing and operations. When payday came, Gene's bonus should have been fifteen thousand dollars, but Ben decided he was going to pay him only seventy-five hundred dollars. When Gene demanded his bonus, Ben remained firm in his decision. Whereupon, Ben remembered, "He took that check and shook it under my nose and said, 'You little son-of-a-bitch, I'm gonna take this and bust you.' And he did." Whether the story is true or not, the story is typical of Gene's determination.[17]

Soon Gene was selling for McCarty Chenille, and when Frank McCarty's ulcer worsened, Gene purchased his first carpet mill in 1949 for forty-five hundred dollars down. As the demand for tufted carpet increased, he built and bought plants. Envisioning global possibilities, he created plants in England and Holland. In 1964 he built the Archer plant in Kensington, Georgia; the plant had nineteen acres under one roof. However, building and acquiring plants was not Gene's major impact on the industry. First of all, Gene was a master salesman. One of the major consultants of the industry, Walter Guinan, said that his dynamic presence—magnificent build, appearance, dress, and driving personality—made him almost irresistible. Dressed in Madison Avenue fashions and with supreme confidence, he would explode into meetings. Distributors would beg the factors not to extend their credit because Gene would offer them such low prices and advertising perks that they could not refuse. There were two ways to run a company—for bottom line or for cash flow. Gene always ran the company for cash flow. A factor would pay as much as 80 percent to 90 percent on the invoice with "hellish interest," but the demand was so great that Gene did not care. He could sell $2 to $3 million in a few days to cover his bills. When they went public in 1968, they were the largest tufted-carpet manufacturers in the world. One of his key managers, Don Browen, believed that possibly Gene's biggest mistake was that when he hit $100 million to $150 million in sales that he "didn't bring in a pencil pusher that would have held onto the profits better."[18]

Others attributed Gene's greatness to his leadership in the industry. Tom Neal asserted, "Gene Barwick was always two years ahead of the industry because he had the vision and he had the guts." In *What You Should Know About Carpet,* Annette Stramesi observed that "'innovation' was a byword in the Monarch (Barwick's trade name) tufting empire. The company was the first to use jute as a primary backing on carpet, first to promote 100% nylon carpet, first to manufacture 100% polypropylene carpet, and first to roller-coat and vulcanize the back of carpet to lock in the pile and make it stand well on the floor."[19]

Many others attributed Gene's tremendous contributions to the technology of the industry and his attendant economic windfall from two major developments—the DuPont 501 nylon yarn and the Zimmer printer. Cotton was first used in the industry because it looked so good, but it matted and soiled quickly. Rayon and viscose had problems with crushing and dyeing. Gene persuaded DuPont to continue the development of Bulked Filament Nylon and worked with them through all the early problems of piling, shedding, and streaking. Once the problems were resolved, Monarch was given a two-year exclusive, and with the cost reduction, resilience, and dyeing possibilities, the profits soared. The Zimmer printer was similar in its impact on the industry. Previously carpet was dyed by throwing sacks of dye into large washing machines or using previously dyed yarn. Austrian Peter Zimmer was successful at printing colors on scarfs and other material. By adapting the concept to a flatbed printer, he could apply as many as four colors to a moving roll of carpet. Gene spent three years and more than a million dollars, but when completed, Buford Talley, Barwick Industries' first president, believed that it was a "hell of a breakthrough" in dyeing.[20]

Finally, Gene sold not just yards of carpet, but the whole tufted industry. He developed traveling roadshows; three planes flew as many as four hundred retailers to his offices and plants; he was the first to use models in the showrooms; and even his yacht in the Caribbean was used to motivate and reward successful individuals. He was "Mr. Carpet" and the "Carpet King." Moreover, he led the industry in wages and benefits. If employees or their parents had worked for a Barwick company for at least a year, scholarships were available as long as they passed their courses; they were also assured summer employment to make school money. He inspired such loyalty that even with the early 1970s housing recession and oil embargo, excessive spending on new ideas and projects, and problems with his factors forced him out of the business, his employees remained true. They had not worked for a company, but for "Mr. Barwick," and they were ready to come back to work for him when things improved. His impact was so great that his portion of the industry's growth is known as the Barwick Era.[21]

The Coronet Carpet Story is the success story of three totally different but achievement-oriented individuals. Born as a dream around the kitchen table of Mrs. B. J. Bandy, floor covering was created by a well-balanced conglomerate: the aggressive New Yorker Bud Seretean, the production-wise Vanderbilt-educated Guy Henley, and the economic-expert Jack Bandy. Their background, previous experience, and temperament were quite different, but they blended their individualities to produce one of the largest carpet companies by 1970. When they were bought out by RCA for $148 million in 1970, Bud became the largest stockholder in that conglomerate. He was the driving genius behind the triumvirate and a leader in the industry.[22]

Born and raised in New York City of Romanian-Jewish immigrant parents, Bud was known as a scrambler and a hustler from the start. In 1976 he told *Modern Floor Coverings,* "It's the challenges that intrigue me, playing a long shot and winning." At age seven he took a route selling *Liberty* magazines, but gave it up in twenty-four hours because selling fifty magazines to earn a jackknife "did not add up." He progressed to shining shoes, working for a tailor, working in his parents' grocery, and delivering for other shopkeepers.[23]

At an early age he was aggressive and resourceful. If the grocery store did not have what was needed, he would sneak out the back door to the nearby A & P and bring the product back. But much of this attitude came from his parents, who made Bud and his three sisters stack the canned goods in the window so that it looked like the store was well-stocked. His mother pawned her $150 engagement ring repeatedly to keep the store in supplies. At the age of thirteen, Bud convinced the supervisor of New York's three stadiums that he was fifteen, so he could sell soda pop and hot dogs. Unfortunately, he ate most of his profit.[24]

He was goal-oriented and one of his goals was to play the trumpet. He played hooky so many times to hear the big bands that he barely graduated from high school. At the City College of New York, he continued his lackluster performance. At this point his life underwent a dramatic change. "I was averaging about zero, going nowhere, nothing in mind beyond blowing a trumpet the rest of my life," recalled Bud. In 1942 he heard that if a person enlisted in the service to fight in the war, he would get a passing grade in all the subjects that he was currently taking. So with no professed patriotism, he entered a new phase of his life. Starting in the Air Corps, he switched to the Engineer Corps and finished the war as a field artillery officer in the 77th Division in Italy. While stationed in Little Rock, Arkansas, military trouble put him on KP duty and the local girl whom he was dating drove off with the company commander, "and she saw me as they drove away." He vividly remembered that "suddenly the whole situation made me very angry, and I made up my mind that from then on I was going to make something of myself." His strong family work ethic, ethnicity, and potential crystallized at the time of this humiliation. He decided to become an officer. After office candidate school he ended up in charge of the post exchange in Italy. It was such an enjoyable experience that he changed his goals to retail and marketing once the war was over.[25]

Using the G.I. Bill, he graduated from Oklahoma State and then earned a master's in retailing from N.Y.U. As a student trainee at Stern Brothers, he determined that he was going to be the president of a department store before he was forty-five. Jobs were scarce, and he was turned down by the major stores. But that did not slow him down. "Rejection," Bud believed, "becomes a force that drives me to do better." As part of the executive training group at Abraham & Strauss, he was paid less, so he worked fifteen hours a day and six or seven days a week to prove that they were underestimating him. At this point his hard work was matched by luck. They needed the "biggest and strongest" man to help in the Labor Day promotions in floor covering. He succeeded, but was told that it would take even an exceptional person a minimum of two years to move from one level to the next. The next day he looked for a new job. When he showed the largest sales increases at Allied Stores, he again ran into the promotional wall. Bud left to become the sales manager with Katherine Rug Mills in Dalton, a small company from which he had purchased carpet.[26]

He had often been excited about the price and value of tufted carpet, and when he saw Barwick's products, he had run "to the workroom to see this new breed of carpet." In his first three years he tripled the sales volume to $6 million and asked to buy into the company. However, the company was owned by Said Shaheen and his brothers, and they would not consider an outsider. At this time Bud was renting a room with the widow Dicksie Bandy, and he would sit around the breakfast table and talk with her son Jack about starting a new company.[27]

It was not the best time to start a new company as the 1953–54 recession created keen competition in the low price merchandise field. Bud decided that there was a niche that they could fill. Tufted carpet was made of cotton and rayon while the woven industry used wool and controlled 80 percent of the carpet market. The Korean War had driven the price of wool up, but the idea of tufted wool carpet seemed a possibility. They started on a shoestring. The sales brochure was made out of construction paper and other companies' advertisements. He used the middle-price bracket and offered a bonded guarantee along with the only wool-tufted product. The samples were made on test machines in Chattanooga. In the near impossible business climate of 1956 he extracted orders from hesitant carpet distributors and the company started. Their plant next to the railroad tracks was so run-down that it shook when trains came by and the floor actually collapsed under one of their major buyers. With Bud selling, Jack Bandy managing the finances, and Guy Henley in charge of the manufacturing, their company grew so rapidly that they had to go public in 1964, the first in the industry to do it. When RCA purchased their company six years later, it had become the best in the industry.

A major degree of success must be credited to the management team of Seretean, Bandy, and Henley. Other companies, under one leader, had splintered from the multiple-business demands when they reached the $100 million level. Yet the drive and goal-orientation of Bud Seretean was at the core of their success and unity. Interestingly enough, Bud was attempting to overcome two perceptions that he believed people saw as his limitations—his age and his religion. Macy's and others had kept him out of their programs because of his mature age of twenty-five, while student organizations at Oklahoma State had avoided him because he was Jewish. Rather than rebelling, he determined to "fight three times as hard as anybody else to prove that he was at least the equal of most other people." One theme seemed to run throughout his life—his commitment to goals. Until his retirement he always carried three legal pads. One pad was used to keep track of responsibilities on which he used a series of stars to indicate the urgency of tasks to be completed. The second pad was to record earnings and projections. The third pad listed board meetings, travels, and other appointments. Goals played the pivotal role in his and Coronet's growth. His favorite quote is from Robert Browning: "A man's reach should exceed his grasp or what's a heaven for."[28]

Although the industry started as a woman's handicraft, the men began to take over as machinery and money arrived. However, a number of strong women played major roles, starting with Catherine Evans Whitener and Dicksie Bandy. Piera Shaheen of World Carpet was one of the tough-willed matriarchs of the industry. Though born in Iowa, she lived in Italy for twenty-one years with her mother. During World War II, her American citizenship destined her for a concentration camp. The underground rescued her and used her university business degree knowledge to control their finances and keep records of their successes for the postwar period. Living with the constant threat of death, injury, or capture, she developed a strong character. She witnessed the cruelty of Nazi firing squads killing young boys. At one point she hid alone in a dark cistern for twenty-four hours with the major underground documents. She later came to America and married Shaheen Shaheen, but she never forgot her Italian ordeal.[29]

Shaheen was the nephew of Said Shaheen, a Palestinian Christian who came to Dalton to buy tufted goods during World War II and stayed. Trained in industrial engineering and business management at Illinois Institute of Technology, Shaheen worked for his uncle as a traveling salesman and then in the home office. In 1954 when Katherine Rug moved to a new location, Shaheen was dismissed. He decided that he would try selling used cars. Piera stubbornly believed that their future was in carpet. When he protested that they had no money, she offered her savings of four thousand dollars to start. However, the business was to be 50–50, not 51–49, as he suggested. The early days were difficult. As his company began to grow, he tried to borrow only four thousand dollars from local banks to secure a Small Business Administration loan of twenty thousand dollars, but they turned him down. However, with Piera running the financial end and Shaheen training the workers, building the machinery, and directing manufacturing, they grew to be the largest privately owned company in the industry, before they sold out to Mohawk Industries. Her knowledge, personal strength, and vision were equal to his in the success of World Carpet.[30]

Possibly the best example of the Horatio Alger story of success was Linda Freeman, president of 1st Choice Carpets. Born into a tobacco farming family in North Carolina, she married before she finished high school and started raising a family and working because her husband was unemployed. Two weeks after she started working at a carpet company, her employer asked her what her goals were. She immediately responded. First she wanted to learn as much as she could as quickly as possible. And with that knowledge she wanted to improve her abilities, her salary, and her benefits.[31]

One year later she started a company with two male co-workers. She was responsible for putting together what the tufted product was, how it would look, how to market it, and how to build an agent and customer base, while her life savings provided the seed capital for the venture. She worked twelve hours a day, and in eleven years they were selling $20 million worth of product, yet she was not allowed a part of ownership. She was told repeatedly that women could not achieve in the industry. Without consulting her, Specialty Carpet was sold to another company whose ethics were questionable. She was not willing to be associated with the production of inferior carpet. At this point she decided that she had enough courage, knowledge, and direction to start her own company. Her success was built on hard work, experience, and a strong positive mental attitude. There was clearly patriarchy in the industry, but an increasing number of females were making impressive incomes in sales, and Pat Durkan worked her way upward to become president and chief operating officer of Durkan Carpet in 1998, which was recently purchased by Mohawk Industries.[32]

Undoubtedly, the most amazing story of the 1980s to the present is the growth and impact of Shaw Industries. In the 1970s they were considered a minor player, but by the turn of the century they dominated the industry and boasted a $4.1 billion sales volume. At the very center of this transformation is the direction and leadership of Bob Shaw. Robert E. Shaw grew up immersed in the developing tufting industry. His father, Clarence Shaw, was in Dalton textiles before tufting machines began to appear. He was the dyer for Lamar Westcott at Westcott Hosiery Mills until it was sold to Real Silk in 1928. When the company went into full-fashion hosiery, there was no further need for a dyer, so Clarence went to work for Washington Hosiery Mills in Nashville, Tennessee. When Cabin Craft was begun, Lamar called Clarence to return as the dyer at Dalton Spread Laundry, which was the commission dyer for Cabin Craft. In 1945 Clarence and John McCarty purchased a commission dye house called Star Dye, which concentrated on spreads, scatter rugs, and robes for a number of local manufacturers. After high school graduation, Bob majored in business at the University of the South at Sewanee, Tennessee. After three years of college, he decided to sell yarn for Bibb Manufacturing Company of Macon, Georgia. From 1952 to 1956 he lived in Chicago and sold string to meat packers as well as other textiles throughout the Midwest. After four years with Bibb, Bob decided to leave the harsher climates for the warmer South. As a chemical salesman for F. H. Ross, a supplier of wet goods, he began to travel the Southeast.[33]

In 1959 his father's serious illness forced him to take a leave of absence to return to Dalton to sell off the family business. When he first returned, he spent the days behind the plant hitting golf balls, while an inventory was being conducted. However, in three weeks time he realized that the family business offered him more than his sales position. Prior to that time Bob had been labeled as a playboy, or as he put it, "young, footloose and fancy free." However, a combination of factors forced him to settle down. He married and fathered a child and his father died.[34]

At this point Bob began a careful, progressive growth in business, always guided by the principle of being the low-cost producer. When Bob began, Star Dye was a small $300,000-a-year business, dyeing scatter rugs. Working with his older brother J. C. (Bud), Bob pooled their money and experience—with the help of Marion Manufacturing interests and John McCarty—to create Star Finishing in 1960, which soon became the largest commission finisher of tufted carpet in the world. They served the finishing needs of the major players of the industry.[35]

Bud Shaw already had been fully prepared by schooling and experience for their paced growth. Bud was a graduate of Georgia Tech in textiles and briefly worked in solution dye for Crown Textiles in Dalton, in carpet mills of Dan River Carpets, and then in Rocky Creek Mills. In 1964 he and a high school friend formed Sabre Carpets in Cartersville. In 1967 the brothers consolidated their holdings and bought an old-line woven carpet company, Philadelphia Carpet. Bob pointed out that their purchase was not part of any great design. "The reason we got involved in Philadelphia was that they were going bankrupt. They owed us $500,000 and our net worth was $700,000 and so we had to take it over. It was not a planned move, it was a forced decision," said Bob. In order to raise the $3.2 million purchase price, Philadelphia Holding Company was created, merging all their interests. In the 1970s, Shaw Industries began a transition. It had entered the business from the supply side (yarn and dyeing) and had to integrate forward into marketing to be a complete business. Needing large sums to expand and unwilling to depend upon the ruinous option of factoring, Shaw went public in 1971. With $7 million from the offering, Shaw concentrated first on yarn supply by buying one plant, creating another, and opening a third for the California market. The west-coast operation provided services in carpet dyeing, shearing, jute, and rubber secondary backings.[36]

In 1977 they made their second major move. The organization had grown so much with the yarn and finishing of Bob and the woven and tufting of Bud that it needed merging. Bud became the chairman of the board, while Bob became president and directed the day-to-day operations. They continued to expand, but the demand forced them to quit selling yarn and providing finishing for others. Then in 1983 they broke with the traditional way of selling carpet. It was a calculated risk. During the previous years, the normal sales sequence had been for carpet mills to either sell their products in bulk to large wholesalers such as L. D. Brinkman & Co. of Dallas, who in turn would mark up prices between 18 percent and 22 percent and sell it to retailers or sell direct to large department store chains like Sears. Shaw began to sell to whoever wanted to buy from them and to only a limited number of wholesale distributors.[37]

The industry questioned his bold strategy and waited "for him to fall on his ass," said Reg Burnett. Their leadership group had recognized a new trend that was taking place in the market and chose to respond drastically. The fastest-growing segment in the market was small specialty carpet retailers. There were about thirty thousand of them with sales less than $2 million a year. Secondly, most consumers were shopping three or four places before buying, looking for the best deal. More placements by Shaw products gave them a greater chance to sell to the cautious buyer. By dealing directly with the small retailer, Shaw's salespeople could undercut wholesalers' marked-up prices. The year before the move, 55 percent of sales went to distributors, but in a few short years 80 percent went to the retailers. In 1980 the company had $213 million in sales and a 9 percent market share; in 1990 they sold $1.48 billion with a 22 percent share. While 28 percent of the industry's output is sold through wholesalers, only 4 percent of Shaw's goes that route. In 1999, Shaw Industries, due to global acquisition and expansion, had grown to a sales volume of $4.1 billion.[38]

Any understanding of the spectacular success of Shaw Industries must begin with Bob Shaw and those close to him. Bob, Bud, and their two sisters grew up in a very supportive but very competitive environment. Bob was the most aggressive of them all. He was little and wiry as he grew up and Bud was always having to get him out of fights. As Bob grew older, he always had to be the best. In sandlot football he had to be the quarterback, even if he was small. His leadership ability, competitiveness, and persistence complemented his excellent business sense. Today he has an infectious, even inspirational, spirit. Because the leadership with which he surrounded himself is first generational in the carpet business, he can make quicker decisions than older, more tradition-bound corporations. Moreover, unlike the other firms that reached $100 million and sold out, Bob has stayed to provide the leadership. Even when Warren Buffet purchased controlling interest in 2000, Bob stayed.[39]

Bob did not begin with a grand design, but he felt that as he put each building block together and stood on it, he could see farther. Ultimately, he reached for the goal of being an international corporation, not just the biggest carpet company. To accomplish this, he believed that he and those working with him had to be ethical. Since the profit margin in the tufted carpet industry is a meager 5 to 6 percent and all pursue the market aggressively, the possibilities for dishonest dealings are always present. Second, he had to have a vision. He thought that most people were locked into a desire for security from the cradle to the grave. Everyone wanted to be rich, but no one wanted to take any risks. As he said, "You are paid for being responsible, but that involves making decisions that could put you out of work. The risk-taker has to take the responsibility on his back. And they've got to be willing to do, as they do in Las Vegas. You're going to push your career to the center of the table, grab the dice and throw them. The entrepreneur is not just a gambler, he is a risk taker. You figure out what the downside is and if you can live with the downside, then you can make decisions." His favorite athletic statement is: "WE PLAY THE GAME TO WIN."[40]

Bob has mixed the Presbyterian ethics of his parents with a sound business sense from experience and focused on tremendous goals. Now he has financially returned his gratitude to the community in the form of support to the medical, academic, cultural and religious needs of Dalton. He has led in community support to make the local hospital superior to any non-metropolitan facility in the state. He has thrown his support and prestige to the Creative Arts Guild, the four-year status for Dalton State College, and the recent move and building of First Presbyterian Church, which is jokingly called Shaw Memorial.[41]

Is this southern paternalism or just southern Christianity? Bob grew up in an environment where business leaders always were involved in community projects. His mentor, Lamar Westcott, accepted only half-pay from the other two owners at Cabin Craft because he wanted to spend half of his time working in the community. Lamar led the Civitan Club in the 1930s to take over and run the financially destitute Hamilton Memorial Hospital and was on the board for most of his active life. The Westcott Psychiatric Center at the hospital and the Westcott Administration building at Dalton State College attest to his involvement. The gymnasium bears the Bandy name and other companies quickly responded to any worthy civic project. Although Gene Barwick rewarded his workers with scholarships, most companies now consider it good business practices to provide GED training on company time as well as college tuition for successful student employees. Women's apparel store owner Harry Saul was a local Boy Scout leader before he began the fourth largest company, Queen Carpet. An early inventor, Mose Painter would share each new invention with his friends at the Elks Club. Many used his creations to become millionaires, although he personally "just had the fun of a millionaire." When I. V. Chandler's Patcraft burned to the ground, his competitor, Odell Edwards of Del Rube Chenille, ran enough yardage to fill Chandler's needs. Julian Saul and Bob Shaw have wrestled each other for portions of the market while playing golf every Saturday. Now Queen is owned by Shaw: Julian is president of Shaw and Bob is chairman of the board. This area of the nation has been characterized as the buckle on the Bible Belt and religious feeling still runs deep. This coupled with a warm community spirit has produced a lingering social consciousness that benefits all.[42]

During the explosion of the carpet industry following World War II, Dalton and particularly Whitfield County experienced significant population growth. Dalton, because it had constraints of city limits, grew at a modest 10+ percent average for the decades after World War II with the 1960s being a low growth period and the 1970s witnessing a new influx of residents. As city property filled with commercial development, many of the middle- and upper-class residents moved beyond its borders. Whitfield County in the postwar years grew at a 22+ percent average with the 1960s exploding at a 31 percent increase and slowing to 19 percent in the 1970s and to 10 percent in the 1980s. Some interesting characteristics stand out in the census records. There was a determined growth pattern in the manufacturing work force so that in 1970, 56.2 percent were involved in manufacturing jobs with the closest other category being professional, managerial white-collar workers at 19.4 percent. By the 1980s the work force had changed only slightly, with approximately 50 percent still in manufacturing. This manufacturing percent was higher than any other county in the state, with the majority of counties in Georgia being in the 20 percent and 30 percent bracket.[43]

	1940	1950	1960	1970	1980	1990
Dalton	10,488	15,968	17,868	18,872	20,939	21,761
Whitfield Co.	26,105	34,432	42,109	55,108	65,789	72,462

The ethnic composition also changed. The black population in Whitfield County remained fairly constant, around two thousand during these years. Most of the people who moved into the area came from surrounding southern states. In the 1970 county census, the largest immigrant group was German with 76 residents. There were no Mexicans listed and only 141 who used Spanish. By 1980 there were 401 Mexicans (total of 526 Spanish speakers) who responded to the census. In these early years, most Mexicans were single males drawn first by job opportunities in the Conagra chicken processing plant. Then the shortage of a labor force in the carpet industry provided new job opportunities. By 2000 the local planning commission estimated that of the 26,000 Dalton residents, there were 13,500 Hispanics. Dalton's interstate location and certain job prospects (unemployment in Dalton is 2.3 percent) have been a magnet.[44]

As the carpet industry matured, two interesting phenomena occurred. First, a concentration of wealth began to be noticeable. The per capita income, fueled by the carpet wealth and inflationary times, jumped from $3,191 in 1970, to $7,383 in 1980, to $15,284 in 1990 in Dalton, and $2,769 to $6,579 to $13,324 when the county totals were noted. However, the number of individuals making $50,000, and above grew from 138 to 763 in the 1970s. Interestingly enough, in the 1980s the narrow city confines forced wealth out beyond the city limits. In the 1990 census, over 20 percent of the county homes claimed an income in excess of $50,000, and 350 households had an income of at least $150,000.[45]

At the same time, wage earners benefited. This second development was the result of two major reasons: the threat of labor unions and the constant demand for laborers. At the end of World War II, there were two strong locals for the Textile Workers Union of America at the local cotton mills. In 1955 they made a concerted attempt to unionize two local carpet mills, but the media was able to focus on the local paper's editor and his "Communist" leanings. This Red Scare hysteria and some local violence led the employees of the major plant, Belcraft, to reject unionization. Local business leaders responded by raising the wages and benefits so that when another vote was taken on unionization at Collins & Aikman, they could point to the lower level of pay and benefits at the cotton mills. Over the years the industry has used this lesson to exclude unions. Also, because there is a limited number of workers in the area, the companies have had to compete financially for the workers.[46] Migrating Mexican laborers, drawn by the higher wages, have now given Dalton the highest Hispanic population in the state after Atlanta.

The wealth that poured into the region benefited all. In the 1970 census, the Georgia average for those living below the poverty line was 16.7 percent, while Whitfield County had only 11.1 percent. Only four Atlanta suburban counties had a lower percentage. By 1989 the *Georgia Statistical Data for Cities and Counties* showed a state poverty average of 11.5 percent, and Whitfield dropped to 7.9 percent. Only 11 suburban areas of Georgia's 169 counties had lower ratings. Moreover, a developing middle class is evidenced by the appearance of multiple residential communities in the county. The 1998 Target Tomorrow study by the Chamber of Commerce identified a strong middle class, and tax rolls reveal a broadened base of affluence.[47]

In contrast to Wilma Dunaway's study of South Appalachia, the tufted-bedspread industry presents evidence of developing capitalism rather than a simple home-craft industry. Local entrepreneurs seized upon the market potentials of the chenille products and quickly produced for a nationwide demand. Although northwest Georgia had a long tradition of subsistence farming, indigenous leadership quickly developed marketing linkage with stores and distributors in the core area of the Northeast and Midwest. These fledgling capitalists were not related to the two small textile mills in town but responded to the new opportunities. Once the industry began to explode, those trained outside the area were drawn in, but the vast majority of Dalton's millionaires were home-grown.[48]

The world-market system paradigm also includes the role of finance in the control of an industry. The core area would provide the finances, while the peripheral fringe provides the cheap labor and raw material. Much of the profit is therefore withdrawn from the area in which it was created. The wage base has been kept low by a determined campaign of the carpet industry in keeping out organized labor. Yet when large corporations attempted to buy into the industry and dictate its directions, they were unsuccessful.[49]

RCA bought Coronet and others followed, but they could not make the industry conform to their business plans, and it proved to be so unprofitable that they had to sell it back to local leadership. Mohawk, the second largest in the industry, moved its New York headquarters, first to Atlanta, and then to Calhoun, just south of Dalton. Actually, the carpet industry reversed the process and Dalton became the core of wealth, technology, and market control. No other industry has been able to do this. However, consolidation has come to the industry and it is dominated by three mega-mills: Shaw, Mohawk and Beaulieu.[50]

The story of the development of the tufted-carpet industry is the story of creative decisions, practical inventions, hard work, and the evolution of an American contribution to the world. Persistence, good work habits, teamwork, and creativity produced new products, styling innovations, and wealth.

At the heart of the industry are the unique individuals who made it happen. While it is impossible to tell it all, it is a story of the men and women, pioneers and newcomers, leaders and line workers, tufters and haulers, friends and rivals.

Sara Alderman Murphy and the Little Rock Panel of American Women: A Prescription to Heal the Wounds of the Little Rock School Crisis

Paula C. Barnes

Sara Murphy's reformist legacy is a jewel in the crown of Arkansas women's history. Her work for social justice began with the Little Rock school crisis and the Women's Emergency Committee. It ended with Peace Links, an organization that confronted Cold War anxieties and fears of nuclear war for both Americans and Soviets. In between she labored to heal the residual wounds of the school crisis. She joined a very determined group of local female elite who set about to ameliorate prejudice and racism in Arkansas. This essay will explore an elite prescription of the Panel of American Women to end the bigotry of the Jim Crow South.

Sara Murphy was born in middle Tennessee and grew up in a fairly well-to-do family. Her father was a faithful Presbyterian and an ardent horse lover who was instrumental in the breed development of the Tennessee walking horse. Her mother was a traditional homemaker who encouraged her daughter to set high goals and develop her talents. With this in mind she attended Peabody College at Vanderbilt University in the wake of the southern Agrarian movement and was shaped by the conservatism of Donald Davidson. Hoping to gain a view of the world outside the South, she chose to attend Columbia University Graduate School in New York City. While an increasing number of southern women were attending college in the post–World War II era, attending graduate school remained a rare option for most women of this generation. It would prove to be the singular most important determinant in her life. Yet she did not stay away from the South long. Taking her master's degree in journalism, she accepted a teaching position in Natchitoches, Louisiana. There she married into a wealthy Cane River family, an area with a rich planter history, including that of a slaveholding former slave woman. In 1950 her husband, Patrick, a lawyer, took a position in Little Rock. They moved to Arkansas, raised a family, and in the midst of some of the most tumultuous days of the twentieth century she became a central figure in the milestone civil rights event known to us today as the Little Rock school crisis.[1]

In the fall of 1957 the Little Rock School District prepared to conform to the landmark *Brown vs. the Board of Education* decision handed down by the Supreme Court in 1954. In accordance with the Blossom plan, named after the School Superintendent Virgil Blossom, Little Rock's Central High School was to be integrated. That fall the school board selected nine highly scrutinized African American students to enter what was regarded as the premier Little Rock high school. Sara Murphy characterized Virgil Blossom as "not enthusiastic about integration . . . [yet he] expected to boost his political and professional stature by [making Little Rock] a model for the entire South." Blossom promoted his plan to integrate Central High through hundreds of meetings, but without encouraging input or heeding advice from the community at large.[2] Although he had shifted his original thinking from elementary school to high school desegregation, Blossom was determined that Little Rock's plan would comply with the Supreme Court's decision gradually, with only one school to be integrated at a time. By this time many middle and upper-middle class white families had moved to the western reaches of Little Rock, and the new Hall High School was under construction to accommodate the burgeoning students. According to the original Blossom plan, Hall High School would not be integrated, leaving what was rapidly becoming a working-class Central High the only school in the district targeted for desegregation.[3]

Gov. Orval Faubus, acting upon political instinct, decided it was in the best interest of the community to prevent the nine African American students from entering Little Rock's Central High School. On the opening day of school, the Arkansas National Guard was mobilized at the school to prevent the nine students from entering and to buffer the school from the hostile crowd outside. Meanwhile, Thurgood Marshall and the NAACP filed suit in federal court and a stalemate ensued. Faubus was called to Pres. Dwight Eisenhower's summer home in Newport, Rhode Island, for consultations. At the end of their meeting it appeared that there was an agreement to allow the desegregation plan to go forward. Upon returning to Little Rock, Governor Faubus removed the National Guard from the school, leaving only the ill-prepared Little Rock police to maintain order, essentially abrogating the agreement made between the governor and the president. Eisenhower, furious with Faubus's defiance but never enthusiastic about the *Brown* decision, was forced to uphold the law by federalizing the Arkansas National Guard and sending the 101st Airborne to restore order around the school and allow the nine students to enter. It was a rough year for all in Little Rock—certainly for the nine students and their mentor, NAACP head Daisy Bates, who withstood many overwhelming threats of violence. Even those who were seemingly on the periphery of the crisis felt the scrutiny of the world on Little Rock. The following school year, Governor Faubus took a more direct approach to end desegregation plans by closing all the district's high schools. The city's economy began to falter and the state's reputation as one of moderation had been bloodied. The overriding question became how to resolve this stalemate and end the nightmare that had become the focus of the growing civil rights movement.[4]

Into the breech stepped Adolphine Terry, a graduate of Vassar, wife of a former New Deal congressman David Terry, daughter of a Confederate veteran, and sister to Pulitzer Prize–winning poet John Gould Fletcher. Mrs. Terry, as she was known to all, had been a leading advocate for numerous municipal—such as the creation of the Little Rock Public Library—and social reforms including anti-lynching activities in central Arkansas and had an immense reputation for getting things done. In 1958 she took it upon herself to organize a group of women to bring the school crisis to an end. After admonishing *Arkansas Gazette* editor Harry Ashmore with a terse "the men have failed . . . It's time to call out the women"; she "called out" a few influential, white-gloved Little Rock ladies to her stately mansion. Sara Murphy did not know Mrs. Terry personally, so she finessed an invitation by way of a mutual friend, Vivion Brewer, in hopes to meet other women of similar thinking about the school crisis and the sanctity of public schools. She had no idea of the potential importance this afternoon tea would hold. That day in early September the Women's Emergency Committee to Open Our Schools (WEC) was formed to turn around what Murphy considered a "miserable mess" and restore order to the educational system in Little Rock. Murphy's assigned task was to recruit new members. She must have been quite effective, for nearly two hundred women attended the second meeting and soon the WEC boasted of over 1,500 official members.[5] The WEC's initial focus was to get the high schools reopened, support the *Brown* decision without coming out in favor of full social integration, and to relieve the city of its now tarnished reputation as a center of racial hatred. The women at the heart of the organization found that it was to be an enormously tough battle in which none were spared the gritty realities of racial politics of the 1950s.[6]

The story of the Little Rock school crisis is a complex one that often requires a score card to keep track of the many players and their ever shifting positions. Little Rock has occupied the minds of many journalists and historians as it has shaped the minds of social theorists and politicians, especially Pres. Bill Clinton. They have looked at the school crisis as a grass-roots starting point of the civil rights movement, a place and time before Martin Luther King Jr. loomed so large over the movement. The crisis has provided numerous constitutional questions and debates and recently has fascinated historians as a significant Cold War story.[7] Many women's historians have regarded Little Rock as a catalyst for feminist activism. Yet it remains unclear how these threads of history come together to explain the larger picture. Perhaps in analyzing the events after the crisis was over, when media attention turned to Mississippi and Selma, can we get a clearer perspective of what Little Rock was all about.

For Murphy the school crisis was an opportunity for "good Southerners" to rise above segregation, prejudice, and racism. Of course she viewed herself as a good southerner, enlightened by education, protected by class and gender, but willing to risk her position to advance the cause of human rights in her community. Throughout the course of school desegregation Murphy worked closely with WEC and its members. In defiance of a slate of segregationist candidates she ran unsuccessfully for a seat on the Little Rock School Board.[8] In 1963 the WEC officially went out of business—believing that its task of opening the schools to allow integration to go forward to be completed. Sara Murphy emerged from the experience as more than a good southerner. Impassioned by the injustices witnessed during the crisis, Murphy understood that much more work was needed. Little Rock and the civil rights movement unleashed ugly old hatreds and racial violence at the same time it unmasked more subtle forms of prejudice naively thought by many to have been dismissed from American society. She began to think that Little Rock could build on its experience to improve upon race relations and social customs of the past. The demise of the WEC meant that a new organization, one more comprehensive in its focus on human rights, must be created. What that new organization was to be would come to Sara Murphy by happenstance.

While attending a national meeting on school boards in Washington, Murphy met Homer Wadsworth, the president of the Kansas City School Board, who commended Murphy and the others for their persistence in the Little Rock case. Their conversation drifted to the unfinished business of the civil rights movement and new ways to promote social justice. Wadsworth told Murphy about an organization established by a local Kansas City woman, Esther Brown, which conducted panel conversations about personal experiences with prejudice and discrimination. Intrigued, Murphy contacted Esther Brown about bringing the concept to Little Rock. Barbara Philips, originally from Kansas City and an activist with the American Jewish Committee, was the midwife of the Little Rock Panel of American Women. Esther Brown knew Philips and chose her to become the conduit between Brown and Murphy to launch the Arkansas program.[9]

The idea was simple: no lecturing, no big names, just average American women from all walks of life quietly discussing the ways in which discrimination—religious, racial, ethnic—had impacted their lives. Panel discussions were held before audiences of various community groups from church to business and other philanthropic organizations. Brown named the organization the Panel of American Women (PAW)—emphasis on "American" to underscore the 1960s popular concept of the cultural melting pot. Eventually the organization had a large national following, incorporating seventy-five chapters.[10]

While these events may seem obvious today, in the 1960s there were real social distances[11]—particularly social distances in the South where Baptists and Methodists often considered themselves planetary worlds apart. Thus the Little Rock PAW came about slowly with the intent to bridge the social distances that were the source of prejudices and discrimination. Murphy gathered a few activists from the WEC days that were interested in organizing the PAW; most were white Anglo-Saxon Protestant (WASP). From this starting point they networked into various religious and ethnic groups, finding Catholics, Jews, Asians, but no black women with whom to work. Ironically, Murphy thought that throughout the turmoil during the school crisis she had associated with only a few middle-class women including NAACP leader

Daisy Bates. By this time, Bates had left Little Rock for Washington, D.C. How would they find an articulate black woman with what Murphy termed "moxey"? From the beginning the women failed to notice that the blacks with whom they were working to help establish PAW, both community and religious leaders, were all men.

Negail Riley, the Methodist chaplain at Philander Smith College and pastor of Wesley Methodist Church, suggested that they speak with his wife, Gwendolyn. Without warning, Sara Murphy, Reverend Riley, and the company of PAW women descended upon Mrs. Riley's home. Murphy's first impression was that Gwen Riley would be perfect. "Would you join us?" she asked. Riley was skeptical, if not initially perturbed with her husband for bringing guests home without advance notice. Riley thought that she had been through enough white scrutiny. In the early 1960s she became the first African American flight reservationist for TWA, and later was interviewed by every top-level executive in the company to become the first African American flight attendant. She quipped that she was the only TWA employee to have met every executive in the company from the president on down. Now a minister's wife, she shared in her husband's calling and her own desire to advance civil rights and warmed to the idea of joining the PAW.[12]

The team was complete with representation from many religious and ethnic groups reflected in the general population of 1960s Little Rock. Murphy made their first assignment to read Lillian Smith's *Killers of the Dream,* a book originally published in 1949 that revealed the destructive nature of segregation to both black and white individuals and southern society as a whole. Together, they wrote their speeches, networked invitations to speak before area organizations, bucked-up their courage, and went out to heal the festering wounds of the school crisis. The programs were an hour long and skillfully choreographed: each panel had a moderator, usually a very safe WASP; the religious or ethnic minorities, from Catholic, to Asian, to Jew presented their stories first. Because the Holocaust was still a fresh memory, the focus was often on the World War II experience, which became the lead-in to the presentation of the black panelist who was the panel capstone. This order created a crescendo designed to take the audience from a distant discrimination to the most obvious form of local racial discrimination. Each presentation was anecdotal and frequently centered on childhood stories or current children's issues. They were not there to be philosophical or in anyway ideologically threatening. The presentations lasted thirty minutes, the last woman to speak was the well-to-do, middle-class woman who presented herself as the recipient of the bounty of American democracy, wishing to extend her good fortune to all. Reflecting on the original speeches, Brownie Ledbetter stated with uncharacteristic embarrassment how "patronizing, knee-jerk liberal" her speech was, "so much so, that it remained on my bedside table to remind me daily of how far we [as a society] have come, and how far we have to go."[13]

The final thirty minutes allowed for the all-important question-and-answer session. Typically there would be a threshold of silence, a silence that served to allow the audience time to reflect and respond. The "most deadly" presentations were the ones when there was no response. At that point the person serving as moderator would prompt questions from the audience. Apparently that rarely occurred. Kathryn Lambright kept a list of the most commonly asked questions during the early panel sessions. Some questions were vaguely hostile—that is hostile commentary dressed up for "polite company" —but overall most were genuine, heartfelt inquiries. The Catholic panelist received questions such as, "Are your creating in Catholic children prejudice when you send them to parochial schools?" and "How do you feel about praying for the conversion of others?" Inevitably a birth control question would be asked. Jewish panelists responded to questions such as, "Isn't Jewish prejudice more prevalent in the North than in the South?" or "Are there any organized anti-Semitic groups in Little Rock?" The most repeated question was: "Is Judaism a nationality, race, or religion?" Asian (then referred to as the Oriental) panelists were asked about the official religion of the state of Hawaii, as well as, "How did that Chinese teacher get her job?" and "Do Orientals experience prejudice?"[14]

Questions posed to the African American (then Negro) panelist centered on housing: "Can a Negro afford to buy a $20,000 house;" schools: "Are white teachers better than black teachers;" or expectations for equality: "Can Negroes participate in (fill in the blank) activity?" At the height of the civil rights movement an audience member might respond with, "We don't have problems with our Negroes here. Why would you come in to stir up trouble?" The response to the "outside agitator question" was typically, "We hope that you continue to have good relationships, but where can you improve?" Eventually someone in the audience would acknowledge that she no longer "owned" the Negroes. More graphic statements such as, "Can you please tell me what Martin Luther King is doing out in the streets with all those niggers?" were not uncommon. Although panelists recoiled from such comments, they agreed that they never felt threatened.[15]

Murphy's original geographic focus for the panel was central Arkansas—specifically Little Rock. The first programs were in local Protestant churches, yet quickly invitations came from all over Arkansas asking the PAW to make presentations at churches, civic clubs, youth groups, and almost every sort of community organization. They traveled as far as Baton Rouge, Louisiana, and made several appearances in Memphis, Tennessee. The Brotherhood of Temple Israel-Memphis nominated the Little Rock PAW for a national Anti-Defamation award, which they won in 1965.[16] Travel expenses, baby sitting costs, meals, and lodging were rarely covered by donations, so that each panelist spent her own money to keep the programs alive. Despite the cost, the travel itself bonded the group and gave them unanticipated opportunities to more deeply understand the nature of prejudice.

In 1964 the Methodist Church of Stuttgart, Arkansas, invited the PAW to give an evening presentation to the congregation. Traveling east from Little Rock into the Arkansas Delta, the women decided to stop for dinner before making their way to the church. They stopped at a diner in downtown Stuttgart where the owner, in a brusque tone, informed the ladies that they would not be able to eat in the front of the restaurant. All dressed up—replete with white gloves and hats—dumbfounded, Murphy did not initially understand the man's intentions. The man pointed to the back door where Murphy and company with their Negro friend could dine. For the first time in their lives these white women felt the real sting of segregation. Outraged and humiliated, they vowed to confront this problem through the best means. When the statement came from the Stuttgart Methodists that they didn't have any problems in their little community, Gwen Riley spoke of the humiliation that she and the others experienced earlier that evening. The congregation was red-faced—"Why no one in our community would treat a black woman dressed as fine as [Riley] in such a way!" According to Murphy, when they returned to Little Rock the women decided to test the recent 1964 Civil Rights Act by visiting the local FBI office. Although they filed a complaint, they were never sure what became of it. They were told that members of the Methodist Church spoke to the restaurant owner, but they never received an official status report from the FBI.[17] Yet several months later, Father Boileau, a white Catholic priest in the Arkansas Diocese, and several black and white parishioners visited the same restaurant and were served without a problem.[18]

Each audience had its own characteristics, and the panels were tailored to meet the anticipated personality of each group. In areas where there were few or no African Americans, the panel was consistently bombarded with the notion that there was no prejudice or discrimination in their community. No blacks in town meant no discrimination. However, the panel was able to gently walk the audience through more subtle forms of ethnic and religious discrimination. The media coverage of the racial violence of the era as witnessed in Birmingham or Selma prompted the greatest amount of fear in these same communities. In communities with a few blacks, a statement might come in the form of what Murphy called the "maid syndrome," that is "the only blacks we know clean our houses, mow our lawns." How could they possibly open their doors to African Americans and risk violence coming to their own communities? Murphy admitted that this was one of the most difficult obstacles at a time when there was "little or no experience between blacks and whites in schools, the work place, or churches."[19]

In retrospect Murphy acknowledged with some laughter that the panel was blind to gender discrimination. "Here we were, all dressed-up, armed to fight the most pressing social ills of the day, but we didn't even see the put-downs we constantly received. For example at the meeting of the Pine Bluff Rotary Club one nice gentleman asked us 'why would pretty young things such as y'all trouble with such ugly issues?'" Further, she noted that they did not always see the class distinctions. It was frequently pointed out to panelists that integration was not their business; it was to be left to working-class whites to work out with poor blacks. "After all," she explained, "that was what the Blossom plan to integrate Little Rock Central High was all about—an effort to keep the new Hall High School lily white. Of course that's what middle class whites would think" and the PAW was not exempt.[20]

Apparently, the Panel of American Women had support in the black community, but was rarely extended invitations to meet with African American organizations. Panelists believed that most African Americans did not need to be reminded of painful everyday exclusions and fear of violence, and Gwen Riley emphatically pointed out that the PAW was not presenting "news" to that community. However, Riley and other black panelists mused in retrospect that the African American community needed to look at its own prejudices as they had done when they became members of the Panel of American Women. It was clear that everyone had a lot to learn from each other.

Indeed, each member had to confront her own prejudices as she took the responsibility to become a member of the PAW. Most of the white panelists suffered from "maid syndrome." Jewish panelist Barbara Philips recalled the first time she went to Gwen Riley's home: "I had never been in black woman's home, it was thrilling, and I knew I had really done something—well it just changed my life forever."[21] Likewise the African American panelists confronted their own blindness to the prejudices their white counterparts had experienced. Saundra Green stated that she had not known to what degree others outside of her own African American community had experienced discrimination.[22]

Time changed racial and ethnic understandings, but of course that did not mean an end to discrimination. The Panel of American Women shifted its discussions to meet the more sophisticated needs of audience participants. Ultimately they dropped the role of moderator. The question-and-answer sessions became less emotionally charged and participants were more concerned with concrete methods to work through integration. They became more tightly focused on developing programs to aid schools. In fact, when they finally received any substantial amount of money it came in the form of a sizeable grant from the Arkansas Department of Education. Did this mean that the Panel of American Women actually helped to mend the social wounds left in the wake of the school crisis? The final analysis is left to anecdotal evidence.

In 1989 the last time the members of the Little Rock Panel of American Women held a reunion, they reflected on their years with the PAW and the present status of race and ethnic relations in Little Rock and around the state. They were all very proud of the work they had done with the PAW. When they began their work southern schools were still embattled over desegregation; separate facilities were still marked in public spaces; and African American voting rights in the South remained hostage to Jim Crow. Jews and Catholics could not buy property in certain neighborhoods nor belong to a number of clubs and organizations. Not quite a generation later, Little Rock's

Central High School was fully integrated, though there were problems between black and white students; separate restrooms and water fountains were almost forgotten; and the African American vote was integral to every election—North and South. An ecumenical spirit was evident around the state with Baptists, Catholics, Methodists, and other mainstream denominations working together on a wide variety of community projects. Some panelists noted, with a touch of irony, that Jews had been admitted to the Little Rock Country Club. In each of the these quarters, the panelists believed that they held a small part in advancing human rights for all—even if that was something as seemingly trivial as membership in the Junior League.

Sara Murphy's assessment was that the PAW was able to poke holes in the power structure, which eventually allowed minorities to become full and active members of the community at large. She especially placed emphasis on the impact the PAW had upon women—for themselves and for the many women they met at panel sessions, it was an early opportunity to witness women speaking out. In turn, Murphy believed, it was a "ripple effect—society can only end its injustices through incremental means." The women who participated in PAW programs in their churches or PTAs were left charged with the power to speak up and take the critical steps to end bigotry within their own communities. Murphy believed that this was an unprecedented opportunity.[23]

Did PAW affect real or measurable change? Were they "invisible revolutionaries," to use civil rights activist Joan Browning's characterization of white women's experience of the civil rights movement? Perhaps it is more accurate to say that they were "preaching to the choir," but it was a choir stunned by rapid social change. The Panel of American Women served initially to help average people cope with the enormity of change brought about by the *Brown* decision and the growing civil rights movement. Despite the emotional interaction between panelists and audience, letters that they kept confirmed that many participants were grateful for opportunities to air concerns and come to greater understandings of complex issues. A Little Rock panelist pointed to the work in Arkansas schools during the 1970s as an indicator of the success of the PAW. Their presentations focused on means to cope with the realities of desegregation—adolescent race relations, white flight, and the proliferation of drug and alcohol—by instituting age-appropriate conflict resolution programs for faculty and students.

A notable failure of the Arkansas Panel of American Women was situated in its reluctance or inability to bring in a new generation to the group. Consequently there was a lack of a newer understanding of social relations and no fresh ideas from those who were younger with a different perspective on the day-to-day realities of integration. The 1964 Civil Rights Acts and the 1965 Voting Rights Act may have provided federal power to end public discrimination or ensure political rights, but legislation did not, and does not, guarantee the end of racism and injustice. All of the panelists believed strongly that the remedy for racism or sexism was constant vigilance and education. Perhaps their quixotic efforts prevented an enduring structure to continue the necessary vigilance to confront the social ills within their own community. Brownie Ledbetter, who continued to work professionally for a number of statewide social justice programs until her retirement in 1999, believed the PAW's greatest failure was that they were "*too romantic* in believing their work could solve the problems of racism, and later sexism within their lifetimes."[24]

Finally, the panelists failed to recognize class issues. Murphy alluded to a vague understanding that the Blossom plan leaned heavily on working-class whites to accomplish the goals of the *Brown* decision. However, the panelists were blind to class issues within their own ranks. Their assumptions about status and equality were expressed by the white panelists who were amused by Gwen Riley's desire not to have to work to help support her family when they were seeking careers outside the home at the height of the second wave of the feminist movement of the 1970s. Why, they thought, would any talented woman *want* to stay home? They were unable to see the socioeconomic implications of having to work and wanting to work outside the home. Although they spoke of the need for a more diverse society with full acceptance of multiculturalism, their authentic model of the social cornerstone remained classically white middle class. They expected that the minorities with whom they worked would want and accept only their vision of success and middle-class achievement.

The Little Rock Panel of American Women began its work late in 1963 and officially ended in 1985. The panel women, as had many American women, moved on to other things. Some were entering new careers, others wanted more time with children and grandchildren. Most continued to volunteer in other activist organizations. Sara Murphy worked closely with Betty Bumpers and Peace Links, the international women's peace organization founded by the first lady of the state of Arkansas, writing speeches and orchestrating similar panel groups incorporating Russian and American women. She firmly believed that the skills learned with the Panel of American Women transferred to the development of Peace Links.

Always optimistic, Murphy offered this summation of the value of the Panel of American Women: "Women have the power to change things, the panel was a very potent and effective group, and [I] took these skills an put them to work for Peace Links, organizing in Arkansas, throughout the United States, and in Russia." She characterized the long-term importance of the PAW's work in a single term "mindshift," indicating the change "needed for the survival of the planet. Not just economic preservation, but environmental, and the basic way human beings interact . . . Women know about nurturing, preserving, affirming life. We absolutely must share [this knowledge] and be heard—it is an imperative. What ever we can do to change organizations and institutions is terribly important. Women can do it together. This I learned working with the Panel of American Women."[25]

It was a brave time for Murphy and the other Little Rock panelists. Credit must also be given to the people of Arkansas who allowed meetings to take place all over the state to simply talk about the problems of prejudice and race. It is unimaginable that this story could have unfolded in neighboring Mississippi without violence and retribution. Southern white female elite such as Sara Murphy began to bridge the chasm between Arkansas whites and blacks.

Notes

Introduction to *The Southern Elite and Social Change: Essays in Honor of Willard B. Gatewood Jr.*
Randy Finley and Thomas A. DeBlack

1. Eugene Genovese, *The Southern Tradition: The Achievement and Limitations of an American Conservative* (Cambridge, Massachusetts: Harvard University Press, 1994), xi.

2. Leon Litwack, *Trouble in Mind: Black Southerners in the Age of Jim Crow* (New York: Alfred A. Knopf, 1998), 280–325.

3. Pete Daniel, *Lost Revolution: The South in the 1950s* (Chapel Hill, North Carolina: University of North Carolina Press, 2000), 47.

4. Gordon S. Wood, *The Radicalism of the American Revolution* (New York: Alfred A. Knopf, 1992), 8.

5. Barbara J. Fields, "Who Freed the Slaves?" in *The Civil War: An Illustrated History*, ed. Geoffrey C. Ward (New York: Alfred A. Knopf, 1990), 178–81.

6. Eric Foner, *Reconstruction: America's Unfinished Revolution* (New York: Harper and Row, 1988), 602–12.

7. Willard B. Gatewood Jr., *Aristocrats of Color: The Black Elite, 1860–1920* (Bloomington, Indiana: Indiana University Press, 1990), 43, 89–90, 235, 305, 310, 348.

In the Shadow of the Revolution: Savannah's First Generation of Free African American Elite in the New Republic, 1790–1830
Whittington B. Johnson

1. Kenneth A. Lockridge, *A New England Town: The First Hundred Years* (New York: W.W. Norton,1970); John Mack Faragher, *Sugar Creek: Life on the Illinois Prairie* (New Haven: Yale University Press, 1986).

2. Gordon S. Wood, *The Radicalism of the American Revolution* (New York: Alfred A. Knopf, 1992), 8.

3. *Columbian Museum and Savannah Advertiser*, 8 January 1802.

4. Thomas Gamble, *A History of the City Government of Savannah* (Savannah: Review Publishing Company, 1901), 87–88.

5. *Population Schedules of the Fifth Census of the United States, 1830: Georgia*, Washington, D.C., 1830.

6. William Harden, *Recollections of a Long and Satisfactory Life* (Savannah, Review Printing Company, 1934), 48–49.

7. Jeremiah Evarts's Diary, 1822, Georgia Historical Society, Savannah, Georgia; Carter G. Woodson, *The Education of the Negro Prior to 1861* (Washington, D.C.: 1919), 215.

8. City of Savannah Tax Digest, 1810, Georgia Historical Society, Savannah, Georgia.

9. City of Savannah Tax Digest, 1820, Georgia Historical Society, Savannah, Georgia.

10. City of Savannah Tax Digest, 1820; Registration of Free Persons of Color of Savannah, 1817–1829, Georgia Historical Society, Savannah, Georgia.

11. Larry Koger, *Black Slaveowners: Free Black Masters in South Carolina, 1790–1860* (Jefferson, North Carolina.: McFarland and Company, 1985), 29–30.

12. The Colonial Office Papers (hereafter cited as CO Papers), 23/87/89. Series 23 contains documents relating to the Bahama Islands. The Department of Archives, Nassau, Bahamas, has the whole series on microfilm, and the public record office, Kew, England, has the originals.

13. Bahamas, Register of Slaves, 1821–34, Department of Archives, Nassau, Bahamas. At the insistence of the home government, the Bahamas legislature passed a slave registry act that mandated the triennial registration of slaves, beginning in 1821. The names of all slaveholders and their slaves are found in these documents.

14. At the time there were in the Bahamas an Anglican catechist, three Baptist preachers, and a Wesleyan Methodist missionary; none were slaveholders. Conversely, the black preachers (all Baptists) in Savannah were slaveholders. Andrew Marshall did not buy another slave after the one he had died.

15. Registration of Free Persons of Savannah, 1826–1835.

16. For a discussion of some of these endogamous marriages see Whittington B. Johnson, *Black Savannah, 1788–1864* (Fayetteville: University of Arkansas Press, 1996), 109–12.

17. The following appears beside Eve Motta's name in the City of Savannah Tax Digest for 1809: "wife of Saunders." Eve was the daughter of London Dolly, a black man. For a discussion of the Dollys, see Austin D. Washington, "The Dollys: An Antebellum Black Family of Savannah, Georgia," *Savannah State College Bulletin, Faculty Research Edition* 26 (December 1972): 101–3.

18. The census did not give separate totals for blacks and mulattoes until much later than the scope of this study. In 1860 mulattoes constituted almost 91 percent of the nonwhite population in Mobile County (Mobile); 76 percent in New Orleans; 75 percent in Charleston; and about 68 percent in Chatham County (Savannah). *Preliminary Report of the Eighth Census, 1860*, Washington, D.C., 1862.

19. Barry W. Higman, *Slave Populations of the British Caribbean, 1807–1834* (Baltimore: Johns Hopkins University Press, 1984), 380.

20. Bahamas, Register of Slaves, 1834; Margaret Clarke's will, 9 March 1868, Great Exuma, Bahama Islands, Department of Archives, Nassau, Bahamas.

21. Johnson, *Black Savannah*, 3. For a discussion of free African Americans in Charleston, see Bernard E. Powers, *Black Charlestonians. A Social History 1822–1885* (Fayetteville: University of Arkansas Press, 1994); for New Orleans see H. E. Strekx,

The Free Negro in Ante-bellum Louisiana (Ruthford, N.J.: Farleigh Dickinson University Press, 1972); moreover, Michael P. Johnson and James L. Roark, *Black Masters* (New York: W.W. Norton, 1984) and David O. Whitten, *Andrew Durnford* (New Brunswick, New Jersey: Rutgers University Press, 1995) are studies of individual large slaveholders in South Carolina and Louisiana, respectively.

22. Ethel M. Christler, "Participation of Negroes in the Government of Georgia" (Master's Thesis, Atlanta University, 1932) 7, 62.

23. Mrs. Pashal N. Strong Sr., "Glimpses of Savannah, 1790–1825," *Georgia Historical Quarterly* 33 (March 1949): 34.

24. Henry N. Sherwood, "Paul Cuffe," *Journal of Negro History* 8 (Apri1 1923): 158.

25. Whittington B. Johnson, *The Promising Years, 1759–1830: The Emergence of Black Labor and Business* (New York: Garland Publishing, 1993), 187.

26. James Porter's Obituary, *Savannah Tribune,* 13 November 1895.

27. CO Papers 23/88/146; Bahama Blue Book of Statistics, 1830; CO Papers 27/28/62.

28. Savannah Georgia City Council Minutes, 1812–1822. Georgia Department of Archives and History, Atlanta, Georgia.

29. Robert E. Perdue, *The Negro in Savannah, 1865–1900* (New York: Exposition Press, 1973), 124–25; Joseph Frederick Waring, *Cerveau's Savannah* (Savannah: Georgia Historical Society, 1973), 66–67.

30. James Simms, *The First Colored Baptist Church In North America* (Philadelphia: J. B. Lippincott, 1888), 80.

31. Richard Houstoun's Estate, 1814, Central Records Office (hereafter cited as CRO), Chatham County Courthouse, Savannah, Georgia.

32. Louis Mirault's Estate, 1827, CRO; St. John the Baptist Catholic Church of Savannah Parish Register, 1796–1816 (hereafter cited as St. John Register). These are the two documents that yield the most information of the literacy of the emigres.

33. James Simms, *The First Colored Baptist in North America* (Philadelphia: J. B. Lippincott, 1888), 57; Mabel Freeman La Far, "The Baptist Church of Savannah, Georgia: History, Records and Register," Georgia Historical Society, Savannah, Georgia, vol.1, 135.

34. St. John Register, 1796–1816.

35. Independent Presbyterian Church Sessional Minutes, 1828–51, Georgia Department of Archives and History, Atlanta, Georgia.

36. Christ Episcopal Church of Savannah Parish Register, 1822–74, Georgia Department of Archives and History, Atlanta, Georgia.

37. First Baptist Church was not formally organized until 26 November 1800. See Margaret La Far, *A Historical Sketch of the First Baptist Church* (Savannah, 1975). The pages are not numbered in this booklet.

38. Registration of Free Persons of Color of Savannah, 1817–1829.

39. Gail Saunders, *Slavery in the Bahamas, 1648–1838* (Nassau, Bahamas: Privately Published, 1985), 88.

40. Henry Bourquin Jr.'s Papers, 1810–12, Georgia Historical Society, Savannah, Georgia.

41. Simms, *The First Colored Baptist Church in North America,* 234–37. Bryan's birth year is usually given as 1716, but in 1800 he gave "sixty-three years old" as his age. See also "Letters Showing the Rise and Progress of the Early Negro Churches in Georgia and the West Indies," *Journal of Negro History* 1 (January 1918): 86–87. That is why I have used the year 1737.

42. George White, *Historical Collections of Georgia* (New York: Pudney and Russell, 1854), 313.

43. "Letters Showing the Rise and Progress," 77–78; Carter G. Woodson, *The History of the Negro Church* (Washington, D.C.: Associated Publishers, 1921), 112.

44. "Letters Showing the Rise and Progress," 79; William Bryan's Will, 1789, CCSC, Deeds, vol. G, 1789–90.

45. "Letters Showing the Rise and Progress," 82–83.

46. "Letters Showing the Rise and Progress," 86–87.

47. CCSC, Deeds, vol. Y, 1892–1805; CCSCD, vol. 2B, 1806–9, Georgia Department of Archives and History, Atlanta, Georgia.

48. Henry Holcombe, *The First Fruits in a Series of Letters* (Philadelphia: Ann Cochran, 1812), 116. Holcombe was the first pastor of the first white Baptist church established in Savannah.

49. Simms, *The First Colored Baptist Church,* 68–69.

50. David Benedict, *A General History of the Baptist Denominations in America, and Other Parts,* 2 vols. (Boston: Manning and Loring, 1813), 2, 191; Edgar G. Thomas, *The First African Baptist Church of North America* (Savannah, Georgia: Privately Published, 1925), 40.

51. For a full discussion of Andrew C. Marshall, see Whittington B. Johnson, "Andrew C. Marshall, A Black Religious Leader of Antebellum Savannah," *Georgia Historical Quarterly* 69 (summer 1985): 173–92.

52. Chatham County Register of Free Persons of Color, 1826–1835. In 1828 Cunningham said he was sixty-four years old, but his tombstone lists his age as eighty-three the year he died (1842), placing his birth year as 1759. I have calculated his birth year on the basis of the information provided in 1828.

53. Henry Holcombe, *The Analytical Repository* 1 (November–December 1802): 188. Emanuel Love, *History of the First African Baptist Church* (Savannah: Morning News Press, 1888), 43.

54. Holcombe, *First Fruits In a Series,* 116.

55. CCSCD, vol. 2D, 1810–12; Chatham County Tax Digest, 1833 (hereafter cited as CCTD).

56. CCTD, 1837.

57. Ruth Blair, ed., Some Tax Digests of Georgia, Georgia Department of Archives and History, Atlanta, Georgia.

58. St. John Register.

59. St. John Register.

60. Louis Mirault's Estate, 1827, CRO.

61. City of Savannah Tax Digest, 1820.

62. City of Savannah Tax Digest, 1820; in 1819, he placed a small house in Greene

Ward on sale, *Daily Georgian,* 4 December 1819.

63. City of Savannah Tax Digest, 1810.

64. City of Savannah Tax Digest, 1813.

65. Richard Houstoun's Estate, 1814.

66. City of Savannah Tax Digest, 1810, 1820.

67. Wayne-Stites-Anderson Papers, Georgia Historical Society, Savannah, Georgia (hereafter cited as W-S-A Papers).

68. "Bill of Clothing for George Anderson," W-S-A Papers; "Bill and Receipt of Willaim H. Nicoll," W-S-A Papers; "Simon Jackson Account," W-S-A Papers.

69. Daniel Huguenin's Will, 1811, CRO.

70. Daniel Huguenin's Inventory Appraisement, 28 September 1811, CRO.

71. Jordan Williams's Will, 26 September 1814; Joseph Dixon's Will, 1 October 1814. Both documents are located in CCSC, Ordinary, Estate Records, Wills, vol. E, 1808–17.

72. Jack Gibbons, CCSC, Deeds, vol. U, 1799–1800.

73. City of Savannah Tax Digest, 1813; Registration of Free Persons of Color, 1817–29.

74. Charles Odingsell's Will, CCSC, Ordinary, Estate Records, Wills, vol. E, 1808–17.

75. For the various residences and occupations that he listed over the years, see the Registrations of Free Persons of Color and the United States Census Reports for the years covered in this study. Moreover, for a full discussion of Anthony Odingsell see Joseph Parsons, "Anthony Odinsells: A Romance of Little Wassaw," *Georgia Historical Quarterly* 55 (summer 1971): 208–21.

"A Model Man of Chicot County": Lycurgus Johnson and Social Change Thomas A. DeBlack

1. Leland Meyer, *The Life and Times of Colonel Richard M. Johnson of Kentucky* (New York: Columbia University Press, 1932), 14–15, 42–44, 47, 337; Lewis Collins, *History of Kentucky,* vol. 1 (Franklin, Kentucky: Kentucky Historical Society, 1966), 255; Reuben T. Durrett, "Bryant's Station," in *The Filson Club Publication,* no. 12 (Louisville: John P. Morton and Company, 1897), 35–42.

2. Ann Bolton Bevins, *The Ward and Johnson Families of Central Kentucky and the Lower Mississippi Valley* (Georgetown, Kentucky: The Ward Hall Press, 1984), 8–27; John Hallum, *Biographical and Pictorial History of Arkansas,* vol. 1 (Albany: Weed, Parsons, and Company, 1987), 159.

3. *Biographical and Historical Memoirs of Southern Arkansas* (Chicago: The Goodspeed Publishing Company, 1890), 1058, 1061.

4. Willard B. Gatewood Jr., "The Arkansas Delta: The Deepest of the Deep South," in *The Arkansas Delta: Land of Paradox,* ed. Jeannie Whayne and Willard B. Gatewood (Fayetteville: University of Arkansas Press, 1993), 6.

5. Thomas Foti, "The River's Gifts and Curses," in Whayne and Gatewood, eds., *Arkansas Delta,* 37.

6. Leona Sumner Brasher, "Chicot County, Arkansas: Pioneer and Present Times."

Special Collections Division, University of Arkansas Libraries, Fayetteville, Arkansas, 3.

7. Alfred Finney and Cephas Washburn, "Mission Among the Cherokees of the Arkansaw," *Missionary Herald* 17 (May–July 1821), excerpted in *Travels in the Old South,* ed. Eugene L. Schwaab (Lexington: University Press of Kentucky, 1973), 1:151.

8. See Walter Prescott Webb, *The Great Frontier* (Austin: University of Texas Press, 1951, 1952), 182–91; Whayne and Gatewood, *The Arkansas Delta,* 8–9.

9. "Flora and Fauna of Chicot County, Arkansas," "Chicot County," WPA Files, Arkansas History Commission, Little Rock, 2; Orville W. Taylor, *Negro Slavery in Arkansas* (Durham, North Carolina: Duke University Press, 1958), 95.

10. Thomas A. DeBlack, "Plantation Arkansas," *Arkansas Democrat Gazette,* 10 August 1997.

11. *Seventh Census of the United States, 1850: An Appendix* (Washington: Robert Armstrong, 1853), ix; Chicot County Tax Assessment Records, 1831, 1–7.

12. United States Land Office, Land Patent Records, 1832–1839; Chicot County Deed Book "A," 277; "Genealogy of the Johnson Family," compiled by Tom L. Johnson, Cleveland, Ohio, typescript; Chicot County Tax Records, 1840, 13.

13. Fred Berry and John Novak, *The History of Arkansas* (Little Rock: Rose Publishing Company, 1987), 60–61; D. A. Stokes, "The First State Elections in 1836," *Arkansas Historical Quarterly* 20 (summer 1961), 140, 142–43; "Genealogy of the Johnson Family;" Ted R. Worley, "The Control of the Real Estate Bank of Arkansas, 1836–1855," *Mississippi Valley Historical Review* 37 (June 1950–March 1951), 413.

14. Chicot County Deed Book "D," 517; Chicot County Tax Records, 1845, no page number; "Genealogy of the Johnson Family;" Chicot County Deed Record Book "C," 112.

15. Taylor, *Negro Slavery in Arkansas,* 113–14; Leona Sumner Brashear, "Chicot County, Arkansas: Pioneer and Present Times," Special Collections Division, University of Arkansas Libraries, Fayetteville, Arkansas, 4–5. The "carpet bag" was described as being "made from a stout piece of carpet, strongly attached, without bottom, just folded together, with a finished top, of lock and key and a handle on each side."

16. Horace J. Ford's Book, journal, Present from Horace F. Walworth, 5 December 1848, Collection of the Arkansas Territorial Restoration, Little Rock, Arkansas, 2 February 1849.

17. Ford's Journal, 20 December 1848.

18. Mel Leavitt, *A Short History of New Orleans* (San Francisco: Lexikos, 1982), 97–98; Erik F. Haites, James Mak, and Gary M. Walton, *Western River Transportation: The Era of Early Internal Development, 1810–1860* (Baltimore: Johns Hopkins University Press, 1975), 130–131, 143; Mrs. Isaac H. Hilliard's Diary, 1849–1850, entry of 28 April 1850, Special Collections Division, University of Arkansas Libraries, Fayetteville, Arkansas.

19. *Seventh Census of the United States, 1850: An Appendix,* ix; Robert B. Walz, "Arkansas Slaveholding and Slaveholders in 1850," *Arkansas Historical Quarterly* 12 (spring 1953): 52–73.

20. *Seventh Census of the United States, 1850, Agriculture,* 556; Manuscript Census Returns, Seventh Census of the United States Census, 1850, Chicot County, Arkansas, Agriculture Schedule, 3–4.

21. *Arkansas State Gazette and Democrat,* 25 April 1851. The Benjamin Johnson mentioned here may have been Robert Ward Johnson's younger brother, Benjamin S. Johnson.

22. *Arkansas State Gazette and Democrat,* 25 April 1851.

23. Elsie M. Lewis, "Robert Ward Johnson: Militant Spokesman for the Old-South-West," *Arkansas Historical Quarterly* 13 (spring 1954): 17; John Hallum, *Biographical and Pictorial History of Arkansas* 1 (Albany: Weed, Parsons, and Company, 1887): 159, 177–78; Michael Dougan, "A Look at the 'Family' in Arkansas Politics, 1858–1865," *Arkansas Historical Quarterly* 29 (summer 1970), 103.

24. Lewis Cecil Gray, *History of Agriculture in the Southern United States to 1860* (Washington, D.C.: The Carnegie Institute of Washington, 1933), 2:1026–27.

25. *Arkansas State Gazette and Democrat,* 16 May 1857.

26. Chicot County Deed Book "I," 221–27.

27. Marion Bragg, *Historic Names and Places on the Lower Mississippi River* (Vicksburg: Mississippi River Commission, 1990), 135–36.

28. Bragg, *Historic Names and Places on the Lower Mississippi River,* 135–36.

29. See information compiled for Nomination to National Register of Historic Homes. Survey and Documentation performed for Arkansas Historic Preservation Society under the direction of Elam L. Denham, University of Arkansas, Fayetteville, 1984. See also Kenneth Story, "A Jewel of the Delta: Lakeport Plantation," *Arkansas Preservation: Newsletter of the Historic Preservation Alliance of Arkansas* (winter 1990): 1; Chicot County Tax Records, 1860, 26.

30. Chicot County Tax Records, 1860, 26; Swannee Bennett and William B. Worthen, *Arkansas Made: A Survey of the Decorative, Mechanical, and Fine Arts Produced in Arkansas, 1819–1870* (Fayetteville: University of Arkansas Press, 1991), 2:134.

31. Thomas Johnson Sherrard, *The Sherrard Family of Steubenville,* ed. Robert Andrew Sherrard (Philadelphia: James B. Rodgers Printing Company, 1890), 287–88, microfilm.

32. Manuscript Census Returns, Eighth Census of the United States, 1860, Chicot County, Arkansas, Agriculture Schedule, 13; Sherrard, *Sherrard Family,* 287–88; Chicot County Tax Records, 1860, 26; 1861, 31; 1862, 26; 1863, 32.

33. Sherrard, *Sherrard Family,* 287–88; Manuscript Census Returns, Eighth Census, 1860, Chicot County, Arkansas, Agriculture Schedule, 13; Chicot County Tax Records, 1860, 26; Manuscript Census Returns, Eighth Census of the United States, 1860, Chicot County, Arkansas, Slave Schedules; Taylor, *Negro Slavery in Arkansas,* 57; Peter Kolchin, *American Slavery, 1619–1877* (New York: Hill and Wang, 1993), 101; Kenneth M. Stampp, *The Peculiar Institution: Slavery in the Ante-Bellum South* (New York: Vintage Books, 1956), 30–31.

34. Sherrard, *Sherrard Family,* 287–88.

35. Manuscript Census Returns, Eighth Census of the United States, 1860, Chicot County, Arkansas, Agriculture Schedule, 13; Chicot County Tax Records, 1860, 26.

36. *Seventh Census of the United States, Agriculture, 1850,* 554–56; *Census of the United States, Agriculture, 1860,* 6–7; *Eighth Census of the United States, 1860, Manufactures,* 331; Jack B. Scroggs, "Arkansas in the Secession Crisis," *Arkansas Historical Quarterly* 12 (autumn 1953): 179–80.

37. *Arkansas State Gazette and Democrat,* 25 August 1854.

38. O. E. Moore to Joseph Medill, *Chicago Tribune,* 29 January 1872, reprinted in *Daily Arkansas Gazette,* 4 February 1872.

39. *Arkansas State Gazette,* 25 February 1860.

40. "Genealogy of the Johnson Family;" Julia J. Johnson died in November 1869, becoming the fifth of the Johnson's ten children to die before the age of ten.

41. Scroggs, "Arkansas in Secession," 181–83; Michael B. Dougan, *Confederate Arkansas: The People and Politics of a Frontier State in Wartime* (University, Alabama: University of Alabama Press, 1976), 15–16. For a full discussion of the life of Thomas Carmichael Hindman see Diane Neal and Thomas W. Kremm, *The Lion of the South: Thomas C. Hindman* (Macon, Georgia: Mercer University Press, 1993).

42. Waddy W. Moore, "Henry Massie Rector, 1860–1862," in *The Governors of Arkansas: Essays in Political Biography,* ed. Timothy P. Donovan and Willard B. Gatewood Jr. (Fayetteville: University of Arkansas Press, 1995), 31; Scroggs, "Arkansas in Secession," 184.

43. James M. McPherson, *Battle Cry of Freedom: The Civil War Era* (New York: Oxford University Press, 1988), 213–21; Scroggs, "Arkansas in Secession," 188.

44. Scroggs, "Arkansas in Secession," 190.

45. David Y. Thomas, *Arkansas in War and Reconstruction, 1861–1874* (Little Rock: Arkansas Division, United Daughters of the Confederacy, 1926), 39; Dougan, *Confederate Arkansas,* 34; Scroggs, "Arkansas in Secession," 190.

46. *Arkansas State Gazette,* 24 November 1860.

47. Scroggs, "Arkansas in Secession," 208–15; Thomas, *Arkansas in War and Reconstruction,* 69–70.

48. Scroggs, "Arkansas in the Secession Crisis," 215.

49. *Journal of Both Sessions of the Convention of the State of Arkansas* (Little Rock, 1861), 55.

50. Scroggs, "Arkansas in Secession," 222–23; Dougan, *Confederate Arkansas,* 462–63. The initial vote was sixty-four in favor of secession and five opposed. All but one of the dissenters, Isaac Murphy of Madison County, changed their votes to make the final tally sixty-nine to one.

51. Thomas, *Arkansas in War and Reconstruction, 1861–1874* (Little Rock: Arkansas Division, United Daughters of the Confederacy, 1926), 96, 99; Richard N. Current, ed., *Encyclopedia of the Confederacy* (New York: Simon and Schuster, 1993), 1:397–99.

52. Memorandum No. 18386, 25 May 1875, Southern Claims Commission Records, barred claim no. 18386 from Record Group 233, 6 January 1873, Records of the U. S. House of Representatives, National Archives, Washington, D. C.

53. Chicot County Tax Records, 1861, 31; Chicot County Tax Records, 1862, 26; Chicot County Deed Records, Book "K," 516–17.

54. McPherson, *Battle Cry,* 383; Thomas, *Arkansas in War and Reconstruction,* 100–101.

55. *The War of the Rebellion: A Compilation of the Official Records of the Union and Confederate Armies,* 70 vols. in 128 books and index (Washington, D. C.: Government Printing Office, 1880–1901), ser. 1, 13:33.

56. Small Manuscripts Collection, Arkansas History Commission, Little Rock, box 4, no. 4a.

57. William L. Shea, "1862: 'A Continual Thunder,'" in *Rugged and Sublime: The Civil War in Arkansas*, ed. Mark K. Christ (Fayetteville: University of Arkansas Press, 1994), 44; McPherson, *Battle Cry*, 420–21; Charles C. Stuart to W. E. Woodruff, 1 April 1863, Woodruff Papers, Arkansas History Commission, Little Rock.

58. Victor M. Johnson's Ledger Book, 1917, p. 5, Special Collections Division, University of Arkansas Libraries, Fayetteville, microfilm.

59. Victor M. Johnson's Ledger Book, 1917, p. 5.

60. Memorandum No. 18386, Southern Claims Commission.

61. Willard B. Gatewood Jr., "Sunnyside: The Evolution of an Arkansas Plantation, 1840–1945," in *Shadows Over Sunnyside: An Arkansas Plantation in Transition, 1830–1945*, ed. Jeannie Whayne (Fayetteville: University of Arkansas Press, 1993), 7; Charles C. Stuart to W. E. Woodruff, Woodruff Papers, 1 August 1863; Susan Read to W. E. Woodruff, Woodruff Papers, 28 November 1862; Susan Read receipt, 19 December 1862, Woodruff Papers; William Woodruff to Alex Jones, Woodruff Papers, 18 March 1863, Special Collections Division, University of Arkansas Libraries, Fayetteville, microfilm.

62. John MacLean to D. H. Reynolds, 10 March 1864, Reynolds Papers, Special Collections Division, University of Arkansas Libraries, Fayetteville.

63. Chicot County Tax Assessment Roll, 1863, 32.

64. For an example of the brutal nature of the war in Chicot County, see Weed Marshall, "Fight to the Finish Near Lake Village, Ark.," in *Confederate Veteran* 19 (April 1911): 169.

65. MacLean to Reynolds, 10 March 1864, Reynolds Papers.

66. Robert L. Kerby, *Kirby Smith's Confederacy: The Trans-Mississippi South, 1863–1865* (Tuscaloosa: University of Alabama Press, 1972), 156, 160.

67. Memorandum No. 18386, Southern Claims Commission.

68. Chicot County Tax Roll, 1860, 26; Chicot County Tax Roll 1861, 31; Chicot County Tax Roll, 1865, 30.

69. For a fuller discussion of this issue, see Carl H. Moneyhon, *The Impact of the Civil War and Reconstruction on Arkansas: Persistence in the Midst of Ruin* (Baton Rouge: Louisiana State University Press, 1994). On the Freedmen's Bureau in Arkansas, see Randy Finley, *From Slavery to Uncertain Freedom: The Freedmen's Bureau in Arkansas, 1865–1869* (Fayetteville: University of Arkansas Press, 1996).

70. Leon F. Litwack, *Been in the Storm So Long: The Aftermath of Slavery* (New York: Alfred A. Knopf, 1980), 411; Records of the Bureau of Refugees, Freedmen, and Abandoned Lands (Washington, D. C.: National Archives, 1971), Register of Contracts and Register of Major Landholders, Field Offices, April 1867 to August 1868; Records of the Bureau of Refugees, Freedmen, and Abandoned Lands (Washington, D. C.: National Archives, 1971), Records of the Assistant Commissioner for Arkansas, Thomas Abel to Gen. John W. Sprague, 31 July 1866 (hereafter cited as FBRAC); O. C. Ord to O. O. Howard, 22 February 1867, FBRAC; Ord to Howard, 22 February 1867, FBRAC; Register of Contracts and Register of Major Landholders, April 1867–August 1868, FBRFO.

71. Moneyhon, *Impact,* 228, 230, 232; Thomas Abel to Gen. John W. Sprague, 30 September 1866, FBRAC; *Agricultural Statistics, 1936* (Washington, D.C.: U. S. Government Printing Office, 1936), 75; Hersey to Ord, 31 January 1867, FBRAC. Moneyhon cites 1866 prices of thirty-seven cents per pound, falling to seventeen and eighteen cents by October 1867. Yearly cotton quotations from various sources often vary considerably considering the market (New York, New Orleans, Memphis) and the grade of cotton.

72. For a full discussion, see Moneyhon, *Impact.* For more information on James Mason, the mulatto who became a political power in Chicot County, see Gatewood, "Sunnyside: The Evolution of an Arkansas Plantation, 1840–1945," in *Shadows Over Sunnyside,* ed. Whayne, 9–10.

73. On the riot, see Thomas A. DeBlack, "A Garden in the Wilderness: The Johnsons and the Making of Lakeport Plantation, 1831–1876," (Ph.D. diss., University of Arkansas, 1995).

74. O. E. Moore to Joseph Medill, *Chicago Tribune,* 29 January 1872, reprinted in *Daily Arkansas Gazette,* 4 February 1872.

75. Bankruptcy Records Act of 1867, RG 21, National Archives, Southwest Region, Fort Worth, Texas, 34–695. For more information on Johnson's reputation, see Register of Contracts and Register of Major Landholders, April 1867–August 1868, FBRFO.

76. Register of Contracts and Register of Major Landholders, April 1867–August 1868, FBRFO.

77. Register of Contracts and Register of Major Landholders, April 1867–August 1868, FBRFO.

78. Manuscript Census Returns, Eighth Census of the United States, 1860, Chicot County, Arkansas, Agriculture Schedule, 13; Manuscript Census Returns, Ninth Census of the United States, 1870, Chicot County, Arkansas, Agriculture Schedule, 19; Chicot County Tax Records, 1869, 16–17.

79. *Biographical and Historical Memoirs of Southern Arkansas,* 1065, 1076–77.

80. Unidentified Newspaper Obituary, Tom L. Johnson, "Genealogy of the Johnson Family."

81. William Faulkner's speech upon receiving the Nobel Prize, 10 December 1950, quoted in John Bartlett, ed., *Familiar Quotations,* 14th ed., (Boston: Little, Brown and Company, 1968), 1039.

"I Go To Set the Captives Free": The Activism of Richard Harvey Cain, Nationalist Churchman and Reconstruction-Era Leader
Bernard E. Powers Jr.

1. *Christian Recorder,* 30 January 1864. The definition of black nationalism used in this essay is set forth by Sterling Stuckey in *The Ideological Origins of Black Nationalism* (Boston: Beacon Press, 1972), 1–2. There the author asserts, "The originators of the ideology . . . [of] black nationalism emphasized the need for black people to rely primarily on themselves in vital areas of life—economic, political, religious, and intellectual—in order to effect their liberation."

2. Kenneth E. Mann, "Richard Harvey Cain: Congressman, Minister and Champion For Civil Rights" *Negro History Bulletin* 35 (March 1972): 65; Daniel A. Payne, *Recollections of Seventy Years* (Nashville: AME Sunday School Union, 1888; reprint, New York: Arno Press, 1968), 332; *Christian Recorder* 16 January 1869.

3. Floyd J. Miller, *Search for a Black Nationality: Black Colonization and Emigration 1787–1863* (Urbana: University of Illinois, 1975), 136–37.

4. Jane H. Pease and William H. Pease, *They Who Would Be Free: Blacks' Search for Freedom, 1830–1861* (New York: Atheneum, 1974), 253–54.

5. Black Abolitionist Papers, 0723–0724 microfilm reel #8 1854.03.27; Pease, *They Who Would Be Free,* 255.

6. Leon Litwack, *North of Slavery: The Negro in the Free States 1790–1860* (Chicago: University of Chicago, 1961), 20–25.

7. Miller, *Search for a Black Nationality,* 173, 179, 182–83, 192; Joel Schor, *Henry Highland Garnet: A Voice of Black Radicalism in the Nineteenth Century* (Westport, Connecticut: Greenwood Press, 1977), 156–57; M. R. Delany and Robert Campbell, *Search for a Place: Black Separatism and Africa, 1860* (Ann Arbor: University of Michigan Press, 1971), 110–11.

8. Miller, *Search for a Black Nationality,* 193, 195, 213–14; Schor, *Henry Highland Garnet,* 180.

9. Miller, *Search for a Black Nationality,* 260–61.

10. *Repository of Religion and Literature* (August 1862), 146–47; *Repository of Religion and Literature* (September 1862), 171. For an exposition of the nationalist ideas of Delany and Garnet see, Stuckey, *Ideological Origins.*

11. Howard Brotz, *Negro Social and Political Thought 1850–1920 Representative Texts* (New York: Basic Books, 1966), 193–96; Benjamin Quarles, *Black Abolitionists* (London: Oxford University Press, 1969), 68, 128, 240.

12. Brotz, *Negro Social and Political Thought,* 194.

13. Earl Ofari, "*Let Your Motto Be Resistance*": *The Life and Thought of Henry Highland Garnet* (Boston: Beacon Press, 1972), 96; *Christian Recorder,* 30 May 1863.

14. Victor Ullman, *Martin R. Delany: The Beginnings of Black Nationalism* (Boston: Beacon Press, 1971), 266–67, 283; Cyril E. Griffith, *The African Dream: Martin R. Delany and the Emergence of Pan-African Thought* (University Park: University of Pennsylvania Press, 1975), 82, 86.

15. *Christian Recorder,* 28 December 1863, 1 January 1864.

16. *The Annual Report of the African Civilization Society Made at the Sixth Annual Meeting Held at New York, May 31, 1865* (New York: George F. Nesbitt, 1865), 1–5.

17. *Christian Recorder,* 12 December 1863, 13 February 1864, 20 February1864, 2 April 20 1864, 20 August 1864; *Annual Report of the African Civilization Society,* 1–5.

18. *Christian Recorder,* 14 November 1863.

19. *Christian Recorder,* 13 February 1864.

20. Daniel Payne, *Recollections of Seventy Years: Daniel Alexander Payne* (New York: Arno Press and the *New York Times*), 151–53; *Christian Recorder,* 7 March 1863.

21. Lewis Woodson's black nationalist ideology is discussed in Miller, *Search for a Black Nationality,* 96–99. His fund-raising plan was directed towards wealthy African

Americans and requested that one hundred men and women each contribute one hundred dollars each, which was no insignificant sum at this time. *Christian Recorder,* 4 April 1863, 25 July 1863, 21 November 1863, 26 November 1864.

22. *Christian Recorder,* 7 March 1863, 28 March 1863, 25 July 1863, 26 November 1864; David Walker was a black abolitionist in Massachusetts in the 1820s. His *Appeal to the Colored Citizens of the World* written in 1829 was one of the most incendiary denunciations of slavery and trenchant expositions of black nationalist ideology in the nineteenth century. See Stuckey, *Ideological Origins,* 8–9.

23. *Christian Recorder,* 30 May 1863, 20 June 1863, 7 May 1864, 7 January 1865.

24. *Christian Recorder,* 16 July 1864.

25. *Christian Recorder,* 16 July 1864; *Minutes of the National Convention of Colored Men Held in the City of Syracuse, N. Y. 1864* (Boston: John Rock and Geo. Ruffin, 1864; reprint, Howard Bell, *Proceedings of the National Negro Conventions 1830–1864,* New York: Arno Press and the *New York Times,* 1969), 25–27, 34–36.

26. *Christian Recorder,* 7 May 1864, 27 May 1865, 3 June 1865, 24 June 1865; Payne, *Recollections,* 162–63.

27. For in depth studies of this process, see Joel Williamson, *After Slavery: The Negro in South Carolina During Reconstruction, 1861–1877* (Chapel Hill: University of North Carolina Press, 1965) and Bernard E. Powers Jr., *Black Charlestonians: A Social History 1822–1885* (Fayetteville: University of Arkansas Press, 1994). "Life of Theophilus G. Steward," Steward Papers, 27 May 1868, reel 2, Schomburg Collection, New York Public Library, microfilm; *Christian Recorder,* 28 April 1866, 21 July 1866, 29 September 1866; *South Carolina Leader,* 21 October 1865; Nancy Ashmore, "The Development of the African Methodist Episcopal Church in South Carolina, 1865–1965" (master's thesis, Furman University, 1964), 24.

28. Powers, *Black Charlestonians,* 205–6; *Christian Recorder,* 28 April 1866; Benjamin Arnett, *The Centennial Budget Containing an Account of the Celebration (November 1887) in the Different Parts of the Church, and the Principal Addresses Delivered in Bethel Church, Philadelphia, Pennsylvania* (Dayton, Ohio: Christian Publishing, 1888), 25–26.

29. *Christian Recorder,* 3 June 1865, 19 May 1866, 2 May 1866.

30. *Charleston Daily Courier,* 14 October 1865; *Christian Recorder,* 24 February 1866; Clarence Walker, *A Rock in a Weary Land: The African Methodist Episcopal Church During the Civil War and Reconstruction* (Baton Rouge: Louisiana State University Press, 1982), 16.

31. *Christian Recorder,* 9 July 1864; Walker, *A Rock in a Weary Land,* 2–3, 7.

32. *Christian Recorder,* 30 June 1866; Peggy Lamson, *The Glorious Failure: Black Congressman Robert Brown Elliott and the Reconstruction of South Carolina* (New York: W.W. Norton, 1973), 54; *The Missionary Record,* 5 July 1873.

33. Rev. Benjamin Franklin Randolph of the Methodist Episcopal church published a newspaper entitled *The Charleston Journal* in Charleston in 1866, but it seems to have started later in the year and had neither the circulation or influence of *The Missionary Record. Christian Recorder,* 13 October 1866, 20 October 1866.

34. Alrutheus A. Taylor, *The Negro in South Carolina During the Reconstruction* (Washington, D.C.: Association for the Study of Negro Life and History, 1924),

40–43; *Journal of The Convention of the People of South Carolina Held in Columbia, S. C. September 1865 Together with the Ordinances Reports Resolutions, etc.* (Columbia: J. A. Selby, 1865), 14, 141–48; Edward McPherson, *The Political History of the United States of America During the Period of Reconstruction* (Solomons and Chapman, 1875; reprint, New York: Negro Universities Press, 1969), 34–36.

35. *Christian Recorder,* 30 September 1865.

36. *Charleston Daily Courier,* 27 March 1867, 8 May 1867, 9 May 1867, 11 May 1867.

37. *Charleston Daily Courier,* 4 November 1867; *Proceedings of the Constitutional Convention of South Carolina Held at Charleston, S.C., beginning January 14th and ending March 17th, 1868,* (Charleston: Denny and Perry, 1868; reprint, New York: Arno Press, 1968), 7, 41–42, 109–110, 136–37, 148, 379 (hereafter cited as *Proceedings*).

38. *Proceedings,* 381, 417–23, 438–39, 452, 506; *The Constitution of South Carolina, Adopted April 16, 1868 and the Acts and Joint Resolutions of the General Assembly,* (Columbia: John W. Denny, 1868), 5.

39. *Proceedings,* 713, 722–23, 732–33, 828–31.

40. *Charleston Daily Courier,* 10 March 1868, 12 March 1868, 28 March 1868, 10 July 1868; Francis Simkins and Robert Woody, *South Carolina During Reconstruction* (Chapel Hill: University of North Carolina Press, 1952), 109–11; *Daily News,* 27 May 1868.

41. William C. Hine, "Frustration, Factionalism and Failure: Black Political Leadership and the Republican Party in Reconstruction Charleston, 1865–1877" (Ph.D. diss., Kent State University, 1979), 140.

42. *Charleston Daily Courier,* 17 November 1868.

43. *Charleston Daily Courier,* 17 November 1868; Walter Fraser, *Charleston Charleston: The History of a Southern City* (Columbia: University of South Carolina Press, 1989), 288.

44. *Charleston Daily Courier,* 12 November 1868, 21 November 1868, 22 December 22 1868, 26–28 January 1969, 8 February 1869, 11 February 1869.

45. *Charleston Daily Courier,* 12 November 1868, 21 November 1868, 22 December 1868, 26–28 January 1969, 8 February 1869, 11 February 1869.

46. *Charleston Daily Courier,* 4 May 1869, 19 July 1869.

47. *Charleston Daily Courier,* 4 May 1869, 15 May 1869, 24 May 1869, 19 July 1869; Hine, "Frustration," 172–75; *Charleston Daily News,* 15 June 1869.

48. Thomas Holt, *Black Over White: Negro Political Leadership in South Carolina During Reconstruction* (Urbana: University of Illinois Press, 1979), ch. 9.

49. Carol K. Bleser, *The Promised Land: The History of the South Carolina Land Commission, 1869–1890* (Columbia: University of South Carolina Press, 1969), xiii, 22–24, 28, 46–47; *Charleston Daily News,* 2 May 1870.

50. *Charleston Daily News,* 29 August 1869.

51. Bleser, *Promised Land,* 65; Walter Edgar, *South Carolina: A History* (Columbia: University of South Carolina, 1998), 387–88.

52. George B. Tindall, *South Carolina Negroes 1877–1900* (Baton Rouge: Louisiana State University Press, 1966), 2, 190.

"This Dreadful Whirlpool" of Civil War: Edward W. Gantt and the Quest for Distinction
Randy Finley

1. *Arkansas State Gazette,* 26 January 1861; E. W. Gantt, *Address of Brigadier General E. W. Gantt, C. S. A.* (Little Rock, Arkansas: no publisher, 7 October 1863), 18–19, 24, 27.

2. John Nicolay and John Hay, *Abraham Lincoln: A History,* vol. 8 (New York: The Century Company, 1890), 440.

3. Marjorie Hood Fischer, *Tennessee Tidbits,* 1778–1914, vol. 1, 137; Bruce Allardice, *More Generals in Gray* (Baton Rouge: Louisiana State University Press, 1995), 95.

4. David Potter, *The Impending Crisis* (New York: Harper and Row, 1976), 18–23, 93; William H. Freehling, *The Road to Disunion: Secessionists at Bay,* vol. 1 (New York: Oxford University Press, 1990), 487–510.

5. Potter, *The Impending Crisis,* 104; Melvin Johnson White, "The Secession Movement in the U.S., 1847–1852 (Ph.D. diss., University of Wisconsin), 66; Thelma Jennings, *The Nashville Convention: Southern Movement for Unity* (Memphis: Memphis State University Press, 1980), 105, 131–32, 219–51; Freehling, *Road to Disunion,* 475–86.

6. Potter, *The Impending Crisis,* 90–105; Jennings, *The Nashville Convention,* 140; Eric H. Walther, *The Fire-Eaters* (Baton Rouge: Louisiana State University Press, 1992), 138–39; Laura White, *Robert Barnwell Rhett: Father of Secession* (New York: The Century Company, 1931), 108; Michael Holt, *The Rise and Fall of the American Whig Party: Jacksonian Politics and the Onset of the Civil War* (New York: Oxford University Press, 1999), 601, 517.

7. Jennings, *The Nashville Convention,* 245.

8. James M. Woods, *Rebellion and Realignment: Arkansas' Road to Secession* (Fayetteville: University of Arkansas Press, 1987), 19, 173; William Lynch, "The Westward Flow of Southern Colonists Before 1861," *Journal of Southern History* 9 (August 1943): 317.

9. 1850 and 1860 Census, U.S., Historical Census Data Browser, Ann Arbor, Michigan (Inter-University Consortium for Political and Social Research); *Washington Telegraph,* 10 May 1854, 11 May 1853.

10. *Washington Telegraph,* 29 January 1851, 19 October 1853, 26 February 1851, 22 October 1856, 14 June 1854, and 16 August 1854.

11. *Washington Telegraph,* 22 August 1855, 11 June 1856, 20 September 1854, 22 August 1855; Charlean Moss Williams, *The Old Town Speaks: Recollections of Washington, Hempstead County, Arkansas* (Houston: The Anson Jones Press, 1951), 302.

12. Charles Sellers, *The Market Revolution: Jacksonian America,* 1815–1846 (New York: Oxford University Press, 1991), 47; *Washington Telegraph,* 6 April 1853; *Washington Press,* 12 June 1886.

13. *Washington Telegraph,* 11 May 1853, 25 May 1853, 16 November 1853, 12 April 1854, 11 October 1854, 6 August 1856, 2 July 1856; Allardice, *More Confederate*

Generals in Gray, 95; *Southern Standard,* 30 March 1858; Williams, *The Old Town Speaks,* 22. Gantt's fiery oratory is noted in a letter by Augustus Garland, reprinted in "Four Unpublished Letters From Augustus Garland", *Arkansas Historical Quarterly* 18 (summer 1959), 184.

14. *Washington Telegraph,* 11 October 1854; Hempstead County Records, Circuit Court Records, books I–K, 1853–67, reel 67, microfilm.

15. Dallas County Tax Records, "Thomas J. Reid," reel 45; Dallas County Records, Marriage Records, book "B," 1854–1875, reel 1; Pulaski County Records, 1870 Census, Second Ward, Little Rock, Arkansas, Household #92.

16. Williams, *The Old Town Speaks,* 174; Hempstead County Tax Records, 1856–1865, reel 75.

17. Woods, *Rebellion and Realignment,* 37, 71; Michael B. Dougan, *Confederate Arkansas: The People and Politics of a Frontier State in Wartime* (University, Alabama: University of Alabama Press, 1976), 14.

18. Dougan, *Confederate Arkansas: The People and Politics of a Frontier State in Wartime,* 14; Woods, *Rebellion and Realignment,* 79.

19. Woods, *Rebellion and Realignment,* 79, 81, 85; Dougan, *Confederate Arkansas,* 17; *Arkansas State Gazette,* 7 April 1860; Diane Neal and Thomas W. Kremm, *Lion of the South: General Thomas C. Hindman* (Macon, Georgia: Mercer University Press, 1993), 59.

20. Woods, *Rebellion and Realignment,* 103–6; *Arkansas State Gazette,* 1 December 1860; David Herbert Donald, *Lincoln* (New York: Simon and Schuster, 1995), 241–56.

21. Woods, *Rebellion and Realignment,* 117, 124; Emory Thomas, *The Confederate Nation* (New York: Harper and Row, 1977), 41, 61; *Arkansas State Gazette,* 1 December 1860; Bruce Catton, *The Coming Fury* (Garden City, New Jersey: Doubleday and Company, 1961), 194–95.

22. *Arkansas State Gazette,* 26 January 1861.

23. James McPherson, *For Cause and Comrade: Why Men Fought in the Civil War* (New York: Oxford University Press, 1997), 19–27.

24. Woods, *Rebellion and Realignment,* 148, 155; Don Montgomery, "The Sons of Southern Sires: Washington, Arkansas and the War Between the States" (unpublished paper, ACC #4592, Washington, Arkansas ,Historical Park), 3.

25. Allardice, *More Confederate Generals in Gray,* 95; Lynda Lasswell Crist, ed., *Papers of Jefferson Davis,* vol. 7: 1861 (Baton Rouge: Louisiana State University Press, 1992), 180.

26. Allardice, *More Confederate Generals in Gray,* 310; *Confederate Military History* (extended ed.), vol. 14 (Wilmington, North Carolina: Broadfoot Publishing Company, 1988), 310; David Burton Coulter, "A Sketch of David Burton Coulter's Life" in *Genealogy of John M. Coulter* (Dr. John W. Coulter: 1953), 146; Eugene A. Nolte, "Downeasters in Arkansas: Letters of Roscoe G. Jennings to His Brother," *Arkansas Historical Quarterly* 18 (spring 1959): 16–17.

27. Nolte, "Downeasters in Arkansas," 13, 15–18.

28. Nolte, "Downeasters in Arkansas," 13, 15–18; Coulter, "A Sketch," 146;

Washington Telegraph, 5 March 1862.

29. *Arkansas State Gazette,* 1 March 1862.

30. David Niven, *The Road to Shiloh: Early Battles in the West* (Alexandria, Virginia: Time-Life Books, 1983), 8.

31. James McPherson, *Battle Cry of Freedom* (New York: Oxford University Press, 1980), 396; Niven, *Road to Shiloh,* 8, 48–49; Nolte, "Downeasters in Arkansas," 19; Coulter, "A Sketch," 147; Brig. Gen. J. P. McCown's Report, 9 November 1861, *The War of the Rebellion: A Compilation of the Official Records of the Union and Confederate Armies,* 70 vols. in 128 books and index (Washington, D. C.: Government Printing Office, 1880–1901), ser. 1, 1:3, 353 (hereafter cited as *WOR*); Allardice, *More Generals in Gray,* 95.

32. Allardice, *More Generals in Gray,* 95; M. Jeff Thompson to Brigadier General Gideon J. Pillow, 7 December 1861, *WOR* 1:8; Polk to Johnston, 30 December 1861, *WOR* 1:3; Gantt to Polk, 21 December 1861, *WOR* 1:8; Coulter, "A Sketch," 148.

33. Polk to Benjamin, 7 December 1861, *WOR* 1:7, 741; Benjamin to Beauregard, 4 March 1862, *WOR* 1:7, 918.

34. Bern Anderson, *By Sea and By River: The Naval History of the Civil War* (New York: Alfred A. Knopf, 1962), 103; James McPherson, *Ordeal by Fire: The Civil War and Reconstruction* (New York: Alfred A. Knopf, 1982), 230; Polk Memo, February 1862, *WOR* 1:8; Niven, *Road to Shiloh,* 158–60, 163–69; McPherson, *Battle Cry of Freedom,* 415; Gen. John Pope's Report, 14 March 1862, *WOR* 1:8, 81–84; General John Pope's Report, 14 March 1862, *WOR* 1:22, 42,; Nolte, "Downeasters in Arkansas," 148; Allardice, *More Confederate Generals in Gray,* 96; Jim Miles, *A River Unvexed: A History and Tour Guide to the Campaigns for the Mississippi River* (Nashville, Tennessee: Rutledge Hill Press, 1994), 47; G. W. Cumming's Report, 10 April 1862, *WOR* 1:8, 112.

35. Minor H. McLain, "The Military Prison at Fort Warren," *Civil War History* 8 (June 1962): 136–37, 139–46; *WOR* 2:3, 640; Lonnie R. Speer, *Portals to Hell: Military Prisons of the Civil War* (Mechanisburg, Pennsylvania: Stackpole Books, 1997), 41–44.

36. Tom Bird, *American POWs of World War II* (Westport, Connecticut: Praeger Press, 1992), xvii.

37. *WOR* 2:4, 447; *Washington Telegraph,* 5 February 1862, 5 November 1862, 22 November 1862.

38. Nolte, "Downeasters in Arkansas," 23; Allardice, *More Confederates in Gray,* 96; Gantt to Polk, 27 August 1862, *WOR* 1:8, 168–69.

39. C. A. Dana to E. M. Stanton, 12 June 1863, *WOR* 1:34, pt. 2, 97.

40. William C. Harris, *With Charity For All: Lincoln and the Restoration of the Union* (Lexington, Kentucky: University of Kentucky Press, 1997), 127.

41. Nicolay and Hay, *Abraham Lincoln,* 410.

42. Gantt, *Address of Brigadier General,* 18, 27.

43. Gantt, *Address of Brigadier General,* 18, 25, 26, 27.

44. Dallas T. Herndon, *Centennial History of Arkansas,* vol. 1 (Chicago: S. J. Clarke Publishing Company, 1922), 286; Earl Shenck Miers, ed., *Lincoln Day by Day: A*

Chronology, 1809–1865, vol. 3 (Washington, D. C.: Lincoln Sesquicentennial Commission, 1960), 226; Jonathan Truman Dorris, *Pardons and Amnesty Under Lincoln and Johnson: The Restoration of the Confederates to Their Rights and Privileges, 1861–1898* (Chapel Hill: University of North Carolina Press, 1953), 36; John Nixon, ed., *The Salmon P. Chase Papers,* vol. 4 (Kent, Ohio: Kent State University Press, 1997), 294; Dana to Stanton, 12 June 1863, *WOR* 1:24, part 1, 97; *Little Rock Unconditional Union,* 1 June 1864; Gantt to G. W. Fair, 6 January 1864, Arkansas History Commission, Little Rock; Nicolay and Hay, *Abraham Lincoln,* 296.

45. *Washington Telegraph,* 28 October 1863, 13 December 1865; Thomas Staples, *Reconstruction in Arkansas 1862–74,* (Gloucester: Peter Smith, 1923), 13; Dorris, *Pardon and Amnesty,* 36; Willard E. Wright, ed., "The Letters of Thomas B. Henley, 1863–1864," *Arkansas Historical Quarterly* 15 (summer 1965): 165; Don E. Fehrenbacher, *Lincoln in Text and Context* (Stanford, California: Stanford University Press, 1987), 147–48.

46. Harris, *With Charity For All,* 85, 127, 132; Thomas A. DeBlack, "1863: We Must Stand or Fall Alone," in *Rugged and Sublime: The Civil War in Arkansas,* ed. Mark K. Christ (Fayetteville, Arkansas: University of Arkansas Press, 1994), 85–96; Donald, *Lincoln,* 471–72; Eric Foner, *Reconstruction: America's Unfinished Revolution: 1863–1877* (New York: Harper and Row, 1988), 35–37; Staples, *Reconstruction in Arkansas,* 13; *Little Rock Unconditional Union,* 3 June 1864.

47. Harris, *With Charity for All,* 199–200, 203; Carl Moneyhon, *The Impact of the Civil War and Reconstruction on Arkansas: Persistence in the Midst of Ruin* (Baton Rouge: Louisiana State University Press, 1994), 159–64; Nicolay and Hay, *Abraham Lincoln,* 296; William L. Shea, "Isaac Murphy, 1864–1868," in *The Governors of Arkansas: Essays in Political Biography,* ed. Timothy P. Donovan, Willard B. Gatewood Jr., and Jeannie M. Whayne (Fayetteville: University of Arkansas Press, 1995), 41–45.

48. *Washington Telegraph,* 17 February 1864; Ruth Caroline Cowen, "Reorganization of Federal Arkansas, 1862–1865," *Arkansas Historical Quarterly* 18 (summer 1959): 146.

49. Harris, *With Charity for All,* 206–7; Leroy P. Graf and Ralph W. Haskins, eds., *The Papers of Andrew Johnson,* vol. 8 (Knoxville, Tennessee: University of Tennessee Press, 1989), 313–14, 351; vol. 7 (1991), 305; Gantt to Seward, 29 June 1864, Amnesty Papers, Arkansas History Commission, Little Rock.

50. *Little Rock Unconditional Union,* 6 July 1865, 23 November 1865, 30 October 1865.

51. George R. Bentley, *A History of the Freedmen's Bureau* (New York: Octagon Books, 1970), 49; *Statutes at Large,* vol. 13 (Boston, Massachusetts: Little, Brown, 1866), 507–8; Charles Sumner, *The Works of Charles Sumner,* vol. 8 (Boston, Massachusetts: Lee and Shepard, 1874), 476.

52. Randy Finley, *From Slavery to Uncertain Freedom: The Freedmen's Bureau in Arkansas* (Fayetteville: University of Arkansas Press, 1996), 11; Randy Finley, "The Personnel of the Freedmen's Bureau in Arkansas," in *The Freedmen's Bureau and Reconstruction: Reconsiderations,* ed. Paul Cimbala and Randall Miller (New York: Fordham University Press, 1999), 93–118; Dawes to Abel, 22 July 1866, Field Office

Reports, Bureau of Refugees, Freedmen, and Abandoned Lands, Record Group 105, Arkansas (hereafter cited as FOR-A); Sweeney Report, 24 January 1865, FOR-A; Sweeney to Bennett, 31 May 1867, FOR-A.

53. "Station Book, 1865–1868," Records of the Assistant Commissioner, Bureau of Refugees, Freedmen, and Abandoned Lands, Record Group 105, Arkansas (hereafter cited as AC-A).

54. Gantt to Sprague, 23 December 1865, FOR-A; *Little Rock Unconditional Union,* 18 January 1866; Gantt to Sprague, 13 January 1866, FOR-A.

55. Gantt to Sprague, 23 December 1865, FOR-A; Register of Contracts, 14 November 1866, FOR-A.

56. John Montgomery to Gantt, 13 November 1865, AC-A; Gantt to R. R. Taylor, 20 January 1866, FOR-A; James Williams to Gantt, 31 March 1866, FOR-A; Gantt Report, 23 April 1866, FOR-A; Sprague to Howard, 20 November 1865, FOR-A.

57. Marriage Certificates, October 1865 to February 1867, Hempstead County, Arkansas, AC-A.

58. Gantt to Sprague, 23 December 1865, FOR-A; Gantt to Sprague, 13 January 1866, FOR-A; Moneyhon, *The Impact of the Civil War,* 210; Gantt to W. A. Britten, 23 December 1865, FOR-A; Register of Complaints, August 1866 to February 1868, Washington, Arkansas, FOR-A.

59. Powell Clayton, *The Aftermath of the Civil War in Arkansas* (New York: The Neale Publishing Company, 1915), 302.

60. Pulaski County Circuit Court Records, 1869; *Arkadelphia Southern Standard,* 11 December 1869; *Arkansas Gazette,* 11 December 1869, 11 August 1866, 4 June 1867; *Daily Gazette* 2 December 1869.

61. Pulaski County Circuit Court Records, 1869–1870; Minutes of the Little Rock Republican Club, 1867–1868, 31 August 1867, Arkansas History Commission, SMC box LXV, no. 4, Little Rock; *Arkansas Gazette,* 28 July 1868; Trelease, *White Terror,* 154; Clayton, *Aftermath of Civil War,* 74–85, 87.

62. *Daily Gazette,* 4 June 1879, 30 July 1872.

63. Allardice, *More Generals in Gray,* 96; Edward W. Gantt, *A Digest of the Statutes of Arkansas Embracing All Laws of a General and Permanent Character (*1874).

64. *Arkansas Gazette,* 11 June 1874.

65. McPherson, *Ordeal by Fire,* 558–59; Carl Degler, *The Other South: Southern Dissenters in the 19th Century* (New York: Harper and Row, 1974), 228–29; Otto H. Olsen, "Reconsidering the Scalawags," *Civil War History* 12 (December 1966): 309.

James Carroll Napier (1845–1940): From Plantation to the City
Bobby L. Lovett

1. Anita S. Goodstein, *Nashville, 1780–1860: From Frontier to City* (Gainesville: University of Florida Press, 1989), 143–45, 152; Acts of the State of Tennessee, 44th General Assembly, 1885 (Nashville: J. C. Mercer, 1885), 240; J. C. Napier Interview, clipping, *Nashville Tennessean,* 1933, in Sarah Shankland, Scrapbook, Tennessee State Library and Archives (hereafter cited as TSLA), manuscript division, Nashville; Bobby L. Lovett, *The African American History of Nashville, Tennessee, 1780–1930: Elites and Dilemmas* (Fayetteville: University of Arkansas Press, 1999), ch. 2.

2. W. C. Napier, 29 June 1869–77, 123 handwritten pages on the Napier family based on W. C. Napier's and Sumner's testimony, Office of Commissioner of Claims, National Archives and Record Service, case no. 8612; *Nashville Globe,* 12 November 1909, 26 November 1909; Davidson County, Circuit Court Minutes, vols. P–Q, 1845–48, Metro Archives, Nashville, (hereafter cited as MAN) for information on W. E. Watkins; Index to Deaths, Nashville, 1894–1913, MAN, for information on Napier; Minute Books, 1839–45, Dickson County, Tennessee, Circuit Court, Historical Records Survey (HRS), Works Progress Administration (hereafter cited as WPA), 1939; for information on Dr. E. W. Napier, see TSLA; Herschel Gower and J. Allen, eds., *Pen and Sword: The Life and Journal of Randal W. McGavock* (Nashville: Tennessee Historical Commission, 1959), 430, for an elite white man's view of antebellum Nashville.

3. J. C. Napier Interview, clipping, *Nashville Tennessean*; Wills, Inventories, Settlements, vol. 19, 1861–65, Davidson County, Tennessee, p. 555; W. E. Watkins Inventory, 30 November 1865, MAN.

4. Dr. E. W. Napier's Will, Will Book "A," Dickson County Records, 1804–56, HRS, WPA, 1936, TSLA; Carol Wells, *Pioneers of Dickson County, Tennessee* (Nacadoches, Texas: Ericson Books, 1988), 100, 102, 164, 173; Jill K. Garrett and I. H. McClain, *Dickson County, Tennessee: Cemetery Records and Obituaries,* 2 pts. (Columbia, Tennessee: published by authors, 1970), pt. 1, 110, 123, 182, 211; Dickson County, Settlements, Administrators, vol. C., May 1848–February 1860, TSLA, includes "Inventory of the Goods and Chattles of E. W. Napier"; J. C. Napier, "Some Members of the Tennessee General Assembly During the Reconstruction and After," *Journal of Negro History* 5 (1920): 115–17, for information on Napier and early times in Nashville.

5. Herbert L. Clark, "The Public Career of James Carroll Napier: Businessman, Politician, and Crusader for Racial Justice, 1845–1940" (D.A. diss., Middle Tennessee State University, 1980), 1–30, 70, 71, 91; Richard A. Polk, "Black Man's Burden in Ohio, 1849–1863" (Ph.D. diss., University of Toledo, 1972), 26; Henry Louis Taylor, ed., *Race and the City: Work, Community and Protest in Cincinnati, 1820–1970* (Urbana: University of Illinois Press, 1993), 47, 49, 80.

6. *Nashville Daily Union,* 4 July 1850, 15 August 1850, 4 September 1850, 18 October 1850, 2 November 1850, 8 November 1850, 11 November 1850, 3 December 1850, 6 December 1850; Clark, "The Public Career of James Carroll Napier," 107; Lovett, *The African American History of Nashville,* ch. 2; Deane Porch, transcribed, *Davidson County, Tennessee, 1850 Census* (Fort Worth, Texas: American Reference Publishing, 1969), 310, 311.

7. See Nashville city directories for locations of Napier residences; see Index for African American Marriages, Davidson County, Tennessee, MAN, 45, for Napier marriages; *Nashville Republican Banner,* 2 October 1859, 18 October 1859, 2 November 1859, 8 November 1859, 11 November 1859, 3 December 1859, 15 December 1859; B. L. Lovett, "African Americans, Civil War, and Aftermath in Arkansas," *Arkansas Historical Quarterly* 54 (1995): 304–58; *The Nashville City Directory, 1859* (Nashville: E. G. Eastman Co., 1859).

8. J. C. Napier Interview, 1933; J. B. Lindsley's Diary, 6 October 1856–1 January

1866, TSLA, MD, contains direct references to Napier; W. C. Napier's Testimony, U.S. Commissioner of Claims; Lovett, *The African American History of Nashville,* ch. 3.

9. W. C. Napier's Testimony, U.S. Commissioner of Claims; Lovett, *African American History of Nashville,* ch. 3; Leroy Graf, ed., *The Andrew Johnson Papers, 1862–1864,* 16 vols. (Knoxville: University of Tennessee Press, 1986), 6:697, 7:159–60, 350, 478–80.

10. William and A. L. Cheek, *John Mercer Langston and the Fight for Black Freedom, 1825–1865* (Chicago: University of Chicago Press, 1996), 85, 86, 87, 117, 135, 295; see B. L. Lovett, "The Negro in Tennessee, 1861–1866: A Socio-Military History of the Civil War Era" (Ph.D. diss., University of Arkansas, 1978); J. C. Napier's Biography, James C. Napier Papers, 1845–1940, Special Collections, Fisk University (hereafter cited as JCN Papers); information on Oberlin College received from Oberlin College Library and Archives, Special Collections, via internet and photo copies, 8 February 2000; John M. Langston, *From the Virginia Plantation to the National Capitol* (Hartford, Connecticut: 1894), 200, 201, 227, 228, 230, 525; see will and inventory for W. E. Watkins, MAN, 1864–65; Daniel A. Payne, *Recollections of Seventy Years* (Nashville: AME Publishing House, 1888), 152, 155, 157; Lindsley Diary, TSLA.

11. Lovett, *The African American History of Nashville,* chs. 4–5.

12. Lovett, *The African American History of Nashville,* chs. 4–5. See certificates and federal commissioners in the JCN Papers; Clark, "The Public Career of James Carroll Napier," 1–20; W. C. Napier's Testimony, U.S. Commissioner of Claims, 1877; Alumni Survey Form for J. C. Napier, 8 May 1908, Oberlin College Archives.

13. J. C. Napier to L. Holland, Nashville, 22 December 1869; biographical sketch, and claims clerk papers, JCN Papers; Clark, "The Public Career of James Carroll Napier," 1–21; May Alice A. Ridley, "The Black Community of Nashville and Davidson County, Tennessee, 1860–1870" (Ph.D. diss., University of Pittsburgh, 1982), 84, 90, 152; Lovett, *The African American History of Nashville,* ch. 9; Mingo Scott Jr., *The Negro in Tennessee Politics and Governmental Affairs, 1865–1965* (Nashville: Rich Printing, 1964), 30, 33, 35, 47, 87, 88; Law School class list, 1871–84, Howard University, Law Library and Moorland Spingarn Research Center.

14. Lovett, *The African American History of Nashville,* chs. 4, 9.

15. Lovett, *The African American History of Nashville,* ch. 9.

16. Lovett, *The African American History of Nashville,* ch. 9; W. C. Napier claim, 1877–80, U.S. Commissioner of Claims; William Gillette, *Retreat From Reconstruction, 1869–1879* (Baton Rouge: Louisiana State University Press, 1979), 28, 29; Brooks D. Simpson, *The Reconstruction Presidents* (Emporia: University of Kansas Press, 1988), 205; Charles R. Williams, *Diary and Letters of Rutherford B. Hayes,* 4 vols. (Columbus: Ohio State University Press, 1925), 4:515–19.

17. Lovett, *The African American History of Nashville,* chs. 4, 9.

18. Biographical sketch, JCN Papers; Clark, "The Public Career of James Carroll Napier," 1–21; Faye W. Robbins, "A World-Within-a-World: Black Nashville, 1880–1915" (Ph.D. diss., University of Arkansas, 1980), 184, 223, 267; file on Nettie DeElla Langston and Ida Morton Napier, Oberlin College Archives; see Nashville city directories, 1878–80; U.S., 1880 Census: Nashville, Fourth Ward, TSLA; *Nashville*

Daily American, 29 September 1878; Lovett, *The African American History of Nashville,* ch. 4; *Union and American,* 7 November 1874, 24 September 1879.

19. T. A. Kercheval's Letter, 2 April 1881, and Negro petition to Garfield in JCN Papers; *Daily American,* 16 December 1882; *Tennessee Star,* 25 November 1887; Lovett, *The African American History of Nashville,* ch. 9.

20. See references to C. D. Warner in speeches for Napier's birthday, C. O. Cashin, JCN Papers; Robbins, "A World-Within-A-World: Black Nashville," 184, 223, 245, 267; *Tennessee Star,* 25 November 1887; *Banner,* 6 October 1887, 8 October 1887, 15 October 1887, 18 October 1887; A. A. Gordon to Nettie Napier, 15 November 1887, Atlanta, JCN Papers. Note: the editor of the *Tennessee Star,* George T. Robinson, a Negro lawyer, was a militant commentator but a friend to J. C. Napier. In 1887 Robinson, a fiery antiprohibitionist, enlisted Napier to represent a Negro family that charged the outspoken prohibitionist pastor, R. T. Huffman of the Mt. Olive Baptist Church, with sexual molestation of their young daughter; Mifflin W. Gibbs, *Shadow and Light: An Autobiography* (Lincoln: University of Nebraska Press, 1995), 202–4, was one of the men, including Frederick Douglass, who was present in New Orleans. Gibbs listed J. C. Napier among the men who "battle for justice and the betterment of their fellow man."

21. John M. Langston, *Freedom and Citizenship: Selected Lectures and Addresses of Hon. John Mercer Langston, LL.D.* (Washington: Rufus Darby Printers, 1883); Lovett, *The African American History of Nashville,* ch. 10 for information on G. W. Cable; Republican Party Certificates, JCN Papers.

22. Lovett, *The African American History of Nashville,* ch. 10; Population Figures, JCN Papers; J. T. Settles to JCN, 16 November 1897, Memphis, JCN Papers; R. F. Boyd to JCN, Nashville, 17 November 1897, JCN Papers; Index to Deaths, Nashville, 1889–96, TSLA; Juanita I. Gill, "The Life of John Mercer Langston, 1829–1897: Prominent Negro Leader" (master's thesis, Tennessee A & I State University, 1954), 11. Note: Elias, Alonzo, and W. C. Napier Sr. apparently were buried at first in the old City Cemetery, but (as were many elite Negro remains) they were removed from that segregated cemetery to the elite, Negro-owned Greenwood Cemetery.

23. Tillman's printed speech, correspondence, telegrams, and condolences including BTW to JCN, New York, 10 April 1908, JCN Papers; *Nashville Globe,* 12 November 1909, 26 November 1909; the author's transcriptions of tombstone headings at Greenwood Cemetery, Nashville.

24. See Louis Harlan, *The Booker T. Washington Papers* (Urbana: University of Illinois Press, 1977–80), including some letters between BTW and JCN.

25. Harlan, *The Booker T. Washington Papers*; Lovett, *The African American History of Nashville,* chs. 5, 10.

26. BTW to JCN and Du Bois, 2 November 1903, 14 December 1903, Tuskegee, JCN Papers; Lovett, *The African American History of Nashville,* ch. 10; Charles Alexander, "The Afro-American Council," *Alexander's Magazine* (July, August 1906): 21–28. According to Giles B. Jackson and D. W. Davis, *The Industrial History of the Negro* (Freeport, New York: Black Heritage Library Collection, 1908, 1971), 201, J. C. Napier served on a panel of judges for exhibits with Mary Church Terrell, the daughter

of elite mulatto Republican leader in Memphis, Robert R. Church. This connection proved helpful to Napier some four years later when he sought another federal position; see also, Benjamin W. Arnett, ed., *Souvenir from the Afro-American League of Tennessee to Hon. James M. Ashley of Ohio* (Philadelphia: AME Publishing House, 1894), which contains photos of some key Negro leaders in Nashville who organized this chapter of the League; Mildred M. Williams, *The Jeanes Story: A Chapter in the History of American Education, 1908–1968* (Atlanta: Southern Education Foundation, 1979).

27. Henry Allen Boyd, "The One Cent Savings Bank of Nashville, Tennessee—Its Organization and Progress," *Alexander's Magazine* 6–7 (1908–9): 266 (this book was written on the fiftieth anniversary of the historical raid of John Brown); *Nashville Globe,* 16 August 1907, 18 February 1910.

28. Paole E. Colletta, *The Presidency of William Howard Taft* (Lawrence: University of Kansas Press, 1973), 30; *Globe,* 22 March 1908, 30 October 1908, 12 November 1909, 26 November 1909; W. H. Taft's Inaugural Address, JCN Papers; *Alexander's Magazine,* 1908–9 issues.

29. *Globe,* 12 November 1909, 26 November 1909; J. S. Stemons, "Mr. Taft and Negro Suffrage," and R. H. Boyd, "The Present Condition of the Negro," *Alexander's Magazine* (1908): 116–18, 211, 252–53; Lovett, *The African American History of Nashville,* ch. 10.

30. JCN to WHT, 9 January 1909, Nashville, *Index to William H. Taft Papers,* 6 vols. (Washington: Library of Congress, 1972), vol. 5; see also letters between Taft and BTW, 2321–24; *Globe,* 29 May 1908, 7 December 1909; BTW to JCN, 29 December 1909, Tuskegee, R. W. Thompson to JCN, Washington, 17 April 1910, *Baltimore Times* clipping, 6 April 1912, JCN Papers; BTW to JCN, 24 May 1910, 7 November 1912, Tuskegee, in Harlan, *Booker T. Washington,* 351–59, 454–55; Henry F. Pringle, *The Life and Times of William Howard Taft,* 2 vols. (New York: Farrar and Rinehart, Inc., 1939), 1:390, 391.

31. JCN speeches and correspondence, April 1910–31 May 1912; JCN Register of the Treasury reports, clippings of *Detroit Informer,* 20 May 1911; *Macon Telegraph,* 10 November 1911; *Macon News,* 9 November 1911, JCN Papers; *Globe,* 7 January 1910.

32. Harlan, *Booker T. Washington,* 351–59, 454–55, 556; L. W. Stark, "Negroes and the Treasury," *Chicago Tribune,* 8 June 1969; clipping in Oberlin College Archives (see www.oberlin.edu/~archive), internet.

33. *National Baptist Union-Review,* 31 October 1914, Nashville; Hooper appointment, JCN speech at NNBL August 1917, JCN Papers; Lovett, *The African American History of Nashville,* ch. 5; Yollette T. Jones, "The Black Community, Politics, and Race Relations in the 'Iris City': Nashville, Tennessee, 1870–1954" (Ph.D. diss., Duke University, 1985), 182; Virginia L. Denton, *Booker T. Washington and the Adult Education Movement* (Gainesville: University of Florida Press, 1993), 140, 159.

34. Books and papers on James Weldon Johnson, who began work at Fisk University in 1931, are in the Special Collections of Fisk; *Washington Evening Star,* 10 June 1932, clipping, President M. C. Johnson to JCN, D. C., 13 June 1932, J. H. Hale to JCN, 29 August 1933, Nashville, Meharry President to JCN, 14 July 1933, Nashville, testimonials to Nettie Napier, 1932, wedding anniversary correspondence,

Carroll Langston to JCN, Oberlin College, 6 September 1934, in JCN Papers; Sondra K. Wilson, ed., *The Selected Writings of James Weldon Johnson,* 2 vols. (New York: Oxford University Press, 1955), 2:417.

35. JCN to President FDR, 10 January 1938, Nashville, JCN to Robert B. C. Howell, 20 April 1938, in the Robert B. C. Howell Papers, TSLA, MD; obituary for Nettie Napier, copy of *The Saint Andrews News* 13 (February 1931), in the JCN Papers; *Globe,* 30 October 1908, 20 January 1939; *Tennessean,* 7 August 1934; J. C. Smith, "Nettie DeElla Langston Napier (1861–1938): Social Reformer, Club Woman, Philanthropist," typescript, Oberlin College Archives; JCN Files, Tennessee State University, Library, Special Collections.

36. Davidson County, Tennessee, Death Certificates, 1938–45, TSLA, for Nettie Langston Napier, 27 September 1938, no. 19056, and for James C. Napier, 21 April 1940, no. 8711; J. C. Napier's Will, Will Book, Davidson County, vol. 57, 2 May 1940, 19 September 1941, 32–33; *Globe,* 1 March 1940, 22 March 1940, 26 April 1940. For sketches on elite Negro leaders, see Bobby L. Lovett and Linda T. Wynn, *Profiles of African Americans in Tennessee* (1996), (see www.tnstate.edu/library), internet.

Robert E. Lee Wilson and the Making of a Post–Civil War Plantation
Jeannie M. Whayne

1. The sources do not agree on Wilson's inheritance. Mabel F. Edrington indicates that he inherited 2,700 acres of swampland in Arkansas from his father, but according to a recent history published by the Mississippi County Historical Society, he inherited only the homestead. Mabel F. Edrington, *History of Mississippi County, Arkansas (*n.p., 1962), University of Arkansas Libraries, Special Collections; "The Wilson Family: R.E.L. Wilson," *The Delta Historical Review* (spring 1998): 1–2.

2. William Henry died in 1883. Josiah had been married before and had two children by that marriage, Viola and Missouri. See Mrs. Charles Elkins, "Wilson Genealogy," manuscript in possession of author.

3. Mrs. Charles Elkins, "Wilson Genealogy."

4. Edrington, *History of Mississippi County,* 383–84.

5. Edrington, *History of Mississippi County,* 384.

6. *American-Lumberman,* 24 June 1899, p. 27. Thanks to Larry Ball at Arkansas State University for alerting me to this article.

7. Mississippi County Real Property Records, 1885, 1922, South Mississippi County Court House, Osceola, Arkansas (hereafter cited as MCRPR). A careful perusal of these records in five-year increments from 1885 to 1930 reveal a steady pattern of acquisition in south Mississippi County until the decade of the 1910s.

8. MCRPR, 1885, 1922.

9. St. Francis Levee Board, *History of the Organization and Operations of the Board of Directors St. Francis Levee District of Arkansas, 1893–1945* (West Memphis, Arkansas: n.p., 1946), 5–9, 11–12.

10. St. Francis Levee Board, *History of the Organization and Operations,* 286–87.

11. *Osceola Times,* 30 November 1901.

12. Edrington, *History of Mississippi County,* 75.

13. Edrington, *History of Mississippi County,* 75–78.

14. *Osceola Times,* 8 July 1908.

15. *Osceola Times,* 30 July 1908. Candidate John Lovewell was running as an independent, having failed to secure the Democratic Party's nomination. See also Edrington, *History of Mississippi County,* 77.

16. Edrington, *History of Mississippi County,* 75–85.

17. Edrington, *History of Mississippi County,* 86.

18. *Osceola Times,* 9 December 1909.

19. *Osceola Times,* 4 March 1909.

20. *Osceola Times,* 4 March 1909.

21. Three other suits to quiet title were filed by the federal government against other defendants. Jeannie Whayne, *A New Plantation South: Land, Labor, and Federal Favor in Twentieth-Century Arkansas* (Charlottesville: University Press of Virginia, 1996), 91.

22. *U.S. v. Lee Wilson and Co.* 214 U.S. 283 (1914). Wilson had purchased these lands from the St. Francis Levee District in several transactions in 1898, 1900, and 1902. According to decree handed down by the federal district court in 1914, "Mr. Wilson bought the lands in section twenty-two on 24 November 1900, and 23 September 1902; those in section twenty-six on 3 June 1898, and 23 September 1902, and those in section twenty-seven on 24 November 1900, and 23 September 1902."

23. *U.S. v. Lee Wilson and Co.* 214 U.S. 283 (1914).

24. The disputed land was all of Township 12, Range 9 (excepting section 16), totaling 14,575.03. See *U.S. v. Lee Wilson and Co. Federal Reporter* 214 (1914): 663, and *Lee Wilson and Co. v. U.S. Federal Reporter* 227 (1917): 829. Wilson owned 8,181 acres of land within that area at the time the United States filed suit in an effort to quiet title and establish once and for all who owned the land; see MCRPR, 1914. For a full elucidation of the controversy and riparian theory, see Jeannie Whayne, "The Power of the Plantation Model: The Sunk Lands Controversy," *Forest and Conservation History* 37 (April 1993): 56–67. See also Whayne, *A New Plantation South,* 64–65, 101–2.

25. One other defendant in a separate case, Ernest Ritter of Poinsett County, also appealed. The Ritter case was decided in 1918 in the government's favor and Ritter apparently relinquished his claim. Whayne, *A New Plantation South,* 90–91.

26. *Lee Wilson and Co. v. U.S.* 245 (1917). See also the decision of the Eighth Circuit Court of Appeals *Lee Wilson and Co. v. U.S.* 4278 (1915).

27. Ritter lost his suit the next year and determined to end his litigation at that point in time. *Lee Wilson and Co. v. U.S.* 4278 (1915).

28. In the words of Rep. William Driver, "on petition of the riparian owners, a survey is to be made, the value of the land to be ascertained by the appraisal and the riparian owner pay the appraised value, that appraised value to include the value of any timber removed, but excluding the value of the improvement placed on the land by the riparian owner." *Congressional Record,* 19 October 1921, p. 6517.

29. Between 1919 and 1922 several entries in the *Congressional Record,* together with Senate reports and House reports issued in this period, reveal an intense interest in

pursuing a congressional remedy for Wilson and other riparian claimants. Senate Bill 5566, which concerned sixty acres claimed by Wilson on Round Lake, was introduced by Joseph T. Robinson. The acreage was within sections 19, 20, 29, 30, in township 11 north, range 10, east. The bill passed and was signed by the president on 1 March 1919. See *Journal of the Senate,* p. 212. House Bill 13400, introduced by William Driver in 1919, involved 1,100 acres in the Golden Lake area, sections 29, 30, 31, 32, township 11 north, range 10 east. This acreage was claimed by Lee Wilson. The bill was later subsumed under House Bill 1318 and joined with other cases. It was supported in the Senate by Joseph T. Robinson. It passed both the House and Senate and was signed by the president on 28 January 1922. Another bill, House Bill 6863, may have also involved Wilson acreage. It too was introduced by Driver in the House and supported by Robinson in the Senate. It passed and was signed by the president on 22 September 1922. See *Journal of the House,* pp. 245, 279, 387, 537, 571, 593. Finally, in 1922 Congress gave the secretary of the interior sole discretion in selling lands to riparian claimants.

30. MCRPR, 1920, 1931.

31. During the first two years of the downturn, Wilson's personal property wealth declined from $128,415 in 1920 to $85,515 in 1922. MCRPR, 1920, 1922.

32. Robert Robinson to J. H. Robinson, 24 April 1912, letter in possession of author. Thanks to Michael Wilson for providing me with a copy of this letter, which he recently received from Randall and Charlotte Gerdes.

33. Edrington, *History of Mississippi County,* 385–86. The name Armorel came from a combination of initials standing for Arkansas (Ar), Missouri (mo), and Robert E. Lee (rel).

34. Edrington, *History of Mississippi County,* 385–86.

35. MCRPR, 1911, 1920.

36. His real property holdings in south Mississippi County changed only marginally, actually declining slightly from 27,226 to 27,184, possibly as a result of the shifting of the Mississippi River. MCRPR, 1911, 1920. For his acquisition of controlling interest in the Blytheville Bank, see an untitled history of that bank written by Velma E. Sample, WPA Records, Arkansas History Commission, Little Rock.

37. John Joiner, Evadale, Arkansas, to Bank of Wilson, 21 February 1919; Johnson Mitchell, Union City, Tennessee, to Bank of Wilson, 24 February 1919, Lee Wilson and Company Archives, Unprocessed Collection, Special Collections Division, University of Arkansas Libraries, Fayetteville (hereafter cited as LWCA).

38. Hollipeter, Shonyo and Company to Bank of Wilson, 5 December 1919, LWCA.

39. Wilson Bank to Hollipeter-Shonyo Company, 8 December 1919, LWCA.

40. L. L. Harwell to R. E. Lee Wilson, 12 March 1919, LWCA. Wilson scrawled his instructions on the bottom of this letter. By the time of his death, Wilson held 608 2–3 shares in Wilson Ward, and may have had an interest in the company at the time of Harwell's suggestion. *Osceola Times,* 20 October 1933.

41. Hanover National Bank to Bank of Wilson, 2 December 1919, 15 December 1919, LWCA.

42. Whayne, *A New Plantation South,* 120.

43. *Osceola Times,* 15 April 1921. For the relationship between the two different Driver families in Mississippi County who did eventually intermarry, see "Driver Family Hold Places in County History: Their Founders, Unrelated, Were Both Leaders in Last Century," no author indicated, WPA Records, Arkansas History Commission.

44. Robert H. Moulton, "Wilson—That's All: A Whole Town is the Result of One Man's Idea," *Illustrated World* 38 (February 1923): 845–47, 942.

45. First National Bank of St. Louis to Bank of Wilson, 25 May 25 1921, LWCA; Bank of Wilson to First National Bank of St. Louis, 27 May 1921, LWCA.

46. Thanks to Michael Wilson for providing me with a copy of an abstract of the town of Wilson. The abstract included a number of transactions dating back to 1851 when a John M. Bass secured title to part of it with a Mexican War warrant. Lee Wilson and his father-in-law secured that segment of what was to become Wilson, Arkansas, in 1896. Wilson subsequently purchased Beall's interest and over the next decade and a half, put together the entire town site. According to a document located in the abstract, the $500,000 loan from American Trust Company was paid in full on 11 March 1936. But the abstract reveals another transaction which might explain Dysart's willingness to take a chance on Wilson. On 19 April 1922, Dysart, who was then employed by William R. Compton Company, advanced Wilson $50,000, payable within sixty days, at an interest rate of 8 percent, on the town site. That note was "satisfied in full" on 20 May 1922, just two days before Wilson negotiated the $500,000 loan with American Trust. See "Abstract of Title," compiled by Prewitt-Rogers Abstract Company, Osceola, Arkansas, 1969, pp. 61–65.

47. Manuscript Census of Population, Golden Lake Township, Mississippi County, Arkansas, 1920. Only 683 of 776 black and white men listed occupations. Of the 93 men who did not list occupations, 46 were black and 47 were white.

48. Manuscript Census of Population, Golden Lake Township, 1920.

49. For "white man's country reference," see *Osceola Times,* 1 January 1904. For references to violence visited upon blacks elsewhere in the Delta, see *Helena World,* 23 February 1898; *Forrest City Times,* 1 April 1904, 10 March 1910, 18 July 1903. Undated *Arkansas Gazette* and *Helena World* newspaper clippings, Trieber Papers, Arkansas History Commission, Little Rock, Arkansas. For an interesting letter from a black man appealing for intervention, see Unsigned Letter to the president, 22 July 1898, Justice Department Records, National Archives, Washington, D.C.

50. Della Abbott to Mary Ann Abbott Dick, 16 February 1916, Abbott Family Papers, copy of letter in possession of author. The names of homesteaders were compiled from the *Modern News,* 8 August 1913, the *Marked Tree Gazette,* 25 September 1914, and the *Hearings of the Committee,* and then they were compared to the Manuscript Census of Population, 1900, 1910, and 1920.

51. Personal Property Tax Records, Mississippi County, 1920, 1931; MCRPR, Mississippi County, 1920, 1931.

52. Tenant housing was notoriously substandard and frequently reported on in *Agricultural Extension Bulletins* and other Extension Agency documents. In one report, the typical housing was described as "unpainted crude shacks made of rough lumber,

with the cracks covered by narrow lath strips. The roof is commonly made of tin, rough boards, or poor-grade shingles." U.S. Department of Agriculture, "Farm Tenancy in Arkansas," Bureau of Agricultural Economics in cooperation with the Arkansas Agricultural Experiment Station, Washington, D.C., August 1941, p. 11–12. See also Deane G. Carter, "Arkansas Farm Housing Conditions and Needs," *Arkansas Agricultural Experiment Station Bulletin* 305 (1934): 1–31. In a report written by Brooks Hays (a future Arkansas Congressmen) on a fact-finding tour of the Arkansas Delta in 1934, Hays reported "that a great many of the tenant homes were in bad repair, and several appeared to be ready to collapse." Brooks Hays, "Memorandum to Mr. Porter," Brooks Hays Collection, Special Collections Division, University of Arkansas Library, Fayetteville, box 82, folder 11, p. 5.

53. Wilson's provisions for medical services to his black workers was not similar from that adopted by the Sunnyside plantation in Chicot County. Wilson charged his workers a monthly amount for "insurance," and they were entitled to visit the Elizabeth Bealle Clinic in Wilson in return. He kept both a white and a black doctor on his payroll. On the other hand, at the Sunnyside plantation a "Dr. Norton charges Italian farmers from $2.50 to $5.00 per visit. He is paid by the company each month while the Italians are paid at the crop settlement, once a year. Investigation proved that on the medical expense advanced by the company, the Italian tenant is charged 10% interest, while the Company is making the monthly settlements with the doctor, gives him only 80% of his fees, retaining out of the doctor's fees 20% as a sort of rebate." Mary Grace Quackenbos, office of the Attorney General, to the Secretary of State, 22 January 1908, p. 91.

54. According to the *Osceola Times,* 22 September 1933, Wilson was "an advocate for higher education. He built the first fine school building erected in this section in the town he owns and shortly afterwards built the finest school building for colored people to be found in the entire state." Photographs of the two schools provide visual evidence of the grandness of the white school and the substantial character of the black school.

55. This practice survived Wilson's death. A photograph taken in 1937 shows Jim Crain—who at that time was co-directing the plantation—inspecting a black family's garden; this photograph appears in the Wilson Collection.

56. D. N. Morris Report, 10 July 1933, LWCA.

57. "Sharecroppers and Renters, Cost Statement," 31 July 1933, LWCA.

58. "Sharecroppers and Renters, Cost Statement," 3 July 1933, 31 July 1933, LWCA

59. "Sharecroppers and Renters Cost Statement," 31 July 1933.

60. George Stith Interview, with author, Gould, Arkansas, 28 March 1983.

61. Memorandum to Mr. Bruton from Margaret Bennett, assistant attorney, office of the General Counsel, 19 June 1934. In this summary of the Arkansas laws written by the legal division of the Department of Agriculture in June 1934, it was found that "every landlord shall have a lien upon the crop grown upon the demised premises in any year for rent that shall accrue for such year, and such lien shall continue for six months after such rents shall become due and payable. Act July 23, 1868, Sec. 1,

p. 245," p 3. Thanks to Pete Daniel for sharing this document with me. See also Erling D. Solberg, "The Legal Aspects of Farm Tenancy in Arkansas," Arkansas *Agricultural Experiment Station Bulletin* 468 (1947): 3–84. Despite a law passed in 1867 (see 14 Stat. 546), which prohibited debt servitude in New Mexico, southerners practiced debt peonage. According to historian Robert Higgs, "despite the date of its enactment, its sponsors did not intend it as a means of protecting southern blacks. This statute lay dormant until it was invoked in the Alabama *Peonage Cases* 123 F 671 (M.D. Ala. 1903). Two years later in *Clyatt v. U.S.* 197 U.S. 207 (1905), the Supreme Court opened the way for further use of this law in the South by holding that it applied to individuals as well as to state-sponsored systems of peonage. At the same time the Court restricted the use of the law to cases where forced labor was the result of debt." Robert Higgs, "Negro Involuntary Servitude in the South, 1865–1940: A Preliminary Analysis," *Journal of Southern History* 42 (February 1976): 44n–45n.

62. According to one study, "the usual practice was to 'furnish' for the 5-month period, March 1 to August 1, with the 4-month period, April 1 to August 1, used less frequently. The average advance in cash or supplies was around $12 per month for the periods mentioned. These advances were usually monthly but were occasionally made every 2 weeks. The furnishing of groceries (rations) or store credit was the predominant practice, while actual cash was loaned in 30 percent of the cases." Glen T. Barton and J.G. McNeely, "Recent Changes in Farm Labor Organization in Three Arkansas Plantation Counties," Preliminary Report, University of Arkansas College of Agriculture, Agricultural Experiment Station, Fayetteville, Arkansas, September 1939, 32, Special Collections Division, University of Arkansas Libraries, Fayetteville, Arkansas.

63. Oscar Fendler Interview, with author, 15 June 1996. According to Mary Grace Quackenbos, Sunnyside planters pursued Italians who fled that plantation. See Quackenbos's report, p. 32.

64. Wilson to W. W. Shaver, 29 November 1932, LWCA.

65. Wilson to Dysart, 29 November 1932. On the same day, Robert E. Lee Wilson Jr. wrote a separate letter to Dysart suggesting that although Branch was probably not speeding, he had been sounding his horn, thus calling attention to himself. He also indicated that he was sending the horn, the shotgun, and Branch's pistol to him. Wilson Jr. to Dysart, 29 November 1932, LWCA.

66. Scipio Jones to R. E. Lee Wilson, 25 May 1932; Wilson to Jones, 27 May 1932, LWCA.

67. For the neoclassical point-of-view, see Gavin Wright, *Old South New South: Revolutions in the Southern Economy Since the Civil War* (New York: Basic Books, 1986); Robert Higgs, *Competition and Coercion: Blacks in the American Economy, 1865–1914* (Cambridge and New York: Cambridge University Press, 1977); and William Cohen, *At Freedom's Edge: Black Mobility and the Southern White Quest for Racial Control, 1861–1915* (Baton Rouge and London: Louisiana State University Press, 1991). For the most extreme expression of this point-of-view, see Stephen J. DeCanio, *Agriculture in the Postbellum South: The Economics of Production and Supply* (Cambridge, Massachusetts: MIT Press, 1974). For a view that stresses the institutional constraints

facing African Americans see Jay R. Mandle, *The Roots of Black Poverty: The Southern Plantation Economy After the Civil War* (Durham, North Carolina: Duke University Press, 1978); Joel Williamson, *Crucible of Race: Black-White Relations in the American South since Emancipation* (New York: Oxford University Press, 1984); J. Morgan Kousser, *The Shaping of Southern Politics: Suffrage Restrictions and the Establishment of the One-Party South, 1880–1910* (New Haven: Yale University Press, 1974); Pete Daniel, *Shadow of Slavery: Peonage in the South* (Chicago: University of Illinois Press, 1972); Harold Woodman, *New South-New Law: The Legal Foundations of Credit and Labor Relations in the Postbellum Agriculture South* (Baton Rouge: Louisiana State University Press, 1995). Some neoclassical economists find institutional constraints problematic: Roger Ransom and Richard Sutch, *One Kind of Freedom: The Economic Consequences of Emancipation* (Cambridge, Massachusetts: Cambridge University Press, 1977).

68. "Mississippi Valley Flood of 1927: Significant Facts," Red Cross Records, RG 200, box 734, file DR 224.08, National Archives, Washington, D.C.

69. "Estimates of Crop Land Flooded and Losses of Livestock by Mississippi Flood—May to July, 1927," Arkansas, p. 1, Red Cross Records, RG 200, box 224, file DR 224.02.

70. "Persons Cared for During the Emergency Period," Red Cross Records, RG 200, box 735, file DR 224.08.

71. Indeed, records in the Red Cross files refer specifically to the northern district of Mississippi County. "Notes of Meeting of Red Cross Representatives with Mr. Hoover and Mrs. Fiser, Marion Hotel, June 6, 1927, Arkansas," RG 200, box 224, DR 224.01, p. 4. See also "Reports Submitted, Hotel Marion," 6 June 1927, Red Cross Records, box 742, file DR 224.6511, p. 3.

72. *Osceola Times,* 20 May 1927.

73. S. E. Simonson, Chairman of Drainage District no. 9 and Sub District no. 3, "Statement of Facts in Dynamiting of Levees," *Osceola Times,* 8 July 1927, p. 4

74. *Osceola Times,* 29 April 1927, 20 May 1927.

75. *Osceola Times,* May 6, 1927.

76. "Short History of the Arkansas Farm Credit Co.," 10 July 1928, Red Cross Records, RG 200, box 742, DR 224.6511, p. 1.

77. "Arkansas Farm Credit Company: Loan Regulations," n.d, Red Cross Records, RG 200, box 742, file DR 224.6511.

78. Farm Ledgers, LWCA.

79. *Osceola Times,* 16 March 1928, 16 December 1932.

80. G. D. Faulkner, "Architecture and Housing in Mississippi Co.," n.d., 4. WPA Records, Arkansas History Commission.

81. Wilson to Judge J. M. Futrell, 24 August 1932, LWCA.

82. Wilson to Wilson Jr., 17 August 1932, LWCA.

83. R. E. L. Wilson to Dr. J. N. Jerome, 28 April 1932, LWCA.

84. Personal Property Tax Records, 1931, 1933.

85. Deed of Trust, 20 March 1933, South Mississippi County Records, Osceola, Arkansas, p. 242. In one note he borrowed $625,000, due 1 January 1935; in the

second note, dated the same day, he borrowed $1,341,138.93, due 1 January 1938. On 21 December 1935, his trustees (Wilson died in September 1933) refinanced the loans with the Prudential Insurance Company and paid off the RFC. Arkansas Deed of Trust, South Mississippi County Records, pp. 637–41.

86. Whayne, *New Plantation South,* 157. See also Pete Daniel, *Breaking the Land: The Transformation of Cotton, Tobacco, and Rice Cultures Since 1880* (Chicago: University of Illinois Press, 1985); and Jack Kirby, *Rural Worlds Lost: The American South, 1920–1960* (Baton Rouge: Louisiana State University Press, 1987).

87. *Blytheville Courier News,* 7 July 1933.

88. *Blytheville Courier News,* 3 June 1933.

89. *Blytheville Courier News,* 30 June 1933, 3 July 1933.

90. *Blytheville Courier News,* 13 July 1933.

91. *Blytheville Courier News,* 25 August 1933.

92. *Osceola Times,* 15 September 1933.

93. Farm Ledgers, LWCA.

94. Farm Ledgers, LWCA.

Reward for Party Service: Emily Newell Blair and Political Patronage in the New Deal
Virginia Laas

1. Emily Newell Blair to Harry Blair, n.d. [September 1932], folder 32, Emily Newell Blair Papers, Western Reserve Historical Society, Cleveland, Ohio (cited hereafter as ENB Papers). On women in politics in the years after gaining the vote, see Kristi Andersen, *After Suffrage: Women in Partisan and Electoral Politics before the New Deal* (Chicago: University of Chicago Press, 1996); Susan Ware, *Beyond Suffrage: Women in the New Deal* (Cambridge: Harvard University Press, 1981); Anna L. Harvey, *Votes Without Leverage: Women in American Electoral Politics, 1920–1970* (New York: Cambridge University Press, 1998); Nancy Cott, "Across the Great Divide: Women in Politics Before and After 1920," in *Women, Politics and Change,* ed. Louise A. Tilly and Patricia Gurins (New York: Russell Sage Foundation, 1990); and Susan Ware, "ER and Democratic Politics: Women in the Postsuffrage Era," in *Without Precedent: The Life and Career of Eleanor Roosevelt,* ed. Joan Hoff-Wilson and Marjorie Lightman (Bloomington: University of Indiana Press, 1984).

2. Ware, "ER and Democratic Politics: Women in the Postsuffrage Era," in *Without Precedent.*

3. For her early life, see Virginia Jeans Laas, ed., *Bridging Two Eras: The Autobiography of Emily Newell Blair, 1877–1951* (Columbia: University of Missouri Press, 1999).

4. ENB, "Letters of a Contented Wife," *Cosmopolitan* 50 (December 1910): 130–38.

5. Among her early articles were, "Every Man His Own Campaign Manager," *Outlook,* 25 February 1911; "Safety Valve," *Lippincott,* May 1911; "A Successful May Fete," *Woman's Home Companion* (May 1911); "Heart of a Wallflower," *Cosmopolitan* (September 1911); and "Evolution of a Lady," *Harper's Bazaar* (December 1911).

6. On the suffrage movement in Missouri, see Mary Semple Scott, ed., "History of Woman Suffrage Movement in Missouri," *Missouri Historical Review* 14 (April/July 1920): 282–384.

7. For a discussion of her career on the DNC, see Virginia J. Laas, "Breaking into Politics: Emily Newell Blair and the Democratic Party in the 1920s," in *Women in Missouri History: In Search of Power and Influence*, ed. Mary Neth, Gary Kremer, and LeeAnn Whites (Columbia: University of Missouri Press, forthcoming) and Kathryn Anderson, "Evolution of a Partisan: Emily Newell Blair and the Democratic Party, 1920–1932," in *We Have Come to Stay: American Women in Political Parties, 1880–1960,* ed. Melanie Gustafson, Kristie Miller, and Elisabeth I. Perry (Albuquerque: University of New Mexico Press, 1999).

8. Jewell Fenzi and Allida Black, *Democratic Women: An Oral History of the Woman's National Democratic Club* (Washington, D.C.: WNDC Educational Foundation, [2000]), 1–23.

9. Among the more important articles that she published in this period are "What Women Have at Stake," *Woman Citizen* (18 October 1924); "Are Women Counting in Politics?" *Saturday Evening Post* (18 July 1925); "Are Women a Failure in Politics?" *Harper's* (October 1925); "Men in Politics as a Woman Sees Them," *Harper's* (May 1926); "Why Clubs for Women?" *Forum* (March 1927); "'Boring from Within': An Answer to 'The Lady and the Tiger,'" *Woman Citizen* (July 1927); "Are Women Really in Politics?" *Independent* (3 December 1927); "Political Platforms," *Outlook* (March 1928); "A New Role for the Donkey: In Which He Might Win leadership and Gain Power," *Century* (May 1928); "Many Roads Lead Women in Politics," *New York Times Magazine* (October 1928); and "Women in the Political Parties," *Annals of the American Academy of Political and Social Science* (May 1929).

10. Mayme Ober Peak, "Women in Politics," *Outlook,* 23 January 1924, 147–50; Ernestine Evans, "Women in the Washington Scene," *Century Magazine,* August 1923, 507–17. See also, Anne Hard, "Emily Newell Blair, Politician," *Woman Citizen (*April 1926).

11. Her two books were *The Creation of a Home: A Mother Advises a Daughter* (New York: Farrar and Rinehart, 1930) and *A Woman of Courage* (New York: Farrar and Rinehart, 1931).

12. ENB to Harry, n.d. [1930], folder 31, ENB Papers.

13. George McGinty to Hon. Royal S. Copeland, 8 January 1931; Sen. Walter F. George to ENB, 10 January 1931, folder 17, ENB Papers.

14. ENB to Harry, n.d. [probably late January 1931], folder 30, ENB Papers.

15. ENB to Harry, 6 February and 14 July 1931, folder 17, ENB Papers.

16. Undated letters, ENB to Harry, folder 32, ENB Papers.

17. ENB to Harry, n.d. [4 March 1932], folder 18, ENB Papers.

18. ENB to Cordell Hull, 10 November 1930, reel 8, folder 53A, Hull Papers, Library of Congress.

19. Eleanor Roosevelt to ENB, 10 March 1930, folder 27, ENB Papers.

20. ENB to Harry, n.d. [17 March 1932], folder 32, ENB Papers.

21. See, for example, ENB to ER, 7 April 1932, and ER to ENB, 12 April 1932,

folder 27, ENB Papers; ENB to Homer Cummings, 11 April 1932 and Cummings to ENB 18 April 1932, folder 18, ENB Papers. For the Missouri situation before the campaign, see Franklin D. Mitchell, *Embattled Democracy: Missouri Democratic Politics, 1919–1932* (Columbia: University of Missouri Press, 1968), 140–46. On the Democratic Party during this period, see Douglas Craig, *After Wilson: The Struggle for the Democratic Party, 1920–1934* (Chapel Hill: University of North Carolina Press, 1992).

22. ER to ENB, 15 July 1932, folder 27, ENB Papers. On the difficulties within the Missouri delegation, see Frederick Gardner to Edward Goltra, 5 July 1932, box 21, Goltra Papers, Missouri Historical Society, St. Louis.

23. ER to ENB, 22 July 1932 and 6 August 1932; ENB to ER, 1 August 1932, folder 27, ENB Papers. ENB to Molly Dewson, 1 August 1932; Dewson to ER, 3 August 1932; ER to Dewson, 4 August 1932, box 14, Dewson Papers, Franklin Roosevelt Library. On Dewson, ER, and the New Deal, see Susan Ware, *Partner and I: Molly Dewson, Feminism, and New Deal Politics* (New Haven: Yale University Press, 1987) and Blanche Wiesen Cook, *Eleanor Roosevelt,* vol. 2, 1933–38 (New York: Viking Press, 1999).

24. ENB to Harry, n.d. [15 September 1932], folder 18 and [30 September 1932], folder 31, ENB Papers.

25. ENB to Harry, n.d. [September 1932], folder 32, ENB Papers.

26. "Report of Women's Division of the Democratic National Campaign Committee, Summary of Lines of Work in 1932 Campaign," box 55, Louis Howe Papers, Franklin Roosevelt Library. The other women speakers were former governor of Wyoming Nellie Tayloe Ross (vice chairperson of the DNC), Florida Congresswoman Ruth Bryan Owen, and New Yorker Frances Perkins. Molly Dewson, "An Aid to an End," 1:67, box 26, Dewson Papers, FDR Library.

27. Eleanore Bailey Johnson to Speakers Bureau, 17 October 1932, folder 18, ENB Papers.

28. ENB to Harry, 30 September 1932, folder 31, ENB Papers.

29. ENB to Dewson, 21 November 1932, box 14, Dewson Papers, FDR Library.

30. See for example, ENB to Lavinia Engle, 13 November 1932, and ENB to Daniel Roper, 28 November 1932, folder 18, ENB Papers; Daniel Roper to ENB, 25 November 1932 and Cordell Hull to ENB, 28 November 1932, box 3, Dewson Papers, FDR Library; ENB to Edward Goltra, 3 December 1932, box 18, Goltra Papers; ENB to Franklin Roosevelt, 29 November 1932, Patronage Correspondence, box 993, DNC Papers, FDR Library.

31. ENB to Molly Dewson, 17 January 1933, box 15, Dewson Papers, FDR Library.

32. ENB to FDR, 17 January 1933, Patronage correspondence, 1932–33, box 990, DNC Papers, FDR Library.

33. ENB to Lavinia Engle, 21 November 1932, folder 18, ENB Papers.

34. ENB to Harry, n.d., folder 18, ENB Papers.

35. ENB to Harry, n.d., folder 32, ENB Papers.

36. ENB to Harry, n.d. [probably February 1933], folder 18, ENB Papers.

37. ENB to Dewson, 21 November 1932, box 14, Dewson Papers, FDR Library.

38. See for example, ENB to Louis Howe, 12 January 1933, box 342, 1932 Correspondence, Democratic National Committee, FDR Library; ENB to Harry, Saturday, folder 32, ENB Papers; Lavinia Engle to Molly Dewson, n.d. [February 1933], box 14, Dewson Papers, FDR Library; ENB to Dewson, n.d. [March 1933], box 13, Dewson Papers; ENB to Eleanor Roosevelt, 1 April 1933, box 1255, ER papers, Series 100, FDR Library.

39. ENB to Harry, n.d., folder 31, ENB Papers.

40. ENB to Dewson, n.d. [probably March 1933], box 13, Dewson Papers, FDR Library.

41. ENB to Eleanor Roosevelt, 1 April 1933, box 1255, Series 100, ER Papers, FDR Library.

42. On Missouri politics, see Mitchell, *Embattled Democracy* and Lawrence H. Larsen and Nancy J. Hulston, *Pendergast!* (Columbia: University of Missouri Press, 1997).

43. Eleanor Roosevelt to Louis Howe, 7 April 1933, box 1255, series 100, ER Papers.

44. Eleanor Roosevelt to Homer Cummings, 10 April 1933, Charlottesville, Virginia, box 80, Cummings Papers, University of Virginia.

45. Cummings to Eleanor Roosevelt, 21 April 1933, box 80, Cummings Papers, UVA. For continued effort on Harry's behalf, see Dewson to Louis Howe, 1 May 1933, box 16, Dewson Papers, FDR Library.

46. ENB to Dewson, n.d., box 16, Dewson Papers, FDR Library.

47. Newell Blair Interview, 14 June 1996, in possession of author.

48. Harry Blair's Résumé, box 80, Cummings Papers, UVA. See also typescripts covering his career in folder 109, ENB Papers.

49. Official File #10, box 1; #10a, box 10, FDR Papers, FDR Library.

50. ENB to Eleanor Roosevelt, 10 June 1933, box 16, Dewson Papers.

51. ENB to Dewson, 10 June 1933, box 16, Dewson Papers.

52. Ewing Mitchell to Homer Cummings, 16 June 1933, folder 2664. See also his letter to Dan Roper, Secretary of Commerce, 1 July 1933, folder 2691, Mitchell Papers, Western Historical Manuscript Collection, Columbia, Missouri.

53. ENB to Mitchell, 11 July 1933, folder 2704, Mitchell Papers.

54. For her central role in securing jobs for women, see Ware, *Partner and I,* 175–96.

55. Molly Dewson to ENB, 25 July 1933, box 16, Dewson Papers, FDR Library.

56. ENB to Dewson, 28 July 1933, box 16, Dewson Papers.

57. Engle to Dewson, 2 August [1933] and 4 August [1933], box 16, Dewson Papers.

58. ENB to Dewson, 28 July 1933, box 16, Dewson Papers.

59. For an overview of the Board's work, see "The Valedictory of the Advisory Board," *The Consumer* 1 (15 October 1935): 11–14, Office Files of ENB, February–November 1935, box 1, entry 363, Records of the Advisory Bodies, Records of the Consumers' Advisory Board, RG 9, Records of the NRA, National Archives. See

also, Bulletin #2, Consumers' Division of the National Emergency Council, Activities of the Consumers' Advisory Board of the NRA and the Consumers' Council of the AAA, box 2, entry 363, Records of Advisory Bodies; ENB to FDR, 18 August 1933, Alphabetical File, 1933–46, roll 48, FDR Papers, FDR Library.

60. "Bulletin #2, Consumers' Division of the National Emergency Council, Activities of the Consumers' Advisory Board of the NRA and the Consumers' Counsel of the AAA, Office Files of ENB, February–November 1935, box 2, Records of Advisory Bodies, Records of the Consumers' Advisory Board, RG 9, NA.

61. FDR Alphabetical File, 1933–48, roll 48. *Consumers' Notes* 1 (March 1935), Office Files of ENB, February–November 1935, Records of the Consumers' Advisory Board, box 1, RG 9, NA.

62. Minutes of the 3 November 1933 meeting of the Consumers' Advisory Board, box 5, Papers of the Women's Division of the Democratic National Committee, 1933–44, FDR Library.

63. ENB, *Bridging Two Eras,* 350.

64. ENB to Dewson, 8 August 1933 and 19 August 1933, box 16, Dewson Papers.

65. 29 December 1933, Homer Cummings' Diary, box 234, Cummings Papers, UVA; Cummings to FDR, 3 January 1934, FDR Alphabetical File, 1933–46, roll 48, FDR Library.

66. ER to Frances Perkins, 19 January 1935; Perkins to ER, 23 January 1935; Dewson to Perkins, 9 January 1935; Dewson to ER, 27 December 1935. All in Series 70, 1935, box 660, ER Papers, FDR Library. See also letters to ENB from Marion Banister and Florence Allen, folder 20, ENB Papers.

67. *Consumers' Research Bulletin,* March 1935, folder 48, ENB Papers, p. 2.

68. ENB to Dewson, 7 January 1934 [1935], box 13, Dewson Papers, FDR Library.

69. Frank P. Graham to Ruth Boynton, 4 July 1935, series 1.1, folder 1935–48, Frank P. Graham Papers, University of North Carolina, Chapel Hill.

70. *Schechter Poultry Corporation v. U.S.,* 295 U.S. 495 (1935).

71. FDR to ENB, 6 March 1936, folder 27, ENB Papers.

72. Harry Blair's Typescript Biographical Sketch, folder 109, ENB Papers.

73. Harry Blair to Homer Cummings, 13 January 1937, box 80, Cummings Papers, UVA.

74. ENB, *Bridging Two Eras,* 351. Her public service was not completed. In fall 1941, she accepted the position of organization director, serving as liaison between the War Department's Women's Interests Section of the Bureau of Public Relations and their Women's Advisory Council. In May 1942 she replaced Oveta Culp Hobby as chief of the Women's Interests Section. The purpose of the section was to provide American wives, mothers, and sweethearts with information on the very different living circumstances of their men who had become soldiers. "History and Function of the Women's Interests Section of the Bureau of Public Relations, War Department," Public Information Division, box 301–K, RG 319, National Archives.

75. ENB to Dewson, 7 January 1934 [1935], box 13, Dewson Papers, FDR Library.

76. ENB, *Bridging Two Eras,* 350.
77. ENB, *Bridging Two Eras,* 357.

"A Generous and Exemplary Womanhood": Hattie Rutherford Watson and NYA Camp Bethune in Pine Bluff, Arkansas, 1937
Fon Gordon

I am especially grateful for the help extended to me by the staff of the John Hay Library, Brown University, Providence, Rhode Island, and the curator of the manuscript's division, Mark N. Brown, Ph.D. The research at Brown University could not have been accomplished without sabbatical leave provided by the department of history, the College of Arts and Sciences, and a grant awarded by the vice chancellor for research and graduate studies, David Watt, at the University of Kentucky, Lexington. My thanks also to Tanya Telfair Sharpe, archivist, Spelman College, Atlanta, Georgia.

1. These works were consulted: Evelyn Brooks Higginbotham, *Righteous Discontent: The Women's Movement in the Black Baptist Church, 1880–1920* (Cambridge: Harvard University Press, 1993) and "African-American Women's History and the Metalanguage of Race," in *We Specialize in the Wholly Impossible: A Reader in Black Women's History,* ed. Darlene Clark Hine, et al. (Brooklyn: Carlson Publishing, 1995), 3–24; Elsa Barkley Brown, "Womanist Consciousness: Maggie Lena Walker and the Independent Order of Saint Luke," in *Unequal Sisters: A Multicultural Reader in U.S. Women's History,* 2nd ed., ed. Vicki L. Ruiz and Ellen Carol DuBois (New York: Routledge Press, 1994), 268–83; Darlene Clark Hine, *Hine Sight: Black Women and the Re-Construction of American History* (Brooklyn: Carlson Publishing, 1994), xxxii, 37–47; and Patricia Hill Collins, *Fighting Words: Black Women and the Search for Justice* (Minneapolis: University of Minnesota Press, 1999) and "When Old Is New Again: Black Women's Motherwork as Political Activism," Mary McLeod Bethune Lecture, University of Kentucky, Lexington, Kentucky, 22 March 2000.

2. See Angela Y. Davis, *Blues Legacies and Black Feminism: Gerture "Ma" Rainey, Bessie Smith, and Billie Holiday* (New York: Pantheon Books, 1998); Patricia A. Schechter, "All the Intensity of My Nature": Ida B. Wells, Anger, and Politics," *Radical History Review* 70 (winter 1998): 48–77; Nell Irvin Painter, *Sojourner Truth: A Life, a Symbol* (New York. W. W. Norton, 1996); Elizabeth Clark-Lewis, *Living in, Living Out: African American Domestics and the Great Migration* (New York: Kodansha International, 1996); Tera W. Hunter, *To 'Joy My Freedom: Southern Black Women's Lives and Labors After the Civil War* (Cambridge: Harvard University Press, 1997); Deborah Gray White, *Too Heavy a Load: Black Women in Defense of Themselves, 1894–1994* (New York: W. W. Norton, 1999); Chana Kai Lee, *For Freedom's Sake: The Life of Fannie Lou Hamer* (Urbana: University of Illinois Press, 1999); Hazel Carby, *Race Men* (Cambridge: Harvard University Press, 1998); Robin D. G. Kelley, *Race Rebels: Culture, Politics, and the Black Working Class* (New York: The Free Press, 1994); Kevin K. Gaines, *Uplifting the Race: Black Leadership, Politics, and Culture in the Twentieth Century* (Chapel Hill: University of North Carolina Press, 1996).

3. "Obituary of Samuel Wilson Rutherford," typewritten, n.d.; Robert H. Rutherford to HRW, 4 December 1928, JBW Papers; Mungo M. Ponton, *Life and*

Times of Henry M. Turner (New York: Negro Universities Press, 1917; reprint, Wesport, Connecticut: Negro Universities Press, 1970), 47.

4. Coincidentally, the photograph on the cover of Stephanie J. Shaw's *What a Woman Ought To Be and To Do: Black Professional Women Workers During the Jim Crow Era* (Chicago: The University of Chicago Press, 1996) pictures the 1907 Spelman College class. Hattie Rutherford Watson, as the only graduate of the college course, is wearing the gown and mortarboard. She is not included in the text.

5. Shaw, *What a Woman Ought To Be and To Do*, 2

6. Jacqueline Anne Rouse, *Lugenia Burns Hope: Black Southern Reformer* (Athens: The University of Georgia Press, 1989), 66; "Hattie Rutherford Watson Résumé, WPA," JBW Papers.

7. Brawley, 197; Jones, 75–76; Nina Mjagkij, *Light In the Darkness: African Americans and the YMCA, 1852–1946* (Lexington: University Press of Kentucky, 1994), 154; John Hope to JBW, 4 February 1924; JBW to R. L. Smith, 16 September 1922; "Hattie Rutherford Watson Résumé, WPA," 26 May 1937, JBW Papers.

8. Waston, *Spelman Messenger*, April 1928, p. 4, SCA.

9. Waston, *Spelman Messenger*, April 1928, p. 5, SCA.

10. Schechter, "All the Intensity of My Nature," 52.

11. NYA, Division of Negro Affairs, "The National Youth Administration Serves Negro Youth," typewritten, n.d., JBW Papers; Mary McLeod Bethune, Director, Division of Negro Affairs, NYA, 30 June 1937, "Annual Report of the Division of Negro Affairs (1 July 1936–30 June 1937)," 12, reel 11, *Bethune Foundation Collection*, pt. 1, ed. John H. Bracey Jr., Sharon Henley, and August Meier (Bethesda, Maryland: University Publications of America, 1995), microfilm copy (hereafter cited as BFC).

12. Elaine M. Smith, "Mary McLeod Bethune and the National Youth Administration," in *Clio Was A Woman: Studies in the History of American Women*, eds. Mabel E. Deutrich and Virginia C. Purdy (Washington, D.C.: Howard University Press, 1980), 150–60; "Summary of the Recommendations of the Conference," 9; "Committee on Education and Recreation," 3; "Letter of Transmittal," MMB to President Franklin D. Roosevelt, 18 January 1937, National Conference on the Problems of the Negro and Negro Youth," reel 12, BFC.

13. William Pickens, "Arkansas—a Study in Suppression," in *These "Colored" United States: African American Essays from the 1920s*, ed. Tom Lutz and Susanna Ashton (New Brunswick, New Jersey: Rutgers University Press, 1996), 38.

14. Nolen M. Irby to HRW, 4 December 1936, JBW Papers.

15. Nolen M. Irby to HRW, 4 December 1936, JBW Papers.

16. MMB to JBW, 24 February 1937, 10 July 1937, 19 September 1938; JBW to MMB, 12 January 1937, 28 September 1938, JBW Papers.

17. "Camp Bethune Staff and Enrollment," typewritten, 1937; "NYA Educational Camp Registration Summary," typewritten, 1937; HRW to L. J. Gurst, 11 March 1937; Carl Buchanan to HRW, 4 September 1937, JBW Papers.

18. Grace Elizabeth Hale, *Making Whiteness: The Culture of Segregation in the South, 1880–1940* (New York: Vintage Books, 1999).

19. Isabella Ferguson to Mr. And Mrs. J. B. Watson, 30 July 1935; Josephine Harreld to M/M JBW, 20 December 1937, JBW Papers.

20. Edward H. Beardsley, *A History of Neglect: Health Care for Blacks and Mill Workers in the Twentieth Century South* (Knoxville: University of Tennessee Press, 1987), 161–62.

21. "Camp Bethune Staff and Enrollment," NYA Educational Camp Registration Summary, JBW Papers.

22. HRW to Florence M. Read, president of Spelman, 6 April 1937, JBW Papers.

23. *Bethune Spotlight* 1 (14 May 1937): 1–7; "Camp Bethune Staff and Enrollment;" NYA Educational Camp Registration Summary," JBW Papers.

24. Chapel assembly, Friday, 21 May 1937, typewritten, JBW Papers.

25. "Monday Night Lectures," *Bethune Spotlight* 1 (14 May 1937): 3, JBW Papers.

26. "Chapel Exercises," *Bethune Spotlight* 1 (14 May 1937), JBW Papers.

27. "Chapel Exercises," *Bethune Spotlight* 1 (14 May 1937), JBW Papers.

28. "Chapel Exercises," *Bethune Spotlight* 1 (14 May 1937), JBW Papers.

29. "Special News," *Bethune Spotlight* 1 (14 May 1937): 5, JBW Papers.

30. "Mrs. Bethune's Message to Camp Girls an Inspiration," *Bethune Spotlight* 1 (14 May 1937): 1, JBW Papers.

31. Wendy Brown, "Jane Mathilda Bolin," in *Black Women in America: An Historical Encyclopedia,* ed. Darlene Clark, et al. (Brooklyn: Carlson Publishing Inc., 1993), 1:145–47.

32. "Our Picture Gallery," *Bethune Spotlight* 1 (14 May 1937): 4–5, JBW Papers.

33. "Student Government in Camp a Good Thing," *Bethune Spotlight* 1 (14 May 1937): 2, JBW Papers.

34. "Social News," *Bethune Spotlight* 1 (14 May 1937): 6, JBW Papers.

35. "Annual Report of the Division of Negro Affairs, 1937," 4, BFC.

36. *Bethune Spotlight* 1 (14 May 1937): 1–4, JBW Papers.

37. HRW to Mrs. Ceola Hannah, 2 March 1937, JBW Papers.

38. HRW to Mr. Sam Moore, 7 May 1937, JBW Papers.

39. Louise Mayo to HRW, 4 October 1937, JBW Papers.

40. HRW to Louise Mayo, 8 October 1937, JBW Papers.

41. HRW to Beatrice Cravens, 3 November 1937, JBW Papers.

42. Willard B. Gatewood Jr., *Aristocrats of Color: The Black Elite, 1880–1920* (Bloomington: Indiana University Press, 1990).

43. HRW to Pine Bluff Business Community, 1 February 1940, JBW Papers.

44. Annual Report of the Division of Negro Affairs, 1937, 12, BFC.

45. Smith, "Mary McLeod Bethune and the National Youth Administration," 162, 165.

46. Kimberle Williams Crenshaw, et al., eds., *Critical Race Theory: The Key Writings That Formed the Movement* (New York: The New Press, 1995); Richard Delgado, ed., *Critical Race Theory: The Cutting Edge* (Philadelphia: Temple University Press, 1995); Derrick Bell, *Faces at the Bottom of the Well: The Permanence of Presumptions of the American Legal Process* (New York: Oxford University Press, 1995).

47. Bernard Sternsher, ed., *The Negro in Depression and War; Prelude to Revolution, 1930–1945* (Chicago: Quadrangle Books, 1969); Harvard Sitkoff, *A New Deal for Blacks: The Emergence of Civil Rights as a National Issue* (New York: Oxford University Press, 1978); John B. Kirby, *Black Americans in the Roosevelt Era: Liberalism and Race*

(Knoxville: The University of Tennessee Press, 1980); Nancy J. Weiss, *Farewell to the Party of Lincoln: Black Politics in the Age of FDR* (Princeton: Princeton University Press, 1983); Patricia Sullivan, *Days of Hope: Race and Democracy in the New Deal Era* (Chapel Hill: University of North Carolina Press, 1996); Roger Biles, *The South and the New Deal* (Lexington: The University Press of Kentucky, 1994).

48. "HRW Résumé/WPA;" HRW to Elwood (Cardozo) and Robert H. Rutherford Sr., 10 November 1962; L. A. Davis to HRW, 20 May 1964; "AM&N College Citation of Service to Mrs. Hattie Rutherford Watson," 25 May 1964, JBW Papers.

49. Florence M. Read to HRW, 16 October 1929, 10 April 1931; John Hope to HRW, 27 June 1935, JBW Papers.

50. "Biographical Sketch of Hattie Rutherford Watson," "HRW Résumé/ WPA," "AM&N College Citation," JBW Papers.

51. HRW to J. P. Whitaker, 16 August 1952; HRW to Elwood and RHR Sr., 26 August 1962, 10 November 1962, JBW Papers.

52. "A Resolution of Appreciation of Mrs. Hattie Rutherford Watson as passed by the Board of Trustees of Spelman College in regular session in New York City on November 15, 1963," JBW Papers.

Tufted Titans: Dalton, Georgia's Carpet Elite
Thomas Deaton

1. This was a common claim, but with worth tied to stock options, facilities, investments, and salaries, it is hard to substantiate.

2. R. E. Hamilton, "Bedspreads are Big Business," *Christian Science Monitor* (15 March 1941): 5, 15.

3. R. E. Hamilton, "Bedspread Bonanza," *Reader's Digest* (April 1941): 42; Thomas M. Deaton, *Bedspreads to Broadloom, The Story of the Tufted Carpet Industry* (Acton, Massachusetts: Tapestry Press, 1993) 19–20; Roy H. Windham, *The Tufting Machine, A Practical Text of Instruction for Machine Fixers* (Rome, Georgia: Southern Craft Co., 1941) 89–117.

4. Lewis Card Interview, Tuftco Machinery, Chattanooga, Tennessee, 21 May 1979; Reg Burnett Interview, 11 February 2000, RBI Associates, Dalton, Georgia.

5. Billie J. Walters and James O. Wheeler, "Localization Economies in the American Carpet Industry," *Geographical Review* (April 1984): 183–91.

6. Randall L. Patton and David B. Parker, *Carpet Capital, The Rise of a New South Industry* (Athens: University of Georgia Press, 1999): 289; Robert McMath, research at Georgia Tech on the history of Dalton Utilities; V. D. Parrott Interview, Dalton Utilities, 21 April 1981.

7. Reg Burnett and Amy Cruse Interview, 11 February 2000; Robert Shaw Interview, Shaw Industries, Dalton, Georgia, 30 May 1991.

8. Ronald V. Gunter, "Launched Tufted Spreads to Save a Country Store," *Chattanooga Times,* 16 March 1967, 14.

9. Gunter, "Launched Tufted Spreads to Save a Country Store," *Chattanooga Times,* 16 March 1967, 14; Larry Kunstler, "A Posthumous Tribute to an Industry Pioneer," *Linens and Domestics* (April 1964): 64.

10. Kunstler, "A Posthumous Tribute to an Industry Pioneer," *Linens and Domestics*, 64; Jack Bandy Interview, Coronet Industries, Dalton, Georgia, 3 July 1979.

11. Jack Bandy Interview, Coronet Industries, Dalton, Georgia, 3 July 1979.

12. Joe and Christine McCutchen Interview, Universal Carpet, Elijah, Georgia, 10 July 1979; Peggy Baugh Jonas, "Early Days of Industry Recalled," *Dalton Daily Citizen-News*, 27 February 1978, 5–6D, microfilm.

13. Deaton, *Bedspreads*, 29–30.

14. *Dalton Daily Citizen-News*, August-December 1945; *An Official History of Whitfield County Georgia 1852–1999* (Fernandina Beach, Florida: Wolfe Publishing, 1999) 107–9.

15. Tom Neal Interview, Lawtex, Dalton, Georgia, 22 April 1981.

16. E. T. Barwick Interview, Barwick Industries, Atlanta, Georgia, 8 April 1980, 26 March 1981, 8 September 1990 Dalton, Georgia.

17. Tom Neal Interview, 22 April 1981.

18. Barwick Interviews; Frank McCarty Interview, McCarty Chenille, Dalton, Georgia, 19 May 1981; Don Browan Interview, Barwick Industries, Eton, Georgia, 13 July 1992.

19. Tom Neal Interview; Annette Stramesi, *What You Should Know About Carpet* (New York: Popular Library, 1973), 186–87.

20. Walter Guinan Interview, Sanford-Bigelow, Atlanta, Georgia, 21 January 1983; Buford Talley Interview, Barwick Industries, Dalton, Georgia, 10 May 1983.

21. Numbers of former employees would volunteer their commitment to Gene Barwick at Barwick Reunion interviews, 8 September 1990; Sandy Sobelman Interview, 18 March 1980, Barwick Industries, Atlanta; Bryan Gibson, 26 May 1981, Dixie Yarns, Rossville, Georgia.

22. Bandy Interview, 3 July 1979.

23. "Bud Seretan" *Retailing Daily*, 5 October 1956, p. 4.

24. "Bud Seretan" *Retailing Daily*, 5 October 1956, p. 4; Bud Seretean Interview, 28 January 1980, Coronet Carpet, Dalton, Georgia; Al Wahnon, "Bud Seretean—The Quintessential Success," *Floor Covering Weekly*, 10 January 1983, pp. 1, 47–48, 87–88.

25. Wahnon, "Bud Seretean," 47–48, 87–88.

26. Wahnon, "Bud Seretean," 47–48, 87–88.

27. Wahnon, "Bud Seretean," 47–48, 87–88.

28. Wahnon, "Bud Seretean," 47–48, 87–88; Isadore Barmash, "RCA's Biggest Shareholder," *New York Times*, 18 April 1971, p. 5. There is a strong Jewish community in northwest Georgia. When Alan *and* Shirley Loberbaum sold Aladdin Industries to Mohawk, they joined the hundred richest families in the United States.

29. Piera Shaheen Interview, 12 March 1994, Dalton, Georgia.

30. Piera Shaheen Interview, 12 March 1994; Shaheen Shaheen, *World Carpets, The First Thirty Years* (Dalton, Georgia: Lee Printing Co., 1984).

31. Linda Edwards Interview, 5 March 1994, 1st Choice Carpet, Dalton, Georgia.

32. Linda Edwards Interview, 5 March 1994, 1st Choice Carpet, Dalton, Georgia; *Patterns*, Spring 2000, Dalton, Georgia, p. 4.

33. "Eye on the Goal," *Floor Covering Weekly*, 14 May 1973; Warren Sims

Interview, 5 October 1990, Shaw Industries, Dalton, Georgia; Shaw Interview, 10 May 1983, 30 May 1991; Frank O'Neill, "The Top 25," *Carpet and Rug Industry, June 1990,* 9–31.

34. O'Neill, "The Top 25," 9–31.

35. O'Neill, "The Top 25," 9–31.

36. O'Neill, "The Top 25,", 9–31.

37. O'Neill, "The Top 25," 9–31.

38. O'Neill, "The Top 25," 9–31.

39. O'Neill, "The Top 25," 9–31.

40. Shaw Interview, 30 May 1991.

41. Shaw Interview, 30 May 1991.

42. Deaton, *Bedspreads,* 73, 138, 142; Mrs. G. L. Westcott Interview, 23 April 1991, Dalton, Georgia; Elaine Taylor, *I've Had a Millionaire's Fun, The Mose Painter Story* (Chattanooga, Tennessee: Painter and Taylor Manuscript Co., 1982); Mose Painter Interview, 12 April 1979, Painter Carpet Co., Dalton, Georgia.

43. *U. S. Census of Population, General Population Characteristics,* U. S. Department of Commerce, Bureau of the Census, 1960, 1970, 1980, 1990; *County and City Data Book, 1972; 1987 Census of Manufactures,* "Weaving and Floor Covering Mills," pp. 28–54, 110–19, Bureau of Census, Washington, D.C., 1988.

44. *1987 Census of Manufactures,* "Weaving and Floor Covering Mills," pp. 28–54, 110–19

45. *1987 Census of Manufactures,* "Weaving and Floor Covering Mills," pp. 28–54, 110–19

46. Douglas Flamming, *Creating the Modern South, Millhands and Managers in Dalton, Georgia, 1884–1984* (Chapel Hill: University of North Carolina Press, 1992), 282–306; Thomas M. Deaton, *The History of Collins and Aikman,* a company history published by and for Collins and Aikman; TWUA was able to unionize Dixie Belle in Calhoun, Georgia, (about twenty miles south of Dalton) but it had a very limited effect on the industry. Randall L. Patton with David B. Parker, *Carpet Capital, The Rise of a New South Industry* (Athens: University of Georgia Press, 1999), 206–32.

47. *Georgia Statistical Abstract Supplement, County and City Data Book,* 1972, 1980, 1990–91, U. S. Department of Commerce, Bureau of Census, Washington, D.C., *Georgia,* p. 91 (1972), table 5, 176, p. 161 (1991). *Target Tomorrow,* Dalton-Whitfield County Chamber of Commerce, 1998; Ken Kessler of North Georgia Area Planning *and* Development Commission believes that strong overtime pay exaggerated these incomes. He thinks that the buying and housing habits of many of the middle class are those of a mill-village attitude. Ken Kessler Interview, 14 April 2000, 16 May 2000, Dalton, Georgia.

48. Wilma A. Dunaway, *The First American Frontier* (Chapel Hill: University of North Carolina Press, 1996), 17–19, 288–300.

49. Dunaway, *The First American Frontier,* 288–300.

50. Big companies have a high cost of doing business, while tufted carpet has traditionally operated on a low-profit margin using the finances of factors, low overhead structures, and independent distribution sources. Even today there is so little national

advertising by even the major mills that product recognition is related to carpet fibers like Anso or distributors like Carpet One. Walter Guinan Interview, 17 May 2000.

Sara Alderman Murphy and the Little Rock Panel of American Women: A Prescription to Heal the Wounds of the Little Rock School Crisis
Paula C. Barnes

1. Sara Murphy (hereafter cited as SM) Interview, by author, Little Rock, August 1992.
2. SM, *Breaking the Silence* (Fayetteville: University of Arkansas Press, 1997), 33.
3. Roy Reed, *Faubus: The Life and Times of an American Prodigal* (Fayetteville: University of Arkansas Press, 1997), 184.
4. Comprehensive documentation of the Little Rock School crisis can be found in the following sources: Numan V. Bartley. *The New South 1945–1980* (Baton Rouge: Louisiana State University Press, 1995); Daisy Bates, *The Long Shadow of Little Rock* (Fayetteville: University of Arkansas Press, 1987); Elizabeth Jacoway and C. Fred Williams, eds., *Understanding the Little Rock School Crisis* (Fayetteville: University of Arkansas Press, 1999); SM, *Breaking the Silence*; Reed, *Faubus;* Beth Roy, *Bitters in the Honey* (Fayetteville: University of Arkansas Press, 1999).
5. Official membership was accorded with the payment of one dollar in dues.
6. SM, *Breaking the Silence,* 27. SM Papers, Special Collections Mullins Library University of Arkansas, Fayetteville.
7. Eleanor Roosevelt acknowledged the Cold War factor of Little Rock during her trip to Moscow in 1958.
8. SM Interviews, July 1989, August 1992.
9. SM Interviews, July 1989, August 1992; Barbara Philips Interview, July 1989.
10. SM, *Breaking the Silence,* 237.
11. *Social distance* is a term used to describe the de facto physical and psychological space between racial, ethnic, and religious groups in any given society.
12. Gwen Riley Interview, by author, Little Rock, July 1989.
13. Brownie Ledbetter Interview, by author, Little Rock, July 1989.
14. Kathryn Lambright's Private Papers, recently contributed to the Butler Center, Little Rock.
15. Kathryn Lambright's Private Papers, Butler Center, Little Rock; SM Interviews, July 1989, August 1992.
16. SM Papers, Special Collections, University of Arkansas.
17. Murphy assumed that a report was never filed and the members of the Methodist Church most likely influenced the restaurant owner to comply with the 1964 Civil Rights Act.
18. SM Interview, July 1989.
19. SM Interview, July 1989.
20. SM Interview, July 1989.
21. Barbara Philips Interviews, by author, Little Rock, July 1989, and St. Petersburg, Russia, April 1995.

22. SM, "Women Panelists Recall Experiences of Last Four Years," *Arkansas Gazette* 7 (May 1967); SM Papers, Special Collections, University of Arkansas.

23. SM Interview, August 1992.

24. Brownie Ledbetter Interview, July 1989.

25. SM Interview, July 1989.

Contributors

Paula C. Barnes is history department chair at Hutchison School in Memphis, Tennessee, and is an adjunct professor at Christian Brothers University. She received her Ph.D. from the University of Arkansas. Forthcoming publications include *Throwing off the Cloak of Privilege: White Southern Women Activists in the Civil Rights Era* and *Betty Bumpers' Arkansas: A View of the World from a Small Southern State.*

James C. Cobb is the B. Phinizy Spalding distinguished professor of history at the University of Georgia. He received his Ph.D. from the University of Georgia and has published *The Selling of the South: The Southern Crusade for Industrial Development, 1936–1990* and *The Most Southern Place on Earth: The Mississippi Delta and the Roots of Regional Identity.* He is currently at work on *From "New South" to "No South": The Great Struggle Within Southern Identity.* He was President of the Southern Historical Association in 1999.

Thomas Deaton is a professor of social sciences at Dalton State College. He received his Ph.D. from the University of Georgia and has published *A Short History of the United States and Georgia* and *Bedspreads to Broadloom: The Story of the Tufted Carpet Industry.* His current research projects include analysis of "Jewish Leadership in the Carpet Industry" and "Dalton Utilities: A Progressive Experiment That Worked."

Thomas A. DeBlack is an associate professor of history at Arkansas Tech University. He received his Ph.D. from the University of Arkansas. He is currently working on a book about the Civil War and Reconstruction in Arkansas and is co-authoring a college-level Arkansas history book.

Randy Finley is an associate professor of history at Georgia Perimeter College. He received his Ph.D. from the University of Arkansas and is the author of *From Slavery to Uncertain Freedom: The Freedmen's Bureau in Arkansas.* He is currently preparing a study of Albany, Georgia, in the 1960s.

Fon Gordon is an associate professor of history at the University of Kentucky. She received her Ph.D. from the University of Arkansas and has published *Caste and Class: The Black Experience in Arkansas, 1880–1920.* She is presently working on southern black women's experiences in the Great Depression.

Whittington B. Johnson is professor of history and acting chair of the history department at the University of Miami. He received his Ph.D. from the University of Georgia. He wrote *The Promising Years, 1750–1830: The Emergence of Black Labor and Business; Black Savannah, 1788–1864;* and *Race Relations in the Bahamas, 1784–1834: The Nonviolent Transformation From a Slave to a Free Society.* He is currently completing research on the aftermath of the abolition of slavery in the Bahamas.

Virginia Laas is an associate professor of history at Missouri Southern State College. She received her Ph.D. from the University of Arkansas. She wrote *Lincoln's Lee: The Life of Rear Admiral Samuel Phillips Lee* (with Dudley Cornish) and *Love and Power in the Nineteenth Century: The Marriage of Violet Blair.* She edited *Wartime Washington: The Civil War Letters of Elizabeth Blair Lee* and *Bridging Two Eras: The Autobiography of Emily Newell Blair.* She is presently at work on a biography of Emily Newell Blair.

Bobby Lovett is professor of history and dean of the College of Arts and Sciences at Tennessee State University. His latest publications include *The African American History of Nashville, Tennesse, 1780–1930: Elites and Dilemmas* and *The Art of William Edmondson.*

Bernard E. Powers Jr. is professor of history and director of history graduate studies at the College of Charleston. He received his Ph.D. from Northwestern University. He is the author of *Black Charlestonians: A Social History, 1822–1885,* a winner of the Association of College Research Libraries Choice Award, Outstanding Academic Book for 1995. He is currently working on the history of the African Methodist Episcopal Church in South Carolina.

Jeannie Whayne is associate professor of history and history department chair at the University of Arkansas. She received her Ph.D. from the University of California at San Diego and is author of *A New Plantation South: Land, Labor, and Federal Favor in Twentieth Century Arkansas.* She also co-edited *The Governors of Arkansas* and is presently at work on a book about Lee Wilson and Company and a documentary series on the Great Depression in Arkansas.

• • •

The editors would like to especially thank Amy Ramsden for her careful and judicious editing of this manuscript. It is a much improved tribute to Professor Gatewood because of her hard work.